COOKS 'ROUND THE GLOBE

SELECTED RECIPES FROM ARTISTS AND FRIENDS OF SAN DIEGO'S AWARD WINNING OLD GLOBE THEATRE

By the Globe Guilders
San Diego, California

OLD GLOBE THEATRE
SIMON EDISON CENTRE FOR THE PERFORMING ARTS

Proceeds from the sale of Cooks 'Round the Globe support the
Old Globe Theatre, San Diego, California.

For additional copies of Cooks 'Round the Globe write:
Cooks 'Round the Globe
Post Office Box 2171
San Diego, California 92112

ISBN: 0-9620130-0-5
Library of Congress Catalog Card Number: 88-81088
Printed in the United States of America

CONTENTS

Cooks 'Round the Globe is published by Globe Guilders, auxiliary of the Old Globe Theatre, Simon Edison Centre for the Performing Arts, San Diego, California.

Cookbook Committee Members

Chairman
Marje Spear

Policy Committee
Katherine Black
Anne Chapman
Jill Holmes
Robin Renert
Lenora Witt

Recipe Staff
Janice Alessandra
Laurie Blackington
Joyce Brower
Marjoree Howard
Barbara Iredale
Billie Lea McKnight
Kathy Newton
Curtis Parker
Sheila Parker
Joe Payson
Carol Sigelman
Carol Stark
Harvey Von Wantoch
Jordine Von Wantoch
Ginny Whitby

Editor
Lois Dechant

Assistant Editor
Lanie Fouch

Editorial Staff
Barney De Selm
Bonnie De Selm
Patricia Eu
Beulah Giovanazzi
Dolly Poet
Ann Pund
Hazel Tow
Kristin Tow
Dixie Unruh
Fran Viertel

Book Design & Production
Suzan Peterson
Peterson Design Studio, Inc.

Cover Illustration
Ralph L. Adloff, M.F.A.

Printing
The Parker Co.
Penguin Printing/Graphics

Typesetting
Typecast Graphics

CRAIG NOEL
Executive Director, Old Globe Theatre

San Diegans have savored his theatrical treats
for more than half a century.

A PINCH OF DIRECTION

I have always been struck with the similarity between preparing a play for the public and preparing a meal. No kidding. When you are thinking about a dinner party, you decide first what you will prepare *(Selecting the Play)* and then spend the better part of one or two days shopping for those ingredients that are perfect for your table *(Audition and Casting)*. There are some dishes you can prepare a day or so ahead, and others that must be done right up to the time your guests arrive and even later *(Rehearsal and Technical Rehearsal)*.

Then you open! It's true, the applause you hear around you as everyone digs in may finally receive different reviews about 2 the next morning, but you must remember that critics, like rich sauces, tend to repeat themselves.

The Globe family is just that—men and women who have been drawn together over many, many years by their love of theatre and their true enjoyment of each other. It's no surprise, then, that the fare that follows should be elegant, in exquisite taste, and full of dramatic surprises. I'm also thrilled to report that the volume covers a considerable range of culinary thrills—picnics to Presidential Banquets.

There are cookbooks you simply read for enjoyment, and others that you actually use. If you knew this group like *I* know this group, you would start at page one and cook your way merrily through the entire lot. Which is just exactly what I intend to do.

Jack O'Brien
Artistic Director
The Old Globe Theatre
Simon Edison Centre for the Performing Arts

HISTORY OF THE
OLD GLOBE THEATRE

The history of San Diego's Old Globe Theatre reflects five decades of inspiration and dedication that have overcome multiple disasters including a near foreclosure, a World War and two destructive fires. The Old Globe today emerges as the longest-established professional theatre in California and the recipient of the 1984 Special Tony Award for "notable past achievements and continuing dedication to theatre artistry."

The name Old Globe applies to the three theatres located at the Simon Edison Centre for the Performing Arts in Balboa Park: the 581-seat Old Globe Theatre, the 225-seat Cassius Carter Centre Stage and the 612-seat outdoor Lowell Davies Festival Theatre. The Globe's status as the oldest professional theatre in the United States with an ongoing commitment to Shakespeare's plays is accorded international recognition. Queen Elizabeth II of England honored the Globe with a 1983 visit and unveiled the bronze Shakespeare sculpture in the theatre lobby.

San Diego's Globe originated as part of the 1935 California Pacific International Exposition when a company of actors gave 55 minute versions of Shakespeare's plays in a re-creation of London's original open air Globe Theatre. When the Exposition closed, the theatre and its auxiliary buildings (the Falstaff Tavern and Ye Olde Gift Shoppe) were sold to a demolition company for $400. Aroused citizens saved the Globe from the wreckers and joined forces under the banner of the San Diego Community Theatre to raise $10,000, a significant sum in Depression days, to renovate the buildings into permanent structures meeting city codes.

On December 2, 1937, the remodeled Old Globe Theatre opened with a production of John Van Druten's "The Distaff Side." In the cast was a young actor named Craig Noel whose career as a director and actor has been devoted to the Globe since that time. World War II brought a halt to Globe activities with the Navy commandeering all buildings in Balboa Park except the Zoo.

Theatre operations resumed in 1947 with director Noel staging William Saroyan's "The Time of Your Life." From 1949-1953 the Globe joined with San Diego State University to present summer Shakespeare productions. In 1954 the San Diego National Shakespeare Festival, solely produced by the Globe, was launched.

A long envisioned second theatre became a reality in 1969 when Cassius Carter Centre Stage replaced Falstaff Tavern as the site for arena productions. The Globe initiated its community outreach programs including Globe Educational Tours, Community Acting Workshops and the Play Discovery Programs.

On March 8, 1978, an arsonist completely destroyed the 43-year-old landmark Old Globe Theatre. Fortunately, other buildings in the complex were spared. The board of directors unanimously vowed to rebuild the theatre, but the immediate need was for a space to produce that summer's San Diego National Shakespeare Festival. The summer opened as scheduled, a mere 100 days following the fire, on a new Festival Stage located in a wooded canyon adjacent to the ruins.

News of the fire elicited an outpouring of financial, personal and moral support from throughout the nation. Most significant was the donation made by Helen Edison in honor of her late husband. In June 1979 the three-theatre complex was named the Simon Edison Centre for the Performing Arts.

In January 1981, while the new theatre was being built, the board of directors established an artistic/administrative triumvirate to lead the complex. Craig Noel was named executive producer. Nationally acclaimed director Jack O'Brien, who had returned to stage eight productions following his 1969 Old Globe Theatre directorial debut, was named artistic director. Thomas Hall, whose credentials carry extensive administrative and production experience, was named managing director.

On January 14, 1982, following a 20-month construction period, a state-of-the-art $6.5 million Old Globe Theatre opened with Noel staging "As You Like It." Events that focused national attention on the new theatre included a live telecast of Thornton Wilder's "The Skin of Our Teeth" for PBS in January 1983 and a critically acclaimed production of Cole Porter's "Kiss Me, Kate" in January 1984.

But the year that had begun so precipitously had its dark side when, on October 29, 1984, arson destroyed the outdoor Festival Stage. Again, the board of directors met in emergency session and vowed to rebuild in time for the summer Festival season. On June 7, 1985, "A Midsummer Night's Dream" opened the new Lowell Davies Festival Theatre named in honor of the long time president of the Old Globe board of directors.

The Globe also celebrated its 50th Jubilee Year during 1985 by establishing the largest subscriber base of any not-for-profit theatre in the nation with more than 50,000 combined winter and summer season subscriptions. Always seeking broader horizons, the Globe is earning new plaudits for producing world premieres that have gone on to become Broadway successes. But let Shakespeare have the last word:

Doubt not but success
Will fashion the event in better shape
Than I can lay it down in likelihood.
MUCH ADO ABOUT NOTHING

APPETIZERS

Helena Carroll, Deborah May, Janie Sell in *Fallen Angels*

CURRY CHEESE DIP

Servings
40-50
Planning
Can make 2
days ahead
Preparing
15 minutes

8 ounces cream cheese,
  softened
½ cup sour cream
1½ tablespoons curry powder

1 tablespoon lemon juice
¼ teaspoon salt, optional
¾ cup chutney, finely
  chopped

Combine cream cheese and sour cream, beating until smooth. Add
curry powder, lemon juice, salt and chutney. Mix well and chill.
Serve either as a dip or as a spread for crackers.

Comment: Goes well with seafood or fruit.

ROASTED GARLIC WITH CHÈVRE

Servings
4
Planning
Serve
immediately
Preparing
10 minutes
Baking
30 minutes

4 whole heads garlic
4 sprigs fresh thyme
4 2-ounce whole chèvre
  (white cheese) rounds

Freshly ground pepper,
  to taste
Baguette loaf, heated and
  sliced

Preheat oven to 350°

Cut each garlic head in half; insert thyme sprig between cut
surfaces. Press halves back together and wrap in foil. Bake 30
minutes.

To serve, place each cheese on small plate with one head garlic
(remove foil); grind pepper over cheese. To eat, squeeze garlic
cloves onto bread sections and spread with cheese.

*Comment: A garlic lover's delight discovered at a small country
inn in France. Serve with cornichons and a robust red wine.*

SMOKY SALMON BALL

Servings
8-10
Planning
Can make
24 hours
ahead
Preparing
20 minutes
Chilling
3-4 hours
Storing
Can freeze
dill version

1 16-ounce can red salmon, drained, skin and bones removed
1 8-ounce package cream cheese, softened
1 teaspoon prepared horseradish
1 tablespoon lemon juice
¼ teaspoon liquid smoke (or more, to taste)
2 teaspoons finely chopped green onions
½ cup finely chopped pecans
3 tablespoons chopped parsley

Combine salmon, cream cheese, horseradish, lemon juice, liquid smoke and onion. Blend well and roll into a ball. Cover and chill. Roll salmon ball in mixture of pecans and parsley.

SMOKY SALMON BALL WITH DILL

Prepare as for Smoky Salmon Ball. Add 1 teaspoon dill, omit horseradish, decrease lemon juice to 1 teaspoon, increase liquid smoke to 1½ teaspoons (or to taste) and substitute ½ teaspoon onion salt for chopped green onions.

The pleasant'st angling is to see the fish
Cut with her golden oars the silver stream,
And greedily devour the treacherous bait.
MUCH ADO ABOUT NOTHING

OLIVE APPETIZERS

Servings
10-12
Planning
Can make
ahead
Preparing
30 minutes
Chilling
4-6 hours
Storing
Can freeze

10-12 colossal-size stuffed
olives, drained
1 8-ounce package cream
cheese, softened

GARNISHES
½-¾ cup finely chopped
almonds
½ cup chopped parsley
½ cup crisp cooked bacon,
crumbled

Pat olives dry with paper towel. In palm of hand, place ball of cream cheese; form cheese around olive, pinching and smoothing until covered. Roll in choice of garnishes. Chill well. (Can be frozen at this point.) To serve, cut in halves or thirds crosswise and lay flat on plate.

Comment: Green and red colors makes this especially attractive for a Christmas party.

CLAM DIP IN BREAD LOAF

Servings
10-12
Preparing
20-25
minutes
Baking
3 hours

2 8-ounce packages cream
cheese, softened
3 6½-ounce cans minced
clams (drain 2)
2 teaspoons Worcestershire
sauce

2 teaspoons lemon juice
2 teaspoons chopped green
onions
6 drops hot pepper sauce
1 round loaf of bread (uncut)

Preheat oven to 250°

Beat cream cheese until smooth. Add drained clams, clams with juice, Worcestershire, lemon juice, green onions and hot pepper sauce; mix well. Slice top off loaf (reserve) and scoop out bread, leaving ½-1 inch shell. Cube bread and reserve. Fill loaf with clam mixture and return top to loaf. Wrap in foil and bake 3 hours.

Comment: Serve with bread cubes and an assortment of crudites and crackers.

SHRIMP BUTTER

Servings
8-12
Planning
Must make
ahead
Preparing
20 minutes
Chilling
3-24 hours

¾ cup butter, softened
1 8-ounce package cream
cheese, softened
4 tablespoons mayonnaise
1 tablespoon minced onion
1 tablespoon lemon juice
3 dashes hot pepper sauce
Salt to taste

12-16 ounces cooked shrimp,
finely chopped

GARNISHES
Whole shrimp
Lemon slices
Parsley

Utensil: small loaf pan or mold, lined with plastic wrap or
waxed paper

Combine butter, cream cheese, mayonnaise, onion, lemon juice, hot
pepper sauce and salt; beat until smooth. Fold in chopped shrimp.
Place mixture in mold and chill at least 3 hours. To serve, remove
from mold and garnish.

Comment: Serve with a variety of fancy crackers or crisp breads.

*I knew a wench married in an afternoon as she went
to the garden for parsley to stuff a rabbit; and so
may you.*

THE TAMING OF THE SHREW

BALBOA CHEESE SPREAD

Servings
12
Planning
Must make
ahead
Preparing
20 minutes
Storing
3-4 days

3 8-ounce packages
  Neufchâtel cream cheese,
  softened
1 8-ounce can unsweetened
  crushed pineapple, partially
  drained

2 tablespoons chopped fresh
  green onion
1 small green pepper, seeded
  and chopped
1 tablespoon seasoned salt
1 cup chopped pecans

In large bowl combine cream cheese, pineapple, green onion, green pepper, salt and pecans. Chill to mellow flavors. Serve with crisp crackers.

Comment: The flavors take on a new dimension, making the ingredients a delightful mystery.

ARTICHOKE SPREAD

Servings
8-12
Planning
Can
assemble
24 hours
ahead
Preparing
15 minutes
Baking
20-30
minutes

1 14-ounce can water-packed
  artichoke hearts, drained,
  chopped
1 cup mayonnaise
¾ cup grated Parmesan
  cheese

1 teaspoon dill (or ½
  teaspoon basil or oregano)
1 clove garlic, crushed
Dash hot pepper sauce

Utensil: 1-quart baking dish
Preheat oven to 325°

Combine artichokes, mayonnaise, Parmesan cheese (reserve 1 tablespoon for garnish), dill, garlic and hot pepper sauce; mix well. Place in dish and sprinkle with reserved Parmesan. (Can refrigerate 24 hours at this point.) Bake 20-30 minutes or until bubbly. Serve hot or cold with crackers. (Recipe may be doubled.)

Comment: Tasters seldom identify artichoke as the main ingredient—the flavor is a surprise.

BEA'S MARINATED ANTIPASTO

Servings
6
Planning
Must make
ahead
Preparing
30 minutes

MARINADE
⅓ cup wine vinegar
⅓ cup white vinegar
⅔ cup oil
¼ cup chopped onion
1 teaspoon salt
1 teaspoon sugar
1 teaspoon basil
1 teaspoon oregano
¼ teaspoon pepper

1½ pounds mushrooms,
   cleaned and sliced
1 14-ounce can artichoke
   hearts, drained
1 7¼-ounce can baby
   carrots, drained
1 cup pitted black olives,
   drained

Marinade: Combine wine vinegar, white vinegar, oil, onion, salt, sugar, basil, oregano and pepper; bring to a boil over medium heat, stirring occasionally. Remove from heat and cool 10 minutes.

In large bowl layer vegetables in this order: mushrooms, artichoke hearts, carrots and olives. Add cooled marinade. Cover and chill several hours or overnight. Toss gently before serving.

Comment: Tasty and attractive.

I warrant there's vinegar and pepper in it.
                                          TWELFTH NIGHT

SPINACH BALLS

2 10-ounce packages frozen
  chopped spinach, cooked
  and squeezed dry
2 cups herb-seasoned bread
  stuffing mix
1 large onion, chopped
4 eggs, beaten

¾ cup butter, melted
½ cup grated Parmesan
  cheese
3 cloves garlic, crushed
¼ teaspoon thyme
¼ teaspoon ground pepper

Utensil: cookie sheet, coated with non-stick spray
Preheat oven to 350°

In large mixing bowl combine spinach, stuffing mix, onion, eggs,
butter, cheese, garlic, thyme and black pepper. Mix well and chill
2 hours. Shape into bite-size balls. (Can be prepared ahead to this
point and refrigerated or frozen.) Bake 25 minutes and serve
immediately.

Comment: Popeye would approve.

Yield
25-30
Planning
Can be
prepared
ahead
Preparing
30 minutes
Baking
25 minutes
Chilling
2 hours
Storing
Unbaked up
to 1 week
or frozen
up to 1½
months

I know a bank where the wild thyme blows,
Where oxlips and the nodding violet grows,
Quite over-canopied with lusty woodbine,
With sweet musk-roses and with eglantine.
                       A MIDSUMMER NIGHT'S DREAM

CRAB WEDGES

Servings
32
Planning
Ready for
oven up to
6 hours
ahead
Preparing
10 minutes
Baking
10-12
minutes

1 8-ounce package cream
  cheese, softened
¼ teaspoon dry mustard
1 tablespoon milk
2-4 dashes cayenne pepper
1 6-ounce can crab meat,
  drained and flaked

2 tablespoons minced chives
2 tablespoons chopped
  almonds
½ teaspoon horseradish
4 English muffins, split in half
  and buttered
Paprika for garnish

Utensil: cookie sheet
Preheat oven to 400°

Beat cheese until fluffy. Mix mustard with milk and add to cheese.
Combine cheese mixture with pepper, crab meat, chives, almonds
and horseradish. Spread mixture on muffins and garnish with
paprika. (Can be prepared ahead to this point and refrigerated.)
To serve, bake 10-12 minutes until lightly browned and cut each
piece into 4 wedges.

MARINATED SHRIMP

Servings
12-18
Planning
Must make
day ahead
Preparing
30 minutes
Marinating
24 hours

2½-3 pounds large shrimp,
  shelled, cleaned and cooked
4 medium onions, cut in
  ¼-inch rings
8-16 bay leaves, depending
  on size
1 clove garlic, peeled

MARINADE
2 tablespoons lemon juice
4 cups tomato juice
½ cup French dressing
¾ cup catsup
2 tablespoons sugar
¼ teaspoon hot pepper sauce

For marinade: Combine lemon juice, tomato juice, French
dressing, catsup, sugar and hot pepper sauce.

In large bowl layer shrimp, onion rings and bay leaves; repeat
layers. Pour marinade over shrimp and place garlic in center.
Cover and refrigerate 24 hours; remove garlic and drain slightly
before serving. (Recipe can be halved or doubled.)

BROOKS' CRAB

Servings
8
Planning
Can
assemble
ahead
Preparing
10 minutes
Baking
15 minutes

2 cups crab meat
1 cup white sauce (recipe
  follows)
1 cup mayonnaise
2 green onions, thinly sliced
⅔ cup seasoned bread
  crumbs
2 tablespoons dry mustard
1 teaspoon white wine
  Worcestershire sauce

1½ teaspoons sherry
1 cup shredded Monterey
  Jack cheese

GARNISH
Paprika
Chopped parsley

Utensils: 8 baking shells
Preheat oven to 350°

Mix crab with white sauce and mayonnaise. Add green onions,
bread crumbs, mustard, Worcestershire sauce and sherry; mix
thoroughly. Mixture should be creamy but not runny. Divide into
shells; sprinkle with cheese. Bake 15 minutes; garnish with
paprika and parsley.

*Comment: Flavors blend to make a delectable appetizer. This could
also serve 4 as a luncheon entrée.*

WHITE SAUCE

2 tablespoons butter
2 tablespoons flour
¼ teaspoon salt

⅛ teaspoon white pepper
1 cup milk

Melt butter over low heat. Blend in flour, salt and pepper; stir
until mixture is smooth. Gradually stir in milk; cook, stirring
constantly, until thickened and smooth.

MEATBALLS CABRILLO

Servings
10
Planning
Can make
meatballs
ahead
Preparing
30 minutes
Frying or
baking
20-30
minutes

2 pounds ground beef
2 eggs, beaten
¾ cup Italian seasoned bread
   crumbs
2 small onions, chopped
½ teaspoon garlic salt

Water chestnut slices,
   optional
Oil for browning, optional
1 18-ounce jar grape jelly
2 12-ounce bottles chili sauce

Utensils: deep skillet or edged baking sheet, chafing dish

Mix beef, eggs, bread crumbs, onions and garlic salt; form into
balls. (For extra crunch, enclose a water chestnut slice in each
meatball.) Brown in skillet or bake in 350° oven 20-30 minutes
until brown. (Meatballs may be refrigerated at this point 1-2 days.)
When ready to serve, melt grape jelly and chili sauce in saucepan
over medium heat. Place sauce and meatballs in chafing dish over
low flame.

Comment: The sauce gives a new definition to "sweet and sour."

Go to, go to; you are a saucy boy.

ROMEO AND JULIET

JACK O'BRIEN & MARSHA MASON

COCKTAIL OPULENCE

Cash in *all* your liquid assets, and then...

Purée in Cuisinart:

1¾ pounds of smoked Nova Salmon
¼ pound melted butter

Add:

Juice of 1 lemon (or more to taste)
3 tablespoons chopped chives
Fresh ground white pepper
¼ pint whipping cream

Later on add (but not to Cuisinart):

4 ounces black caviar

Blend to a smooth paste. Put ½ mixture into a small terrine.
Spread the top with 4 ounces black caviar and cover with the
remaining mixture. Refrigerate overnight, or 'til needed. Turn out
carefully on a plate and serve with dark thin bread.

JACK O'BRIEN, Artistic Director
Old Globe Theatre since 1981. Nationally known for directing broad array of theatre, classical to
contemporary, including world premieres, opera, television and on Broadway.

MARSHA MASON
Four-time Academy Award nominee. Starring roles on Broadway, off-Broadway, numerous regional
theatres as well as film. Viola in "Twelfth Night" at Globe.

GÂTEAU DES QUATRE FROMAGES

Servings
16
Planning
Can make 3
days ahead
Preparing
30 minutes
Chilling
3 hours

4 ounces ripe Brie cheese
   with rind
4 ounces Gruyère or Swiss
   cheese, grated
4 ounces blue cheese
3 8-ounce packages cream
   cheese, softened

2 tablespoons sour cream
6-8 ounces pecans, chopped
Red and green apple slices,
   dipped in lemon and water
Minced parsley
Finely chopped pecans, for
   garnish

Utensil: 9½-inch quiche pan or 9-inch spring form pan, lined with foil

In large bowl mix Brie, Gruyère and blue cheeses with 2 packages cream cheese until smooth. In medium bowl blend remaining package cream cheese with 2 tablespoons sour cream. Spread sour cream mixture in bottom of pan and sprinkle with chopped pecans; add 4-cheese mixture and spread evenly. Cover with plastic wrap and refrigerate at least 3 hours.

When ready to serve, invert pan onto serving plate and peel off foil. Garnish with minced parsley, chopped pecans and apple slices. Serve with crackers.

Comment: Watch and see how this "cheesecake" performs its disappearing act. Amazing!

Why, my cheese, my digestion, why hast thou not served thyself in to my table so many meals?
                                                TROILUS AND CRESSIDA

CAVIAR SPREAD

Servings
12
Planning
Must make
ahead
Preparing
15 minutes
Chilling
Minimum 2
hours

1 8-ounce package cream
cheese
2 ounces black lumpfish
caviar
2 green onions, minced

2 hard-cooked egg yolks,
finely chopped
Lemon or lime wedges
Crackers

Place cream cheese block on plate and coat with onion, pressing
lightly to adhere. Cover onion with caviar, again pressing lightly,
and sprinkle with egg yolks. Cover and refrigerate at least 2 hours.
Serve with crackers and lemon or lime wedges to squeeze over
caviar.

Comment: You thought you didn't like caviar? Try this!

CAVIAR MOUSSE

Servings
12
generously
Planning
Make 2-3
days ahead
Preparing
30 minutes
Chilling
At least 4
hours

¼ pound unsalted butter,
melted
2 7-ounce cans water-packed
white tuna, drained
1 teaspoon chopped green
onion tops
1 6-ounce jar herring tidbits
in wine, drained

1 4-ounce jar black caviar,
divided
¼ teaspoon garlic powder
½ teaspoon sugar
1 4-ounce jar red caviar

Rye bread rounds

Utensils: blender, 1-pint mold or small bread pan

In blender gradually process butter with tuna to paste consistency.
Add onion, herring, 1 heaping teaspoon black caviar, garlic
powder and sugar; blend until smooth. Pack into mold; chill.
Unmold when ready to serve; coat with remaining black caviar and
top with red caviar. Serve with rye bread rounds.

Comment: Delicious.

ALMOND-STUFFED MUSHROOMS

Servings
6
Planning
Can make
ahead
Preparing
30 minutes
Baking
10 minutes

1 pound large mushrooms,
  cleaned
4 tablespoons butter, divided
1 tablespoon lemon juice
½ teaspoon seasoned salt

1 tablespoon grated onion
4 tablespoons minced parsley
2 tablespoons mayonnaise
½ cup chopped toasted
  almonds

Utensils: large skillet, non-stick baking sheet
Preheat oven to 350°

Remove stems from mushrooms; chop and set aside. Sauté
mushrooms lightly in 2 tablespoons butter and lemon juice; remove
mushrooms and place, cavity side up, on baking sheet. Add
remaining butter and sauté stems; add salt, onion, parsley,
mayonnaise and almonds. Fill caps with mixture and chill
(overnight if desired). To serve, bake 10 minutes.

Comment: A happy hour favorite.

MARINATED MUSHROOMS

Yield
25-30
pieces
Planning
Can make
1-2 days
ahead
Preparing
15 minutes
Cooking
3 minutes
Marinating
6 hours or
overnight

1 pound small mushrooms,
  cleaned
Water
1 bunch green onions,
  including tops, chopped

2 cloves garlic, minced
1 8-ounce bottle Italian salad
  dressing

Utensil: large saucepan

Bring water to boil. Add mushrooms and bring back to rolling boil.
Immediately take pan off heat and drain. Mix mushrooms with
onions, garlic and dressing. Refrigerate until well chilled.

*Comment: Excellent as cocktail or buffet fare, or as a tasty
addition to a green salad.*

OLD ENGLISH STUFFED MUSHROOMS

¾ pound medium mushrooms, cleaned
7 tablespoons oil, divided
1 tablespoon finely chopped onion
⅓ cup finely chopped Italian cotto salami

⅓ cup sharp Cheddar cheese spread
1 tablespoon catsup
½ cup soft buttered bread crumbs

Yield
15-20
Planning
Can assemble ahead
Preparing
30 minutes
Baking
10 minutes

Utensils: skillet, greased cookie sheet
Preheat oven to 425°

Remove mushroom stems and mince. Brush mushroom caps with 6 tablespoons oil and place, cavity side up, on cookie sheet. In skillet heat remaining oil and add ⅓ cup mushroom stems, onion and salami; sauté until onion is transparent. Add cheese and catsup; mix well. Mound mixture in mushroom caps and top with bread crumbs. Bake 10 minutes and serve immediately.

Comment: Delectable and delicious.

Appetite, an universal wolf...
TROILUS AND CRESSIDA

MANGO DAIQUIRIS DE MULEGÉ

Servings
4
Planning
Serve
immediately
Preparing
3-5 minutes

3-4 cups ice cubes
3 tablespoons powdered
  sugar
Juice of 2 large limes

2 canned mangoes plus
  ¼ cup syrup
4 jiggers white rum
Mint sprigs for garnish

Utensil: blender

In covered container place ice cubes, powdered sugar, lime juice, mangoes, syrup and rum; blend to sherbet consistency. Serve in chilled glasses and garnish with mint.

Comment: A hot weather triumph.

SANGRITA

Yield
1¼ quarts
Planning
Can make
ahead
Preparing
15 minutes
Chilling
2-4 hours

1 32-ounce can tomato juice
Juice of 3 oranges
Juice of 2 limes
1 small onion, chopped
1 teaspoon sugar

¼ teaspoon hot chili powder
  (or ¼ teaspoon hot pepper
  sauce)*
Salt and pepper to taste
Lime slices for garnish
Tequila, optional

Utensils: blender, serving bowl

Combine tomato, orange and lime juices, chopped onion, sugar, chili powder, salt and pepper. Blend until smooth. Chill well.

When ready to serve, float lime slices in bowl. A shot of tequila is a traditional accompaniment.

*Comment: If brave enough, omit chili powder (or hot pepper sauce) and add 4 fresh hot chiles. Serve in bowl that won't melt!

SOUPS

photo by Robert Burroughs

Associate Artist Sada Thompson and Joan Snyder in *Catsplay*

BROCCOLI CHEESE CHOWDER

Servings
8-10
Preparing
30 minutes
Cooking
20 minutes

2 pounds fresh broccoli
3 cups chicken broth
3 cups milk
1 cup chopped cooked ham
2 teaspoons salt

¼ teaspoon pepper
1 cup light cream
½ pound Swiss cheese,
    grated
½ cup butter

Utensil: large kettle with cover

Prepare broccoli and cook 10 minutes, covered, in 1 cup chicken broth. Remove broccoli from broth; cool and chop coarsely. Add remaining broth, milk, ham, salt and pepper to hot broth in kettle. Bring to boil over medium heat, stirring constantly; add cream, cheese, butter and chopped broccoli. Heat to serving temperature but do not boil.

CREAM OF CHICKEN & MUSHROOM SOUP

Servings
4-6
Planning
Can make
ahead
Preparing
30 minutes
Cooking
20 minutes

3 tablespoons butter
¼ cup finely chopped onion
1 pound mushrooms, sliced
⅓ cup flour
4 cups chicken broth
1½ cups half-and-half

½ cup dry white wine
½ teaspoon hot pepper sauce
2½ cups diced cooked chicken
¼ teaspoon tarragon
Chopped parsley for garnish

Utensil: large kettle

Melt butter over medium heat. Add onion and cook until tender; add mushrooms and cook 10 minutes. Blend in flour and cook 1 minute. Stir in chicken broth, half-and-half and wine. Cook, stirring constantly, over medium heat until mixture thickens and comes to a boil. Add pepper sauce, chicken and tarragon. Simmer uncovered 20 minutes. Garnish with parsley.

Comment: Sada Thompson suggests this heartwarming soup for a chilly evening.

HAM & SPLIT PEA SOUP

Servings
8
Planning
Make broth
day ahead
Preparing
Day 1: 30
minutes;
Day 2: 30
minutes
Cooking
Day 1:
3½-4
hours; Day
2: 1 hour

FIRST DAY
3-4 pound picnic ham
Water
1 bay leaf
1 onion, quartered
8 peppercorns

½ cup split peas
4 cups water

SECOND DAY
Reserved ham broth
3 cups water
Drained, soaked peas
1 onion, chopped
1 tablespoon oil
1 carrot, peeled and diced
1 stalk celery, diced
1 potato, peeled and diced
1 large dry red pepper pod
Diced ham

Utensil: large stock pot

First day: Cover ham with water; add bay leaf, onion and peppercorns. Cook over medium heat 3½-4 hours until tender. Remove ham from broth. Strain broth and refrigerate overnight. Remove fat from ham. Dice ham; reserve. Soak split peas in water overnight.

Second day: Skim fat from broth. Drain peas. Sauté onion in oil until transparent. Add to ham broth: water, peas, onion, carrot, celery, potato and red pepper. Bring to boil; lower temperature, cover and simmer 1 hour or until tender, stirring occasionally. When ready to serve, remove pepper and add ham; heat to serving temperature.

Comment: Comforting and substantial.

TWO-DAY BEEF SOUP

Servings
6
Planning
Must make
broth day
ahead
Preparing
Day 1:
1 hour;
Day 2:
20 minutes
Cooking
Day 1:
2 hours;
Day 2:
20 minutes
Storing
Refrigerate
Chilling
Overnight

FIRST DAY
3½ pounds meaty beef
    shanks
2 stalks celery with leaves,
    chopped
1 onion, chopped
1 bay leaf
1 teaspoon basil leaves
1 quart water
1 cup sauterne or other dry
    white wine
2 teaspoons salt

SECOND DAY
1½ cups sliced celery
1 onion, sliced
1 cup sauterne or other dry
    white wine
1 teaspoon salt
1 cup sliced carrots
2 16-ounce cans tomatoes
1 15-ounce can white kidney
    beans
1 8-ounce can garbanzo beans

Utensil: large soup kettle with cover

On first day combine meat, celery, onion, bay leaf, basil, water, wine and salt; cover and simmer 2 hours. Cool. Remove fat, bones and gristle from meat; cut meat into bite-size pieces. Strain broth to remove vegetables and bay leaf; return meat to broth, chill overnight.

On second day remove and discard surface fat; reheat broth with meat. Add celery, onion, wine, salt, carrots, tomatoes, kidney beans and garbanzo beans. Simmer 20 minutes and serve.

Comment: This hearty soup needs only a loaf of fresh whole-wheat bread, a green salad and a good red wine to make a memorable meal.

Double, double toil and trouble;
Fire burn, and cauldron bubble.
MACBETH

BLACK BEAN SOUP

Servings
6
Planning
Can make
2-3 days
ahead
Preparing
25 minutes
Cooking
2-2¼ hours

1 pound black beans (about
  2½ cups)
1-2 smoked ham hocks
1 bay leaf
5 whole cloves
2 cloves garlic, mashed
1 large onion, sliced
2 celery stalk tops, coarsely
  chopped
1 carrot, coarsely chopped

1 small dried red pepper,
  seeds removed
1 14½-ounce can beef broth
4-5 cups water
½ cup sherry
Salt and pepper to taste
Plain yogurt or sour cream,
  optional
Fresh cilantro or parsley
  sprigs, optional

Utensil: large soup kettle

Sort through dry beans; rinse well and drain. Cover beans with
water in a large kettle and bring to a boil; boil for 5 minutes, then
turn off heat and let soak 1 hour. Drain and return to kettle.

Add ham hocks, bay leaf, cloves, garlic, onion, celery tops, carrot,
dried red pepper, broth and water. Bring mixture to boil, reduce
heat and simmer until beans are tender, 1½-2 hours.

Remove ham hocks, dried red pepper, cloves and bay leaf. Prepare
ham bits to add to soup later by discarding skin, bones and fat.
Puree bean-vegetable mixture in food mill or food processor and
place mixture in large sauce pan. Add sherry, salt and pepper.
Bring to boil, reduce heat, add ham bits and simmer gently 15
minutes.

Serve topped with dollop of yogurt or sour cream and sprigs of
cilantro or parsley.

*Comment: Smooth and rich, this soup is an ideal candidate for a
one-dish Sunday supper.*

POTAGE PERRIGORDINI

Servings
8
Planning
Can make
day ahead
Preparing
10-15
minutes
Cooking
30 minutes

1 cup chopped onion
¼ cup unsalted butter
2 teaspoons finely chopped
  parsley
½ teaspoon ground
  cardamom
½ teaspoon sugar
3 10-ounce packages frozen
  peas

2 tablespoons flour
4 cups chicken broth
1 10-ounce package frozen
  chopped spinach, thawed
½ cup diced ham
¼ cup brandy
Croutons, optional

Utensil: large Dutch oven

Sauté onion in butter until limp; add parsley, cardamom, sugar
and peas. Cover and cook slowly until peas are quite soft; remove
from heat. Combine flour with small amount chicken broth; add to
mixture with remainder broth. Return to heat and stir constantly
until mixture reaches boiling point. Add spinach and continue
cooking over medium heat, about 5 minutes. Meanwhile, soak ham
in brandy. When ready to serve, add ham and top with croutons, if
desired.

Comment: This excellent soup comes from an old family recipe.

*An you'll come to supper to-night, you may; an you
will not, come when you are next prepared for.*
                                                    OTHELLO

TRADITIONAL FRENCH ONION SOUP

Servings
8
Planning
Can make
ahead
Preparing
45 minutes
Cooking
Stock 3½
hours; soup
30 minutes
Broiling
3 minutes

STOCK
3 pounds beef short ribs
1 veal knuckle
4 chicken wings
2 chicken feet
1 large onion, sliced
2 leeks, sliced
2 stalks celery including
    leaves, sliced
1 carrot, sliced
4 sprigs parsley
1 tablespoon chopped turnip
1 small bay leaf
1 tablespoon salt
6 peppercorns
Pinch of thyme
3 quarts water

SOUP
5 large Bermuda onions,
    sliced in rings
3 tablespoons butter or
    margarine
2 teaspoons flour
2 quarts soup stock
2 teaspoons salt
¼ teaspoon pepper
8 1-inch slices French bread,
    toasted
8 tablespoons grated Gruyère
    cheese
8 tablespoons grated
    Parmesan cheese

Utensils: large stock pot, oven-proof soup bowls
Preheat broiler

Stock: In stock pot add short ribs, veal knuckle, chicken wings
and feet, onion, leeks, celery, carrot, parsley, turnip, bay leaf, salt,
peppercorns, thyme and water. Cover, bring to slow boil and
simmer 3½ hours; remove surface foam after ½ hour. Strain, chill
and reserve.

Soup: Cut onion rings in half. Melt butter in stock pot; add onions
and sauté, covered, until transparent. Sprinkle flour over onions
and cook 1 minute, stirring constantly. Remove fat from reserved
stock. Pour stock over onions; add salt and pepper. Cover and
simmer ½ hour. Pour into 8 oven-proof soup bowls. Top toast
slices with 1 tablespoon each Gruyère and Parmesan. Float slices
in soup bowls. Place under broiler 3 minutes or until cheeses
brown.

Comment: This will transport you to Paris.

SADA THOMPSON

KABISSUPPE (SWISS COUNTRY CABBAGE & RICE SOUP)

3 tablespoons butter or
   margarine
4-5 cups shredded cabbage
1 large onion, thinly sliced
4 14½-ounce cans chicken
   broth
1 teaspoon salt

⅛ teaspoon freshly ground
   pepper
⅛ teaspoon ground nutmeg
½ cup long grain rice
1 cup shredded Swiss or
   Gruyère cheese

Melt butter in 4-quart kettle. Rinse cabbage in cold water and drain, leaving a little water clinging. Add cabbage and onion to kettle. Cover and cook over medium heat, stirring often, until cabbage is golden and almost tender, about 10 minutes.

Add broth, salt, pepper and nutmeg; simmer, covered, 10 minutes. Add rice; continue simmering, covered, 15-20 minutes, or until rice is tender. Stir frequently to keep rice grains separated. Taste and add more salt and pepper if necessary. Serve in deep soup plates; pass cheese to sprinkle. Makes 6 servings.

SADA THOMPSON, Associate Artist of the Globe
Winner of Tony, Emmy and Obie awards for starring roles on Broadway, television and film. Mrs. Antrobus in Globe's nationally televised production "The Skin of Our Teeth."

SPANISH SAUSAGE & LENTIL SOUP

Servings
8-10
Planning
Can make
ahead
Preparing
40 minutes
Cooking
2 hours
Storing
Can freeze

2 tablespoons olive oil
1 pound sweet Italian
   sausage links
7 ounces smoked ham
2 large onions, finely chopped
1 large green bell pepper,
   finely chopped
1 large carrot, finely chopped
2 cloves garlic, minced
1 bay leaf
¾ teaspoon fresh thyme

½ teaspoon ground cumin
8 cups chicken stock (rich
   homemade preferred)
1 16-ounce can peeled
   tomatoes
1¼ cups dried lentils, rinsed
   and sorted
12 large spinach leaves,
   washed, trimmed, shredded

Utensil: 6-8 quart stock pot with lid

Heat oil. Add sausage and cook until fat is rendered; remove
sausage and drain all but 2 tablespoons drippings. Add ham,
onions, pepper and carrot; cook covered 15 minutes, stirring
occasionally. Add garlic, bay leaf, thyme and cumin; cover and
cook 5 minutes. Cut sausage into thin slices and return to pot.
Add stock, tomatoes and lentils. Reduce heat to low; cover and
simmer gently 2 hours until lentils dissolve. (Soup can be prepared
ahead at this point and refrigerated for 3 days or frozen up to 3
months.)

When ready to serve, discard any surface fat and adjust seasoning
with salt and pepper. Simmer until warmed through. Add spinach.

*Comment: A wonderful wintertime soup that pairs well with
Spanish Rioja or California Barbera.*

SMOLENSK BORSCHT

Servings
8
Preparing
30 minutes
Cooking
1 hour

2 quarts water
4 teaspoons instant beef
  bouillon granules
2 cups minced cabbage
1 cup minced onion
2 cups minced beets
1 cup minced carrots
1 whole bay leaf
1 teaspoon whole savory

1 teaspoon rosemary leaves
1 teaspoon dill weed
1 teaspoon white pepper
1 teaspoon paprika

GARNISH
Sour cream
Chopped green onions

Utensils: large kettle with lid, cheesecloth bag

Bring water and bouillon to slow boil; add cabbage, onion, beets
and carrots. Place bay leaf, savory, rosemary and dill in
cheesecloth bag and add to kettle; add pepper and paprika. When
soup returns to a boil, reduce heat and simmer 1 hour. Discard
cheesecloth bag. Serve with a dollop of sour cream and a sprinkle
of green onions.

*Comment: For an authentic Russian meal, add black bread and
vodka.*

**The tears live in an onion that should water this
sorrow.**
                              ANTONY AND CLEOPATRA

SEAFOOD CHOWDER

Servings
6-8
Planning
Can make
1-2 days
ahead
Preparing
30 minutes
Cooking
1 hour

10 stalks celery, chopped
1 medium onion, chopped
½ cup oil
1 pound boneless turbot or
   cod, cut into pieces
1 pound shrimp, salad-size

1 pound crab meat
1 46-ounce can V-8 juice
1 46-ounce can tomato juice

Utensil: large Dutch oven with lid

Brown celery and onion in oil until translucent; add fish, shrimp
and crab. Cover and cook on medium heat 15 minutes. Add V-8
and tomato juices; cover and simmer 45 minutes.

*Comment: Sourdough bread is a must to serve with this main dish
soup, akin to San Francisco's cioppino.*

EASY GOURMET SOUP

Servings
6-8
Planning
Can make
ahead
Preparing
5 minutes
Cooking
10 minutes

1 10¾-ounce can condensed
   tomato soup
1 15-ounce can regular-
   strength green pea soup
1 cup chicken broth

1 cup cream or half-and-half
½ cup sherry
1 7-ounce can crab, drained
   and flaked
Dash onion salt

Utensil: large saucepan

Mix together and heat tomato and pea soups, chicken broth and
cream; add sherry, crab and onion salt. Continue heating until
crab is hot. (Can make ahead, chill and gently reheat.)

Comment: Lovely and luscious.

TACO SOUP

Servings
6-8
Planning
Can make
day ahead
Preparing
30 minutes
Cooking
30 minutes

1 pound lean ground beef
1 large onion, chopped
1 cup sliced celery
½ cup chopped red bell pepper
½ cup chopped green bell
  pepper
1 15-ounce can kidney beans,
  drained
1 16-ounce can tomatoes,
  chopped with juice

3 10½-ounce cans beef broth
6 10½-ounce cans water
¼ cup chopped fresh parsley
1 jalapeño pepper, chopped,
  optional
1½ tablespoons chili powder
1-2 teaspoons ground cumin
½ teaspoon pepper
1-2 cloves garlic, minced

CONDIMENTS
Chopped green onions
Chopped cilantro or parsley
Grated Cheddar cheese

Tortilla chips
Sliced avocado
Salsa
Sour cream

Utensil: large soup pot

Brown ground beef. Add onion, celery, green and red peppers to
pot; sauté until onion is translucent. Add kidney beans, tomatoes,
broth and water. Bring to boil, stirring continuously. Turn to
simmer and add parsley, jalapeño, chili powder, cumin, pepper
and garlic. Simmer ½ hour or until vegetables are tender. Serve in
heated bowls and offer condiments to add to individual servings.

*There is measure in every thing, and so dance out
the answer.*
                        MUCH ADO ABOUT NOTHING

CREAM OF JALAPEÑO SOUP

Servings
10
Planning
Partially
make ahead
Preparing
30 minutes
Cooking
4 hours

2 green bell peppers, seeded
   and diced
2 carrots, peeled and diced
1 large onion, diced
3-4 jalapeño peppers, seeded
   and diced
½ pound butter
1 cup all-purpose flour

1½ quarts chicken broth,
   heated
1 pint cream
½ cup grated sharp Cheddar
   cheese
½ cup grated Monterey Jack
   cheese

Utensil: large heavy kettle with lid

Sauté green peppers, carrots, onions and jalapeños in butter; gradually add flour, stirring after each addition until smooth and absorbed. Slowly add chicken broth, stirring until mixture boils; lower heat, cover and simmer 3 hours. (Can be made ahead to this point and refrigerated overnight.) One hour before serving add cream, Cheddar and Jack cheeses; cook uncovered over low heat, stirring occasionally. Do not boil.

Comment: A contrast in flavors, mellow yet spicy.

Marion Ross

COGNAC TOMATO SOUP

1½ quarts vegetable broth (made with cubes)	2 tablespoons brown sugar
1 teaspoon sweet basil	1 tablespoon lemon juice
12 ounces tomato paste	1 tablespoon Worcestershire sauce
¼ cup Cognac	¼ cup butter
1 cup light cream	¼ cup flour
¼ cup condensed milk	

Add basil to broth, simmer. Add tomato paste, Cognac, cream and condensed milk. Stir 'til blended and simmer very gently for a short while; add brown sugar, lemon juice and Worcestershire sauce.

In medium skillet heat butter 'til it bubbles. Stir in flour. Cook roux over very low flame for a few minutes. Add some hot soup. Stir with whisk until sauce is smooth. Pour back into soup. Stir with whisk, heat gently without bringing to boil.

MARION ROSS, Associate Artist of the Globe
Emmy-nominee for Mrs. Cunningham of television's "Happy Days." Globe credits include "Summer and Smoke."

CARROT VICHYSSOISE

Servings
6
Planning
Can make
ahead 12
hours
Preparing
30 minutes
Cooking
30 minutes

5 cups chicken broth
6 tablespoons butter
2 cups sliced green onions
   (without tops)
4 tablespoons flour
4 cups peeled, sliced carrots
1 teaspoon salt

$1/8$ teaspoon white pepper
$1/2$ cup sour cream

GARNISH
Sour cream
Chopped chives

Utensils: large sauce pan, blender

Heat chicken broth; set aside and keep warm. Melt butter, add
onions and sauté 5 minutes; stir in flour. Gradually add hot broth
and bring to a boil. Add carrots, salt and pepper; simmer 30
minutes. Purée in blender and stir in sour cream. Serve hot or
cold; garnish with sour cream and chives.

Comment: Hot or cold, it's appetizing and appealing.

MINNESOTA WILD RICE SOUP

Servings
6-8
Planning
Can make
ahead
Preparing
30 minutes
Cooking
30 minutes
Storing
3-4 days in
refrigerator

6 medium russet potatoes,
   peeled and cooked
1 quart reserved potato water
1 medium onion, chopped
1 quart half-and-half
1 14½-ounce can chicken
   broth

2 cups cooked wild rice
½ teaspoon nutmeg

CONDIMENTS
1 cup crisp crumbled bacon
1 cup shredded Cheddar
   cheese
½ cup chopped parsley

Utensil: 3-4 quart stock pot

Mash potatoes; add potato water, onion, half-and-half, chicken
broth, wild rice and nutmeg. Heat at simmering (not boiling)
temperature 30 minutes. Serve in mugs and pass the condiments.

Comment: Wonderful winter fare.

TECATE TOMATO SOUP

4 cups tomato juice
½ cup oil
½ cup wine vinegar
¼ cup lime juice
1 clove garlic, thinly sliced
2 tablespoons sugar
1 teaspoon dry mustard
1 tablespoon rosemary leaves
Pinch crushed thyme
Pinch oregano
Pinch basil

¼ cup chopped pimiento
  stuffed olives
¾ cup milk
Salt to taste
½ cup very thinly sliced
  pimiento stuffed olives for
  garnish
½ cup diced, seeded
  cucumber for garnish

Servings
8
Planning
Can make
up to 2
days ahead
Preparing
20 minutes
Chilling
12-48 hours

Combine tomato juice, oil, vinegar, lime juice, garlic, sugar, mustard, rosemary, thyme, oregano, basil and chopped olives. Gradually stir some tomato juice mixture into milk; return to remaining tomato juice mixture. Chill overnight or up to 48 hours. To serve, strain into chilled bowl or tureen; season with salt to taste. Garnish with sliced olives and cucumber.

Comment: Unusual, zesty and simplicity itself.

CHILLED AVOCADO SOUP

Servings
6-8
Planning
*Must make
ahead*
Preparing
20 minutes
Chilling
4-24 hours

4 medium avocados, peeled
   and diced
2 cups chicken broth, chilled
   with fat skimmed
1 tablespoon lime juice

½ teaspoon salt
1 large clove garlic, crushed
Dash hot pepper sauce
1½ cups heavy cream
Lemon slices for garnish

Utensil: blender

In blender purée avocados and chicken broth, small amounts at a
time, adding lime juice, salt, garlic and hot pepper sauce. Add
cream and blend well until mixture is smooth and creamy. Chill
thoroughly (4 hours minimum). Serve in chilled soup bowls or glass
mugs and garnish with lemon slices.

*Comment: This smoothie has a gorgeous color and mellow taste.
Delightful summer fare.*

CUERNAVACA CURRY SOUP

Servings
4-6
Planning
*Can make
day ahead*
Preparing
5 minutes
Cooking
15 minutes

2 tablespoons butter
1 tablespoon curry powder
4 cups chicken broth
2 egg yolks, beaten

1 cup half-and-half
1 avocado, peeled, pitted and
   sliced into thin crescents
Pimiento for garnish

Melt butter in large saucepan; stir in curry powder and chicken
broth. Simmer uncovered 10 minutes. Mix egg yolks with half-and-
half. Stir 1 tablespoon of hot broth into egg yolk mixture; then stir
egg yolk mixture into broth. Heat, stirring constantly, until mixture
simmers. Immediately put pan in an ice bath to cool rapidly and
prevent curdling. Chill well.

When ready to serve, thin with more half-and-half if necessary.
Ladle into chilled bowls and garnish with avocado and pimiento.

Comment: A surprise of tastes and textures.

COLD CUCUMBER SOUP

Servings
4-6
Planning
Must
partially
make ahead
Preparation
30 minutes
Cooking
30 minutes
Chilling
2-24 hours

¼ cup butter
2 large cucumbers, peeled
 and diced
½ large white onion, finely
 chopped
1 bay leaf
1 teaspoon salt
1 tablespoon flour
3 cups chicken broth
Green food coloring

1 large cucumber, peeled,
 seeded and grated
1 cup half-and-half
3 tablespoons lemon juice
1½ teaspoons dill weed
¼ cup Chablis wine

GARNISH
Sour cream
Snipped chives or dill weed

Utensils: soup pot, sieve

Melt butter. Add 2 cucumbers, onion, bay leaf and salt; sauté until
cucumbers are soft and onion golden. Blend in flour and chicken
broth; cover and simmer ½ hour. Remove bay leaf and sieve
mixture. Chill well.

Skim fat. Add 1-2 drops green food coloring, grated cucumber,
half-and-half, lemon juice, dill weed and Chablis. Serve in chilled
cups; garnish with sour cream and snipped chives or dill weed.

Comment: The perfect starter.

GAZPACHO

Servings
12
Planning
Must make ahead
Preparing
1 hour
Chilling
4 hours minimum
Storing
Up to 24 hours

2 medium cucumbers, peeled
   and chopped
1 large onion, peeled and
   chopped
5 medium tomatoes, chopped
1 medium green bell pepper,
   seeded and chopped
1 teaspoon crushed garlic
   cloves
1 cup water
3 cups V-8 juice
½ cup red wine vinegar

3-4 teaspoons salt
4 tablespoons olive oil
1 tablespoon tomato paste

CONDIMENTS
1 medium cucumber, peeled,
   seeded and finely chopped
2 medium tomatoes, finely
   chopped
½ green bell pepper, seeded
   and finely chopped
1 cup croutons

In large bowl combine cucumbers, onion, tomatoes and green pepper. Add garlic, water, V-8, vinegar and salt; stir well. Using a whisk, add oil and tomato paste. Cover and chill at least 4 hours. Serve with condiments.

Comment: Perfected in Madrid.

BREADS

photo by Paul Black

Kandis Chappell in *Intimate Exchanges*

BLUE RIBBON MEXICAN CORN BREAD

Yield
2 loaves
Planning
Can make ahead
Preparing
30 minutes
Rising & resting
2½-3 hours
Baking
30 minutes
Storing
Freeze

½ cup oil
1 teaspoon salt
1 tablespoon sugar
1 medium onion, finely chopped
1 cup buttermilk
1 cup cornmeal
2 packages active dry yeast
½ teaspoon baking soda
2 eggs

2 canned jalapeño peppers, minced
1 tablespoon canned pimiento, minced
1 cup cream style corn
1½ cups sharp Cheddar cheese, grated
5-5½ cups all-purpose flour
¼ cup butter, melted, divided

Utensils: two 5 x 9 inch loaf pans, greased and dusted with cornmeal
Preheat oven to 400°

In large saucepan combine oil, salt, sugar, onion and buttermilk; heat to lukewarm. Add cornmeal, yeast and baking soda. Add eggs and beat until blended. Add peppers, pimiento, corn and cheese; blend well. Add 4 cups flour, 1 cup at a time, until well mixed. Turn dough onto floured board and knead in remaining 1-1½ cups flour until dough is elastic.

Grease bowl with melted butter. Add dough; cover and let rise about 1½ hours until doubled. Divide dough and fold to fit pans. Allow to rise again until doubled. Bake 10 minutes, remove from oven and brush with butter; return to oven and bake additional 20 minutes. Remove and brush again with butter (optional). Cool before cutting.

Comment: Perfect with chili—and wonderful toasted.

Good morrow, gallants! want ye corn for bread?...
I HENRY VI

COTTAGE CHEESE DILL BREAD

Yield
1 loaf
Planning
Can make
ahead
Preparing
2 hours
Baking
40-50
minutes
Storing
Freeze

1 cup creamed cottage cheese
1 medium onion, finely
   chopped
3 tablespoons margarine
3 tablespoons sugar or honey
¼ cup water

2 tablespoons dill weed
1 teaspoon salt, optional
1 egg
2-2½ cups bread flour or
   unbleached flour
1 package rapid rising yeast

Utensils: electric mixer; 1½-2 quart casserole, oiled
Do not preheat oven

In saucepan mix cottage cheese, onion, margarine, sugar or honey,
water, dill weed, salt and egg. Heat to 115°. Pour into mixer
bowl; add 1 cup flour and yeast. Beat 2 minutes at low speed; add
1 more cup flour and beat 2 minutes at high speed. Work in
remaining flour by hand or with dough hook of heavy duty mixer.
Continue beating until dough is very stiff; beat 1 more minute.

Transfer dough to warm, oiled bowl. Cover with plastic wrap and
let rise until doubled, about 1 hour. Stir down and transfer to
casserole. Cover and allow to rise until doubled. Place on bottom
oven rack, set temperature to 350° (do not preheat) and bake
40-50 minutes.

Comment: A very light-textured dill bread with a wonderful flavor.

An honest maid as ever broke bread.
                              THE MERRY WIVES OF WINDSOR

PARKER HOUSE ROLLS FROM NEW MEXICO

Yield
10 rolls
Planning
Can make ahead
Preparing
15 minutes
Rising & Resting
30 minutes
Baking
10-15 minutes

1 cup milk
1½ tablespoons sugar
½ teaspoon salt
2 tablespoons butter

1¾ cups all-purpose flour
2 packages active dry yeast
Butter pats

Utensil: cookie sheet, greased
Preheat oven to 400°

Heat milk, sugar, salt and butter until lukewarm. Mix flour with yeast and add milk mixture. Beat well and put in a warm place for 15 minutes. Turn out on a well floured board; flour hands as necessary and pat to ¾-inch thickness (dough will be soft and sticky). Cut dough with a well floured biscuit cutter (minimum 2 inches in diameter) and fold over a pat of butter. Place on greased cookie sheet and let rise 15 minutes. Bake 10-15 minutes.

Comment: This is not a typical "Parker House" roll. It's crisp on the outside, soft on the inside, and has a texture somewhere between biscuit and bread. Makes great little sandwiches.

Dogberry: An honest soul, i'faith, sir; by my troth, he is as ever broke bread.
MUCH ADO ABOUT NOTHING

MITCHELL'S WHOLE-WHEAT BREAD

Yield
2 large loaves, or 2 smaller loaves and 12 breadsticks
Planning
Can make ahead
Preparing
30-45 minutes
Rising & resting
1½-1¾ hours
Baking
30-40 minutes
Storing
Freeze

3¾ cups all-purpose flour
3¾ cups whole-wheat flour
3 packages active dry yeast
2 teaspoons salt
¼ cup light brown sugar
¼ cup dark brown sugar
3 tablespoons cornstarch

1 cup cracked wheat
1 cup sunflower seeds
¼ cup margarine, melted
3 cups very warm water
3 tablespoons melted
   margarine for topping

Utensils: two 5 x 9 inch bread pans, non-stick or well
buttered
Preheat oven to 350°

Combine all-purpose and whole-wheat flours, yeast, salt, light
brown sugar, dark brown sugar, cornstarch, cracked wheat and
sunflower seeds.

Blend very warm water with melted margarine; add flour mixture,
½ cup at a time. Turn onto well floured board and knead 10
minutes, adding additional flour as required to keep from sticking
(try to use equal amounts all-purpose and whole-wheat flours).
Place in well greased bowl; cover and let rise until doubled (about
1½ hours). Turn onto well floured board and cut into 2 pieces;
knead each piece 4-5 minutes. Shape and put in bread pans. (Pans
should be approximately ⅔ full. If there is too much dough for the
pans, cut off excess dough and make breadsticks.) Make 4 razor
slashes diagonally across each loaf. Let rise until doubled (about
45 minutes). Bake 30-40 minutes or until golden. Remove from
oven; brush tops and sides with melted margarine.

For breadsticks: Take a walnut-size piece of dough and roll
between palms until it reaches ¼-inch in diameter. Place on
buttered baking sheet and let rise until doubled. Bake 20-25
minutes in a 325° oven or until golden brown.

Comment: Guaranteed!

CONNIE HEDGES' ITALIAN BREAD

1 package active dry yeast
½ cup lukewarm water
4 cups water

1 teaspoon sugar
1 tablespoon salt
12 cups all-purpose flour

Utensils: cookie sheets, greased
Preheat oven to 350⁰

Dissolve yeast in lukewarm water 5 minutes. Place in large mixing bowl with 4 cups water, sugar and salt; mix until salt and sugar are dissolved. Stir in 5 cups flour, beat 300 strokes and allow to rise until doubled (about 1 hour).

Add remaining flour, 1 cup at a time, until dough can no longer be stirred (or balls up, if using electric mixer). Turn onto floured board and knead, adding flour as required to keep from sticking. Knead dough until smooth and elastic. Return to bowl and allow to rise until doubled (about 1 hour).

Turn onto floured board; knead until elastic again and cut into 4 equal portions. Shape into long loaves and place on cookie sheets. Allow to rise until doubled. Slash tops and bake 40-50 minutes or until golden brown and loaves sound hollow when tapped.

Comment: Great texture and flavor. Makes a super garlic bread.

Yield
4 loaves
Planning
Can make
ahead
Preparing
40 minutes
Rising &
resting
3 hours
Baking
40-50
minutes
Storing
Freeze

Age cannot wither her, nor custom stale
Her infinite variety: other women cloy
The appetites they feed; but she makes hungry
Where most she satisfies.
                    ANTONY AND CLEOPATRA

56   Breads

FRANCES' FRENCH BREAD

Yield
2-3 loaves
Planning
*Can make
ahead*
Preparing
30 minutes
**Rising &
resting**
3-4 hours
Baking
*30-40
minutes*
Storing
Freeze

2 packages active dry yeast
2 tablespoons sugar
1¾ cups warm water
   (110-115°)
1½ teaspoons salt

5-6 cups all-purpose flour
¼ cup shortening, melted
3 egg whites, stiffly beaten
¼ cup butter, melted, for
   topping

Utensil: baking sheet, greased
Preheat oven to 375°

In large bowl mix yeast and sugar; add warm water and stir to
dissolve. Add salt and 2 cups flour; beat thoroughly. Stir in
shortening and egg whites. Add 3 cups flour, ½ cup at a time.
Turn onto floured board and knead until dough is smooth and
elastic, adding remaining flour as needed. Place in lightly greased
bowl. Cover and let rise until doubled (1-2 hours).

Punch down and let rise again until doubled (1-1½ hours). Turn
onto floured board and shape into 2 or 3 long loaves. Place on
baking sheet and make 5-6 razor slashes across tops. Cover and
let rise in a warm place until doubled (about 45 minutes). Brush
tops and sides with melted butter. Bake 30-40 minutes or until
loaves are golden brown and hollow sounding when tapped. May
be brushed with butter once or twice during baking period.

*Comment: A different French bread, with a tender crust and
smooth texture.*

The vines of France and milk of Burgundy.
                                                    KING LEAR

DELIGHTFUL BREADSTICKS

½ cup butter or margarine
1 teaspoon oregano
1 teaspoon basil

⅛ teaspoon garlic powder
1 package breadsticks
   (15-18 count)

Utensil: broiler pan or edged cookie sheet
Preheat oven to 200°

Melt butter in pan. Add oregano, basil and garlic powder; stir to mix evenly. Lay breadsticks in pan and bake 1 hour; give breadsticks one-quarter turn every 15 minutes. Serve warm.

(Recipe can be doubled or tripled. Leftovers can be frozen; reheat frozen breadsticks 15 minutes at 200° and watch to prevent too much browning.)

Comment: These bring rave reviews. Serve with soups or salads.

Yield
*15-18
breadsticks*
Planning
*Can make
ahead*
Preparing
15 minutes
Baking
1 hour
Storing
Freeze

CHASEN'S CHEESE BREAD

1 cup butter
1 cup grated Parmesan
   cheese

1 clove garlic, minced
1 baguette French bread,
   sliced very thin

Utensil: cookie sheet
Preheat oven to 250°

Melt butter; add cheese and garlic. Dip bread slices (one side only) into mixture and place, buttered side up, on cookie sheet. Bake 10-15 minutes. (Can make ahead and serve at room temperature.)

Servings
12
Planning
*Can make
ahead*
Preparing
10 minutes
Baking
*10-15
minutes*
Storing
*In airtight
container
several
days*

REFRIGERATED BRAN MUFFINS

Yield
6 dozen
Planning
*Must make
at least 12
hours ahead*
Preparing
20 minutes
Baking
25 minutes
Storing
*Batter will
keep 6
weeks in
refrigerator*

2 cups boiling water
6 cups bran cereal
1 cup butter or margarine
1½ cups sugar
4 eggs
1 quart buttermilk

5 cups unbleached flour
5 teaspoons baking soda
1 teaspoon salt
2 cups chopped dates or
   dried figs
2 cups nuts, optional

Utensils: muffin tins, greased
Preheat oven to 375°

In bowl pour boiling water over cereal; let stand. In large bowl blend butter, sugar and eggs; add bran mixture and buttermilk. Sift flour with baking soda and salt; add to bran mixture. Stir in fruit and nuts. Place in airtight container and chill at least 12 hours. Fill muffin cups ½ full and bake 25 minutes.

Comment: Have these wonderful bran muffins fresh every day, as many or as few as you want.

CRANBERRY COFFEE CAKE

Servings
12
Planning
*Can make
ahead, but
best fresh*
Preparing
10 minutes
Baking
*25-30
minutes*
Storing
*Several
days*

1½ cups cranberries, fresh or
   frozen
3 tablespoons butter
1 cup sugar, divided
1½ cups all-purpose flour

2 teaspoons baking powder
½ teaspoon salt, optional
1 egg, beaten
½ cup milk
3 tablespoons butter, melted

Utensil: 8 x 8 inch baking pan, ungreased
Preheat oven to 400°

Place cranberries in pan and dot with 3 tablespoons butter; sprinkle with ½ cup sugar. In bowl sift flour, ½ cup sugar, baking powder and salt. Add egg, milk and 3 tablespoons melted butter; mix until blended and spread over cranberries. Bake 25-30 minutes or until inserted toothpick tests clean.

Comment: Perfect for Christmas morning.

DOUGLAS W. SCHMIDT

DIETETIC MIDNITE
MUFFINS YO' MAMA *

A perfect late night snack when you need to unwind after, say, a
tedious, frustrating 14-hour technical rehearsal but you're
watching your weight, and anyway, Pizza Hut is closed, but you
REALLY NEED SOMETHING IN YOUR MOUTH. Try a few of these
little cuties before bedtime.

First you need to have on hand:

¾ cup hot water
½ cup molasses
¼ cup low fat milk
2 cups whole-wheat flour
1 cup all-purpose flour
¾ cup sugar

3 tablespoons baking powder
1 teaspoon baking soda
1 teaspoon salt
1½ cups coarsely chopped
   dry roasted pecans

Combine well all the wet stuff (water and molasses first, then the
milk) in a medium bowl.

Sift together all the dry stuff and mix in nuts in another bowl.

Fold wet into dry *just* until all the flour is damp—don't get carried
away.

Grease up your tin, spoon in the muck and bake at 300° for
about as long as David Letterman or a little less (keep checking).
Then, as they say, butter 'em while they're hot. Ladies and
Gentlemen: the reason they invented the word voilà!

*The discerning chef may think he's seen a similar recipe in
another author's cookbook. But I assure you, dear reader, if he
was using my dietetic formula he couldn't possibly have become
so FAT.*

DOUGLAS W. SCHMIDT, Associate Artist of the Globe
Scenic artist. Winner of top awards for Broadway, opera and television as well as numerous Globe
productions.

ANNE'S POGO

½ cup butter, margarine or
  shortening, melted
2 cups warm water
½ cup sugar, divided

2 teaspoons salt
1 package active dry yeast
6-7 cups all-purpose flour
Melted butter for topping

Utensil: non-stick baking sheet or pizza pan
Preheat oven to 350°

In large bowl combine margarine, yeast, 1 tablespoon sugar and
warm water. When mixture bubbles, stir in remaining sugar, salt
and 1½ cups flour; mix until batter becomes smooth. Add
additional flour, 1 cup at a time. When dough becomes too sticky
to stir, turn onto floured board; add remaining flour and knead 10
minutes. (Dough will be softer than regular bread dough.)

Place in lightly oiled bowl, cover with cloth and let rise in warm
place until doubled (about 1 hour). Punch down and let rise a
second time (about 1 hour). Remove and place on floured board
and flatten with hands to 1½-inch thickness. Pierce closely all
over with fork. Cover and let rise until doubled (about 20 minutes).
Shape dough with palms into a circle 12-14 inches in diameter.
Place on sheet and bake 30 minutes. Remove to wire rack and
brush with melted butter.

*Comment: A Serbian recipe, originally called pogača, this bread
has a sweet taste and dense texture. Excellent for toast, including
French toast, or croutons.*

**He that keeps nor crust nor crum,
Weary of all, shall want some.**
                              KING LEAR

MOTHER JARNBERG'S COFFEE BREAD

2 packages active dry yeast
½ cup warm water
2 teaspoons sugar
2 cups milk, scalded
½ cup shortening
1½ cups sugar
3 teaspoons salt
9 seeds cardamom, crushed
  or 2 teaspoons ground

7-9 cups all-purpose flour
2 eggs
¼ cup butter, melted and
  cooled
Cinnamon and sugar for
  topping

Yield
3 loaves
Planning
Make ahead
Preparing
1 hour
Rising
3½ hours
Baking
45 minutes
Storing
Freezes well

Utensils: three 4½ x 8½ inch loaf pans, greased
Preheat oven to 350°

In small bowl, soften yeast in warm water; blend in 2 teaspoons sugar. In large bowl, combine milk, shortening, ¾ cup sugar, salt and cardamom; cool. Add 3 cups flour to milk mixture, then add yeast. Knead briefly on floured board. Place dough in greased bowl and turn over to grease top. Cover and let rise about 1 hour.

Mix eggs with remaining ¾ cup sugar and cooled butter; add to dough. Add 4-6 cups flour and knead on floured board until smooth and satiny. Return to bowl, cover and let rise 1½ hours.

Divide dough into three parts and place in loaf pans. Sprinkle with cinnamon and sugar. Cover and let rise 1 hour; bake 30-45 minutes or until loaves sound hollow when tapped.

Comment: A winner! Great toasted and buttered—and for French toast.

BLUE RIBBON SOURDOUGH BREAD

Yield
2 loaves
Planning
Can make
2-3 days
ahead
Preparing
1 hour
Rising
2½ hours
Baking
35 minutes
Storing
Can be
frozen

5½-6 cups all-purpose flour
¼ cup sugar
2 teaspoons salt
¼ cup warm water
1 package active dry yeast
2 servings prepared instant
  mashed potatoes or 1 cup
  homemade
¾ cup milk

¼ cup melted butter or
  margarine
2 eggs
1 cup sourdough starter
  (page 63)
1 egg, beaten
Cornmeal
Poppy seeds, optional

Utensil: large cookie sheet, greased and dusted with cornmeal
Preheat oven to 350°

In a large bowl, combine 2 cups flour, sugar and salt. Dissolve yeast in warm water. Prepare instant mashed potatoes; stir in milk, butter, eggs and sourdough starter. Beat until smooth. Add yeast and potato mixture to dry ingredients in bowl and beat until well blended.

Stir in remaining flour, ½ cup at a time, until the dough becomes stiff (about 1½ cups). Turn out on a floured board and knead until smooth. Add more flour as required to prevent sticking (¼ cup at a time). Enough flour has been added when a finger pushed into the dough comes out clean.

Place dough in buttered bowl and turn to coat all sides. Cover and let rise in a warm place until doubled in bulk (about 1½-2 hours). Punch dough down. Divide in half, then divide each half into thirds. Roll each piece to form a rope about 24 inches long. Pinch three of the ropes together at one end. Braid ropes, making sure that holes exist between braids to allow for dough expansion.

Transfer braided loaves to baking sheet. Allow loaves to rise until almost double (about 45 minutes). Brush each loaf with beaten egg and sprinkle with poppy seeds, if desired.

Bake 25 minutes, then check. If necessary, bake another 5-10 minutes or until bread is golden brown. Cool on wire rack.

Comment: The blue ribbon was awarded at the San Diego County Fair.

SOURDOUGH STARTER

1 package active dry yeast
2 cups warm bottled spring
  water

2 cups all-purpose flour
1½ teaspoons sugar

Sourdough preparation has one taboo: metal. Use only wooden or plastic mixing spoons. Use only glass, plastic or crockery mixing bowls. Bearing this in mind, dissolve the yeast in ½ cup water in a large jar or bowl. Add flour, sugar and remaining water and stir until well blended. Let stand, partially covered, in warm place (70°-80°) 4 to 5 days, stirring mixture down each day. It's ready when fermented (it bubbles). Use at once or refrigerate until ready. Always stir down before using.

To keep starter going, always reserve at least 1 cup batter for future use, discarding the excess. To reserved starter, add 1 cup all-purpose flour and 1 cup lukewarm water and let stand overnight until fermented and bubbling. Store in refrigerator.

HONEY WHEAT CHEESE BREAD

1½ cups water
1 cup small-curd creamed
  cottage cheese
½ cup honey
¼ cup butter
3 cups whole-wheat flour

2 tablespoons sugar
3 teaspoons salt
2 packages active dry yeast
1 egg, beaten
4 cups unbleached flour
Butter for topping

Yield
3 loaves
Planning
Can make ahead
Preparing
30 minutes
Rising
1½ hours
Baking
45-50 minutes
Storing
Can freeze

Utensils: three 5 x 9 inch loaf pans, greased
Preheat oven to 350°

Heat together: water, cottage cheese, honey and butter. Beat in whole-wheat flour, sugar, salt, yeast and egg. Beat well. Add 3½-4 cups unbleached flour and knead on floured board about 10 minutes. Place in greased bowl, cover with towel and let rise about 45 minutes. Punch down, shape into three loaves, place in pans and let rise another 45 minutes. Bake 45-50 minutes. Remove from pans and butter tops.

JANKA'S INSTANT BREAD

Yield
2 loaves
Planning
Can make
ahead
Preparing
45 minutes
Rising &
Resting
45 minutes
Baking
20-30
minutes
Storing
Can be
frozen

2 packages active dry yeast
½ cup warm water
¼ cup sugar
¾ cup dry milk powder
1¾ cups warm water

1½ teaspoons salt
6 tablespoons oil
6 cups flour (rye, all-purpose,
    wheat or combination)
Butter for topping

Utensils: two 5 x 9 inch loaf pans, lightly greased
Preheat oven to 375°

Mix yeast, water and sugar and let stand until bubbly, about 10
minutes. Mix together dry milk, water, salt and oil. Add yeast
mixture and dry milk mixture to 3 cups flour; stir well. Add 3
more cups flour and stir; dough will be stiff. Let rest 15 minutes.

Knead lightly on floured surface, adding more flour if necessary.
Shape into 2 loaves and let rise 20 minutes. Make razor cut down
center of bread. Bake 20-30 minutes until golden brown and
hollow sounding when thumped. Butter tops after removing from
pan.

Comment: Fast and easy, hearty and tasty.

BATTLESHIP BREAD

Yield
3 loaves
Planning
*Can make
ahead*
Preparing
40 minutes
Rising &
resting
2-3 hours
Baking
40 minutes
Storing
Freeze

10-12 cups all-purpose flour
3 tablespoons cornstarch
3½ cups very warm potato
    water
2 tablespoons sugar

3½ teaspoons salt
2 tablespoons margarine
1 package active dry yeast
¼ teaspoon turmeric
Melted butter for topping

Utensils: three 5 x 9 inch non-stick bread pans
Preheat oven to 350°

Mix flour with cornstarch. In large mixing bowl combine potato
water, sugar, salt, margarine, yeast and turmeric; beat well. Add
flour mixture, ½ cup at a time; mix well until dough leaves sides
of bowl.

On a floured board knead dough 10 minutes, adding flour as
necessary until dough no longer sticks to hands. Place in greased
bowl, cover and let rise in a warm place until doubled (1½-2
hours). Remove and place on floured board; cut into 3 pieces.
Knead each piece 4-5 minutes and place in bread pans. Make 4
razor slashes across each loaf and let rise until doubled (1½-2
hours). Bake 40 minutes; butter tops and sides.

Comment: This is a winner!

These our ships...
Are stored with corn to make your needy bread.
                                        PERICLES

MITCHELL'S DINNER ROLLS

Yield
30 rolls
Planning
*Can make
ahead*
Preparing
1 hour
**Rising &
resting**
2 hours
Baking
15 minutes
Storing
Freeze

4-5 cups all-purpose flour
¼ cup sugar
¼ cup nonfat dry milk
1 package active dry yeast
1 tablespoon cornstarch
1½ teaspoons salt
⅛ teaspoon cardamom

1¼ cups warm water
**½ cup butter or margarine,
    melted**
1 extra large egg
**½ cup butter or margarine,
    melted, for topping**

Utensil: 14 x 17 inch baking pan, non-stick or well buttered
Preheat oven to 350°

In a large bowl blend 4 cups flour, sugar, dry milk, yeast,
cornstarch, salt and cardamom. In another large bowl mix warm
water, melted butter and egg. Add dry mixture, ½ cup at a time,
to warm water mixture. Add more flour, as necessary, until dough
leaves sides of bowl. (Dough will be soft.)

Put dough into greased bowl, cover with light cloth and let rise in
a warm place until doubled (about 1 hour). Turn onto floured
board and cut into 3 equal pieces. With rolling pin, flatten each
piece into 10-inch circle ¼-inch thick.

Generously brush tops with 1 tablespoon melted butter. Cut each
piece into 10 pie-shaped wedges. Starting with wide end, roll each
wedge toward the point and curve slightly to resemble cattle
horns. Place on pan in 3 rows of 10 horns. Cover and let rise in a
warm place until doubled (about 1 hour). Bake 15 minutes; rotate
pan halfway through baking. Remove and brush lightly with
melted butter.

Baking tip: The final appearance of these rolls will depend on the
ambient temperature during the rising period. A cooler
temperature will cause the rising time to be longer, but the rolls
will maintain their original shape better. A warmer temperature
(100°-115°) will allow faster rising, but the dough will spread out
more and the lines of the rolls will become softer (or more
rounded). This is simply a matter of technique; the quality and
flavor are not affected.

Comment: These rolls are fantastic.

BIJOU'S FAVORITE DOG BISCUITS

2 cups whole-wheat flour
½ cup cornmeal
⅔ cup water
**1 tablespoon chicken or beef
   bouillon granules, optional**

Utensil: cookie sheets
Do not preheat oven

Combine flour, cornmeal, water and bouillon granules if using. Mix thoroughly, using hands. Roll to ¼-inch thickness and cut into shapes with decorative cutters. (The dogs will not notice the shapes, but their owners will.) Place in cold oven and set temperature to 350°. Bake 35-45 minutes or until browned and toasty. (They will be very hard.)

Comment: Bijou, the Old Globe's resident dog, suggests that you "gift" your friends' canines with these at Christmas.

Yield
5 dozen
Planning
*Can make
ahead*
Preparing
15 minutes
Baking
*35-45
minutes*
Storing
*Airtight
container*

BIJOU NOEL
Golden Retriever, recognized as a canine Kim Novak. Friend of all artists and world renowned, Bijou is
the "jewel" her name implies and a true devotee of the theatre.

MONKEY BREAD

Servings
10-12
Planning
Can make
ahead
Preparing
30 minutes
Rising &
resting
2-2½
hours
Baking
50-60
minutes

2 envelopes active dry yeast
1 cup lukewarm water
1 cup shortening
¾ cup sugar
1½ teaspoon salt

1 cup boiling water
2 eggs, beaten
6 cups all-purpose flour
½ cup butter, melted

Utensils: two 9-inch tube pans (or tube pan and 5 x 9 inch loaf pan)
Preheat oven to 350°

Dissolve yeast in lukewarm water. Mix shortening, sugar and salt; add boiling water, stir and cool to lukewarm. Add eggs to shortening mixture and stir. Add 2 cups flour and yeast mixture, alternately, to shortening mixture; continue adding flour, ½ cup at a time, until mixture becomes too stiff to stir. Turn onto floured board and knead until elastic, adding flour as necessary to keep from sticking. Form into long, narrow loaf; cover and let rise until doubled (1-1½ hours). To assemble, pinch off and dip various size dough pieces in melted butter; place in pans, layer on layer, until each pan is half full. Let rise again until doubled. Bake 50-60 minutes or until browned.

Comment: A holiday favorite.

KANDIS CHAPPELL

CHOCOLATE CHIP BANANA BREAD

1 teaspoon soda
4 tablespoons sour cream or
   plain yogurt
¼ pound butter or margarine
   (1 stick)
¾ cup sugar

2 eggs
1 cup mashed bananas*
1 6-ounce bag semisweet
   chocolate chips
Pinch of salt
1 teaspoon vanilla

Please Note:
Please add 2¼ cups
all purpose flour to
Kandis Chappell's
recipe on page 69.

Mix together soda and sour cream or yogurt and set aside. Cream butter with sugar until light and fluffy. Add eggs, one at a time, beating well after each addition. Add flour and sour cream mixture alternately to butter mixture. Stir in bananas and chocolate chips. Add vanilla and salt.

Place mixture in a greased and floured loaf pan and bake in a 350° preheated oven for about 40-45 minutes or until a cake tester inserted in center comes out clean. (You can use 3 baby loaf pans. Test at 35 minutes.) This bread freezes well.

Note: Riper bananas give this bread a better flavor than "young" bananas. In fact, for super results, use almost rotten bananas! I often have a bunch of awful, black bananas rotting away in my kitchen. If you can stand the sight and the fruit flies, these old beauties give the bread a strong, rich banana flavor and even give the impression the recipe includes a liqueur! Delicious!

KANDIS CHAPPELL, Associate Artist of the Globe & Callaway Fellow
With Globe since 1964. Her lead and character portrayals, encompassing a variety of styles and periods, have earned kudos at the Globe and other major Western regional theatres.

BANANA NUT BREAD

Yield
2 loaves
Planning
Can make
ahead
Preparing
15 minutes
Baking
50-55
minutes

1 cup butter, softened
2 cups sugar
1 teaspoon vanilla
2 teaspoons lemon juice
4 eggs
2 cups mashed bananas

1 teaspoon salt
3½ cups sifted flour
2 teaspoons baking soda
2 teaspoons baking powder
1 cup sour cream
1 cup chopped nuts

Utensils: two 5 x 9 inch loaf pans, greased and floured
Preheat oven to 350°

In large bowl blend butter and sugar. Add vanilla, lemon juice, eggs and bananas; blend until creamy. Sift together salt, flour, soda and baking powder. Add sifted ingredients and sour cream, alternately, to banana mixture; beat batter after each addition. Fold in nuts. Pour into 2 loaf pans and bake 50-55 minutes.

Comment: A very special cake-like bread.

BORREGO BREAD

Yield
1 loaf
Planning
Can make
ahead
Preparing
15 minutes
Baking
50-60
minutes

3 cups biscuit mix
1 egg
1 cup buttermilk
½ cup sour cream
2 tablespoons sugar

1 cup grated Swiss cheese
1 cup sliced pimiento-stuffed
olives
¾ cup chopped walnuts

Utensil: 5 x 9 inch loaf pan, greased
Preheat oven to 350°

Combine biscuit mix, egg, buttermilk, sour cream and sugar in mixing bowl and beat 1 minute to blend thoroughly. Gently stir in cheese, olives and nuts; spoon into pan. Bake 50-60 minutes or until wooden pick tests clean.

Comment: Try this for breakfast, toasted and buttered.

MEATS

Joanna Gleason in *Into the Woods*

CHARLES HAID

BUTTERFLY STEAKS AEOTEAOROA

4 pork butterfly steaks
2 cups sourdough
  breadcrumbs
1 egg
¼ cup milk
Flour (wheat)
2 tablespoons Parmesan
  cheese

2 tablespoons parsley
1 tablespoon butter
1 tablespoon olive oil
1 garlic clove (chopped)
Salt & pepper
2 large taro leaves (or
  banana, Ti or ginger leaves)

Pound steaks 'til flat. Mix flour, salt, garlic & pepper. Beat egg &
milk together. Add cheese & chopped parsley to crumbs. Coat
steaks in flour, then egg & milk mix, then breadcrumbs.
Refrigerate for 30 minutes. Fry in oil & butter at medium heat for
5 minutes each side. Serve on taro leaf.

From New Zealand.

CHARLES HAID
Following major Shakespearean roles at Globe, starred on television's long-running police drama "Hill
Street Blues."

OVEN-BAKED STEAK

Servings
6-8
Preparing
15 minutes
Broiling
2-3 minutes
Baking
15-20
minutes

3 pounds boneless sirloin
   steak, 2 inches thick
1 tablespoon oil
½ teaspoon salt
½ teaspoon mixed Italian
   seasoning

3 tablespoons butter, melted,
   divided
1 clove garlic, minced
1 large shallot, chopped
½ cup red wine
2 ounces brandy or Cognac

Utensil: range-to-oven pan
Preheat oven to broil, lower to 375°

Pat steak dry with paper towels and rub both sides with oil. Place
in broiler and quickly brown both sides; remove. Sprinkle both
sides with salt and Italian seasoning; brush with 2 tablespoons
butter.

Reduce heat to 375° and return meat to upper third of oven. Bake
15-20 minutes, turning once, until meat registers 125° or is rosy
rare. Remove meat to heated platter.

Remove excess fat from baking pan; add garlic, shallot and 1
tablespoon butter. Sauté 1 minute over high heat. Add wine and
scrape pan to loosen meat particles. When liquid is syrupy, add
brandy and warm briefly; ignite (MAKE CERTAIN EXHAUST FAN
IS OFF). Slice steak; pour juices over meat and serve.

Comment: A memorable main dish.

STEAK SUPRÊME

¼ cup butter or margarine
3 medium onions, sliced
½ pound fresh mushrooms, sliced
½ cup chopped green bell pepper
¾ cup chili sauce
½ cup tomato juice

1½ teaspoons garlic salt
¼ cup sliced ripe olives
½ teaspoon pepper
1 teaspoon Worcestershire sauce
1½-2 pounds round steak, 1-inch thick

Servings
6
Planning
Can make
ahead
Preparing
25 minutes
Baking
1 hour 40
minutes

Utensil: shallow baking dish
Preheat oven to 425°

Melt butter. Add onions, mushrooms, green pepper and simmer 5 minutes. Blend in chili sauce, tomato juice, garlic salt, pepper, Worcestershire sauce and olives. Place steak in baking dish and pour sauce over it. Bake 10 minutes. Reduce temperature to 350° and continue baking for 1½ hours.

Comment: A great family dish.

The capon burns, the pig falls from the spit,
The clock hath strucken twelve upon the bell;
My mistress made it one upon my cheek:
She is so hot because the meat is cold;
The meat is cold because you come not home;
You come not home because you have no stomach;
You have no stomach having broke your fast;
But we that know what 'tis to fast and pray
Are penitent for your default to-day....
Methinks your maw, like mine, should be your clock
And strike you home without a messenger.
                    THE COMEDY OF ERRORS

Servings
4-6
Planning
Must
marinate
ahead
Preparing
10 minutes
Barbecuing
10 minutes
Marinating
24 hours

CHEESE-CRUSTED STEAK

2 flank steaks (1-1½ pounds each)

TOPPING
1½ teaspoons paprika
2 teaspoons Dijon mustard
1 teaspoon Worcestershire sauce
1 cup grated Cheddar cheese

MARINADE
1 teaspoon lime juice
2 tablespoons olive oil
1 tablespoon crumbled oregano
1 tablespoon crumbled basil
3 garlic cloves, finely minced
2 tablespoons wine vinegar
1 cup dry red wine

Utensil: large baking dish
Preheat barbecue or broiler to high heat

For marinade: In a large jar combine lime juice, oil, oregano, basil, garlic, vinegar and wine; blend thoroughly.

Lightly score steaks; place in baking dish and cover with marinade. Chill 24 hours.

For topping: Combine paprika, mustard, Worchestershire and cheese.

Barbecue steaks 5 minutes; turn and coat top with cheese mixture. Continue barbecuing 5 minutes for medium rare. Slice steaks on diagonal and serve.

Comment: This calls for a dry red wine such as Cabernet Sauvignon.

TOM LACY

SAN DIEGO SHEPHERD'S PIE

Brown:
3 pounds ground beef (drain thoroughly and let cool)

Mix together in a large bowl:
1 cup salsa ranchero (a hot Jalapẽno, tomato, onion sauce)*
1 cup kernel corn
1 cup sliced black pitted olives
½ cup chopped pimiento
2 teaspoons chili powder

Add browned beef, mix thoroughly.
Pack mixture flat in bottom of 7 x 12 oven dish or equivalent size casserole.

Boil:
6 large russet potatoes (scrubbed, cut up, with *skins left on)*

Mash potatoes with:
¼ pound butter, softened or cut up
1 cup sour cream
Splash of milk
Salt to taste
(If mashed in food processor, it will make 2 batches)
Spread mashed potatoes over meat mixture. They will rise high over sides of dish, so don't make them too soft.

Sprinkle:
1 cup shredded Cheddar cheese over top

Heat in 350° oven for 20-30 minutes.
Brown cheese topping in broiler.
Dish can be made a day ahead and refrigerated, or frozen. Thaw. Heat in 350° oven 30 minutes. Brown topping.
Serves 8-10 for brunch or after theatre. (Try it with coleslaw on the side, and Mexican beer.)

*Dish can be made with a milder sauce, but not by me.

TOM LACY, Associate Artist of the Globe
Noted for his multiple comedy and character portrayals at Globe. He also has acted on television as well as on and off-Broadway.

FLANK STEAK WITH MARINADE

Servings
2-4
Planning
Must
marinate
ahead
Preparing
15 minutes
Broiling
7-10
minutes
Marinade
6 hours to
2 days in
refrigerator

1-1¾ pounds flank steak

MARINADE
½ cup olive oil
¼ cup red wine vinegar
¼ cup lime juice
¼ cup finely chopped onions
2 cloves garlic, minced
2 teaspoons Worcestershire
  sauce

2 teaspoons soy sauce
1 teaspoon sugar
1 teaspoon oregano leaves
¼ teaspoon basil leaves
4 drops hot pepper sauce
2 teaspoons dry mustard
½ teaspoon black pepper

Utensil: barbecue grill
Preheat grill to medium

For marinade: In glass pan mix oil, vinegar, lime juice, onions, garlic, Worchestershire, soy, sugar, oregano, basil, hot pepper sauce, mustard and pepper.

Place steak in marinade and cover. Chill at least 6 hours or up to 2 days. Grill until medium rare. Slice diagonally across grain and serve.

Comment: Savory and succulent. Pray for leftovers to make great sandwiches.

Arviragus: I am weak with toil, yet strong in appetite.
Guiderius: There is cold meat i'the cave: we'll browse on that.

CYMBELINE

ENGLISH PUB SKILLET O' BEEF

Servings
6
Planning
Can make
24 hours
ahead
Preparing
20 minutes
Cooking
2 hours

1½ pounds London broil or
   top round steak
3 tablespoons flour
½ teaspoon ground thyme
1 teaspoon salt
¼ teaspoon coarsely ground
   pepper

3 tablespoons oil
3 cups beef bouillon
1 tablespoon Worcestershire
   sauce
1 cup thinly sliced fresh
   mushrooms
1 cup pearl onions, blanched

Utensil: deep 10-inch skillet with lid

Trim fat from meat and cut into 1-inch cubes. Mix flour, salt,
pepper and thyme in a plastic bag; add beef and shake to coat
meat evenly. Heat oil in skillet on medium high heat and brown
meat cubes a few at a time. Add beef bouillon and Worcestershire
to skillet; stir and bring to boil. Cover skillet, turn heat to low and
simmer 1½-2 hours until meat is tender. Add mushrooms and
pearl onions; simmer another 15 minutes.

BAJA BARBECUE SAUCE

Yield
5½ cups
Planning
Make ahead
Preparing
15 minutes
Storing
Refrigerate
up to 6
weeks

¾ cup firmly packed dark
   brown sugar
¼ cup steak sauce
1 cup chili sauce
1½ cups catsup
2 tablespoons Worcestershire
   sauce
1 tablespoon oil

½ cup wine vinegar
¼ cup lime or lemon juice
¾ cup beer
¼ cup prepared mustard
1 tablespoon ground black
   pepper
¼ teaspoon hot pepper sauce

Combine sugar, steak sauce and chili sauce; mix to dissolve sugar.
Add catsup, Worcestershire sauce, oil, vinegar, lime or lemon juice,
beer, mustard, pepper and hot pepper sauce. Stir to mix; cover
tightly and store in refrigerator until ready to barbecue.

SAVORY TENDERLOIN

Servings
4-6
Planning
Serve
immediately
Preparing
10 minutes
Roasting
40-45
minutes

1 whole beef tenderloin
(about 2 pounds)

2 tablespoons butter,
softened

SAUCE
¼ cup chopped green
onions
2 tablespoons butter
2 tablespoons soy sauce

1 teaspoon Dijon mustard
Dash ground pepper
¾ cup dry white or sherry
wine

Utensil: shallow pan
Preheat oven to 400°

Spread meat with butter; place in pan and roast 20 minutes.

Meanwhile, sauté green onions in butter until tender; add soy
sauce, mustard, pepper and wine. Heat just to boiling point and
pour over meat.

Return meat to oven. Continue roasting, basting often: 20 minutes
for rare or 25 minutes for medium rare. (For a larger tenderloin,
use a meat thermometer to check degree of doneness.)

*Comment: Frequent basting is the secret of this moist, flavorful
roast.*

Suffolk, the new-made duke that rules the roast.
II HENRY VI

MEAT LOAF DE SELM

2-3 eggs
2 teaspoons salt
½ teaspoon ground white
 pepper
2 teaspoons marjoram
2 teaspoons Italian herbs
2-3 pounds lean ground beef

1 pound pork sausage
1 medium-large onion,
 chopped
2-3 cups Italian seasoned
 bread crumbs
2-3 cups milk

Servings
10-12
Planning
*Can make
ahead*
Preparing
*20-30
minutes*
Baking
2 hours
Storing
Freeze

Utensil: edged baking pan
Preheat oven to 350°

In large bowl beat eggs with wire whisk and combine with salt,
pepper, marjoram and Italian herbs. Add beef, sausage and onion;
mix lightly. Add bread crumbs and milk, small amounts at a time,
and blend until mixture reaches firm, mush-like consistency. Shape
into loaf, place on pan and cover with foil. (At this point meat loaf
can be frozen, wrapped in foil. Thaw 4 hours before baking.) Bake
covered 1 hour; remove from oven, pour off fat and bake
uncovered 1 more hour.

*Comment: This meat loaf stars in innumerable roles: as a
companion for cold salad luncheons, as the lead for a buffet
supper, or as the hero of a sandwich.*

**About the sixth hour; when beasts most graze, birds
best peck, and men sit down to that nourishment
which is called supper.**
LOVE'S LABOUR'S LOST

ISLAND CHILI

Servings
8
Planning
*Make day
ahead*
Preparing
30 minutes
Cooking
*40-50
minutes*

5 tablespoons oil, divided
3½ pounds beef top round, in
 ½-inch cubes
5 cloves garlic, minced
2 cups chopped onion
4 tablespoons chili powder
1½ teaspoons oregano
1½ teaspoons ground cumin
1 teaspoon crushed red
 pepper

1 14-ounce can beef broth
1 cup red wine
1 28-ounce can whole
 tomatoes, drained, chopped
1 6-ounce can tomato paste
1 tablespoon salt
1 teaspoon sugar
1 15-ounce can kidney beans,
 optional

Utensil: large stock pot

Heat 3 tablespoons oil and brown meat in small batches; remove
meat. Add remaining 2 tablespoons oil; sauté garlic and onion
until limp. Stir in chili powder, oregano, cumin and red pepper;
mix until onions are coated. Add broth, wine, tomatoes, paste, salt
and sugar. If using kidney beans, add at this point. Return meat to
pot, cover and simmer 40-50 minutes. Cool and refrigerate several
hours or overnight; reheat to serve.

*Comment: An émigré from Hawaii, this chili traditionally is served
over rice. Cornbread, green salad and beer round out the meal.*

*Say, can you fast? your stomachs are too young;
And abstinence engenders maladies.*
                                    LOVE'S LABOUR'S LOST

CHILI

Sauté 6 onions and 4 cloves (or more) garlic in olive oil. It helps to chop onions & garlic first. A lot of olive oil if you're thin and less if you lean to port-ly. Add about 3 pounds ground round or chuck *very* lean. Brown. Add 1 or 2 cans Hunt's tomato sauce. Stir. Add soy sauce about ¼ cup. Little wine, optional. Simmer gently.

Add ½ bottle chili powder, generous pinches of basil, oregano, cumin seeds and less generous pinches of cayenne pepper and allspice. Stir. Add 4 or 5 cans kidney beans, maybe even 6 cans. Stir and simmer as long as you want. Make sure you eat this with someone you've known and loved for a very long time. Enjoy.

I never cook from recipes so leave me alone already?!

MICHAEL LEARNED
Multiple Emmy Award winning actress. Familiar to audiences for her starring role on television's "The Waltons," she portrayed Cleopatra at the Globe.

Servings
4
Planning
Serve
immediately
Preparing
30 minutes
Searing &
roasting
10 minutes

SUPRÊME ENTRECÔTE JONATHAN

1 8-ounce jar Pacific oysters,
  drained
3 pounds top sirloin steak,
  2 inches thick
2 tablespoons butter
1 clove garlic, crushed

4 tablespoons finely chopped
  green onion tops
2 tablespoons dry vermouth
1 2-ounce jar black caviar
6 tablespoons chopped
  parsley

Utensils: large skillet, wooden toothpicks, 8 x 11 inch pan
Preheat oven to 400°

Rinse oysters, pat dry and set aside. Trim all excess fat from
sirloin; cut into 4 pieces about 3 x 4 inches each. Cut a 2 x 3 inch
pocket into one side of each piece, leaving a ½-inch edge on the
other sides.

Heat butter over medium-high heat; add crushed garlic and sauté
briefly. Add oysters and sauté 1 minute per side. Place oysters on
platter; sprinkle with onion tops, cover and keep warm.

Bring the remaining butter-garlic sauce to high heat and sear
steaks 1½-2 minutes per side. Remove from heat and insert 1-2
oysters with onions in each steak pocket; close with toothpicks.
Put steaks in baking pan; place in oven and roast 4 minutes.
Remove and sprinkle with vermouth. Spread caviar generously
over steak tops; garnish with parsley and serve immediately.

Comment: A special occasion dish to team with Champagne!

That's meat and drink to me, now.
                    THE MERRY WIVES OF WINDSOR

BEEF STROGANOFF

Servings
6
Planning
Can
partially
make ahead
Preparing
1 hour
Cooking
40-50
minutes

2 pounds tenderloin or
   sirloin, trimmed and cut in
   2-inch strips ¼-inch thick
½ cup flour
1 teaspoon salt
⅛ teaspoon pepper
½ cup butter or margarine,
   divided
1 medium onion, finely
   chopped

2 cups beef broth
½ pound mushrooms, sliced
1 cup sour cream
3 tablespoons tomato paste
1 teaspoon Worcestershire
   sauce

Cooked rice or noodles
½ cup chopped fresh parsley
   for garnish

Utensil: heavy 10-inch skillet with cover

Shake meat strips, a few at a time, in bag containing flour, salt
and pepper. Heat ⅓ cup butter and brown strips on both sides in
batches of 20; remove each batch to warm platter. Add onion and
sauté until tender. Return meat to skillet and add beef broth.
Cover and simmer 25-30 minutes or until meat is tender. Sauté
mushrooms in remaining butter and add to beef. Remove skillet
from heat (may be refrigerated 1-2 days at this point).

When ready to serve, return to heat; stirring constantly, slowly add
sour cream, tomato paste and Worcestershire sauce. Continue
cooking and stirring until serving temperature is reached. (Do not
let mixture come to a boil.) Serve over rice or noodles; garnish
with chopped parsley.

Comment: A gourmet cook's rendition of a perennial favorite.

Servings
4
Planning
Serve
immediately
Preparing
30 minutes
Broiling
5-7 minutes

FILLET DE MONTICELLO

4 beef fillets (each ½ pound
and 2 inches thick, cut
from small end of tenderloin)
4 tablespoons fine-textured
liver pâte (about 2 ounces)
1 tablespoon celery salt
1 teaspoon pepper
3 tablespoons clarified butter

SAUCE
⅓ cup finely chopped shallots

¼ cup finely chopped celery
leaves
¼ cup finely chopped carrots
1 tablespoon flour
¾ cup Madeira
1 cup chicken stock
3 tablespoons clarified butter
12 large mushroom caps, cut
into ¼-inch slices
6 cooked artichoke hearts,
quartered

Utensils: medium-size skillet, large skillet, broiler pan
Preheat broiler

Cut pocket 1½ x 1½ inches through middle of each fillet. Stuff
each pocket with 1 tablespoon pâte and press edges together to
seal. Combine celery salt and pepper and evenly coat fillets with
mixture. In medium-size skillet over moderately high heat, melt
butter and sauté fillets 2 minutes on each side or until browned.
Remove fillets to warm platter.

For sauce: Using same skillet over moderate heat, add shallots,
celery leaves and carrots. Sauté 2-3 minutes until vegetables are
slightly tender. Sprinkle flour over vegetables, reduce heat slightly
and cook 2-3 minutes, stirring frequently. Add Madeira and
chicken stock; bring to boil over moderate heat. Stirring frequently,
cook sauce 5 minutes or until reduced to about 1 cup. In a large
skillet set over moderate heat, warm butter and add mushroom
slices; sauté for 2 minutes. Add the artichoke hearts and heat
through. Keep warm over low heat.

Without turning, broil fillets 5-7 minutes to desired degree of
doneness in pan placed 5 inches from broiling element. Remove
fillets to heated platter. Pour meat juices into sauce, add
mushroom and artichoke mixture and reheat briefly.

To serve, place one fillet on each plate and top with sauce
mixture.

Comment: Superb!

JOE'S KEFTETHES

Yield
24 patties
Planning
Can make
ahead
Preparing
45 minutes
Frying
10-15
minutes

1¼ cups finely chopped onion
2 tablespoons butter
2 eggs
½ teaspoon white pepper
¼ teaspoon black pepper
¾ teaspoon salt
¾ teaspoon garlic powder
1½ cups herb-seasoned
   stuffing mix
⅓ cup half-and-half

3½ tablespoons finely
   chopped fresh mint leaves
2½ tablespoons finely
   chopped fresh parsley
2 pounds ground round lean
   beef
½ cup flour
½ cup Italian bread crumbs
½ cup olive oil

Utensil: large skillet

Sauté onion in butter until golden brown; set aside. In large bowl
mix eggs, white and black peppers, salt and garlic powder.
Moisten stuffing mix with half-and-half; add mint, parsley, egg
mixture, beef and onion. Mix well by hand.

Roll mixture into balls the size of a small lemon. Combine flour
and bread crumbs; coat balls. Flatten balls into patties. Heat olive
oil in skillet and fry patties until golden brown.

(Patties may be prepared a few hours ahead and stored in
refrigerator. Use wax paper to separate layers. Mixture may also
be formed into cocktail-size meatballs to serve as appetizers.)

Comment: A taste thrill.

Please you to dine with us.
THE MERCHANT OF VENICE

PORK SAN JOAQUIN

Servings
4
Planning
Serve
immediately
Preparing
10 minutes
Cooking
50 minutes

2 tablespoons olive oil
Salt and pepper to taste
4 loin pork chops, ½ pound
   each
1 medium onion, chopped
2 cloves garlic, chopped
1½ teaspoons cumin

½ teaspoon coriander
½ cup dry white wine
2 cups canned whole
   tomatoes, crushed
½ teaspoon thyme
¼ cup chopped fresh cilantro

Utensil: 12-inch saute pan

Heat oil. Salt and pepper chops; brown over medium heat 3-4
minutes per side. Remove chops and lower heat. Add onion and
sauté until tender. Add garlic, cumin and coriander; cook 1 more
minute. Add wine, tomatoes, thyme and cilantro; stir well. Return
chops and juices to pan. Cover and simmer until chops are tender
(40-45 minutes); remove cover during last 10 minutes to reduce
sauce.

Comment: Succulent fare that harks back to hacienda days.

Small cheer and great welcome makes a merry feast.
THE COMEDY OF ERRORS

JONATHAN McMURTRY

BRAISED VIENNESE PORK ROAST

3 pounds boneless pork loin
roast
¼ cup bacon or salt pork
drippings
1 cup chopped onion
1 cup chopped carrot
1 teaspoon paprika
¾ cup chicken broth

2 tablespoons all-purpose
flour
½ cup sour cream
¼ teaspoon caraway seeds
1 teaspoon chopped capers
1 tablespoon loosely chopped
parsley

Brown roast in ovenproof skillet or Dutch oven in bacon drippings
(or salt pork)—set aside. Cook onions and carrots in remaining
drippings until tender—don't let them brown, however. Blend in
paprika by stirring. Put the roast on top of vegetables. Add
chicken broth. Bake covered at 350° for 1½-2 hours (meat
thermometer 170°).

Remove roast and keep warm. Strain pan drippings (throw away
vegetables). Skim off excess fat—add water, if necessary, to
measure 1⅓ cups. Return to Dutch oven. Blend flour into sour
cream and then gradually stir into pan drippings. Cook & stir until
thickened and bubbly. Add caraway seeds, capers & parsley. Serve
with roast. A wonderful gravy for mashed potatoes.

*For the perfect accompaniment, serve a fresh fruit salad on
Boston lettuce with Poppy Seed Dressing (see page 220).*

JONATHAN McMURTRY, Associate Artist of the Globe
Popular actor who has performed nearly 100 roles at Globe since 1961, ranging from classical to
contemporary, dramatic and comedy.

VEAL PARMIGIANA

Servings
4-5
Planning
Serve
immediately
Preparing
30 minutes
Baking
45 minutes
Storing
Refrigerate
or freeze
per
directions

4-6 boneless veal cutlets
  (about 1 ½ pounds)
4 tablespoons oil
½ pound mozzarella cheese,
  sliced

BREADING
1 egg, beaten
½ teaspoon salt
¼ teaspoon pepper
½ cup bread crumbs
3 tablespoons grated
  Parmesan or Romano
  cheese

SAUCE
2 green onions, chopped
1 6-ounce can tomato paste
2 tablespoons oil
1 tablespoon sugar
1 teaspoon salt
1 teaspoon oregano
1 teaspoon basil
¼ teaspoon ground black
  pepper
1 cup white wine

Utensil: shallow baking pan
Preheat oven to 350°

For sauce: Sauté onions in tomato paste and oil for 5 minutes.
Add sugar, salt, oregano, basil, pepper and wine; bring to boil,
lower temperature and simmer 30 minutes.

For breading: Mix egg with salt and pepper. Mix bread crumbs
and grated cheese. Dip veal first into egg mixture and then bread
mixture, coating both sides.

Heat oil and brown breaded veal on both sides. Remove to baking
pan and cover with sauce. Bake 30 minutes. (Can be refrigerated
or frozen at this point.) Cover with mozzarella and bake another
15 minutes.

*Comment: This is a grandmother's time-tested and true recipe.
Boneless, skinless chicken breasts (flattened to ¼-inch fillets) can
substitute for veal.*

CÔTÉ DE VEAU

Servings
6
Planning
Assemble
up to 8
hours ahead
Preparing
30 minutes
Baking
30 minutes

6 veal chops
Butter
Salt and pepper to taste
6 tablespoons Cognac, divided

6 ¼-inch slices Monterey
    Jack cheese
½ cup sour cream
½ pound mushrooms, sliced

Utensils: skillet, shallow pottery or glass baking dish
Preheat oven to 400°

Sauté veal in butter until browned. Arrange in baking dish and add salt and pepper. Pour 3 tablespoons Cognac over chops; cover with cheese slices. Deglaze skillet with remaining Cognac; add sour cream and mushrooms, cooking until heated through. Pour over chops and bake 30 minutes.

Comment: Easy and elegant.

BARBECUED SPARERIBS

Servings
4
Planning
Can
prepare day
ahead
Preparing
10 minutes
Cooking
30 minutes
Baking
30-40
minutes

2-3 pounds pork spareribs,
    cut into 2-rib portions

BARBECUE SAUCE
½ cup catsup
2 teaspoons salt
¼ cup vinegar

2 teaspoons Worcestershire
    sauce
½ teaspoon liquid smoke
¼ teaspoon chili powder
½ teaspoon dry mustard
6 tablespoons dark brown
    sugar

Utensil: 9 x 9 inch baking pan
Preheat oven to 325°

Boil spareribs in water to cover 30 minutes. (Meanwhile make barbecue sauce.) Place in baking pan and cover with sauce. Bake 30-40 minutes.

For barbecue sauce: Combine catsup, salt, vinegar, Worcestershire, liquid smoke, chili powder, mustard and sugar.

LAMB WITH JUNIPER SAUCE

Servings
6-8
Preparing
30 minutes
Roasting
1½-2 hours

STUFFING
2 tablespoons butter
½ cup chopped onion
½ cup sliced mushrooms
1 stalk celery, chopped
3 ounces seasoned bread
  stuffing (½ package)
Pinch of rosemary or thyme
1 egg, beaten
Stock or water, optional

4-5 pound lamb leg, boned
  and butterflied
1 clove garlic, peeled and
  halved
1 teaspoon salt
1 teaspoon pepper
2 teaspoons whole juniper
  berries, crushed

BASTING SAUCE
½ cup beef broth
½ cup red wine
1 clove garlic, crushed
2 tablespoons whole juniper
  berries

GRAVY
Pan juices
1-2 tablespoons flour
Remaining basting sauce
Stock or water
2 tablespoons red currant
  jelly

Utensils: Medium frying pan, large roasting pan, small
saucepan
Preheat oven to 400°; lower to 350°

For stuffing: Melt butter and sauté onion. Add mushrooms and
celery; cook until soft. Mix with stuffing. Add rosemary or thyme;
bind with egg. If texture is too dry, add stock or water as needed.

For basting sauce: Combine broth, red wine, garlic and juniper
berries; bring to boil. Reduce heat and simmer 10 minutes.

Lay lamb flat and spread stuffing across surface. Roll up and tie
securely with butcher's twine. Rub all exposed meat surfaces with
garlic clove. Combine salt, pepper and crushed berries and press
into meat. Roast uncovered 20 minutes in 400° oven. Lower to
350° and, basting every 10-15 minutes, roast until meat
thermometer registers desired degree of doneness: rare
130°-135°, medium 160°-165° or well done 175°-180°. Place
lamb on serving platter and keep warm.

For gravy: Skim all but 1-2 tablespoons fat from pan juices. Place pan over heat and stir in flour to make roux; cook, stirring constantly, until dark brown. Add remaining basting sauce and stock or water to make a thin sauce. Stir in currant jelly and adjust seasoning. Place in gravy bowl and serve with lamb.

Comment: Serve with barbecued vegetables, pilaf and a California Cabernet. Have poached pears for dessert.

LOUISE'S BRISKET

5 pound beef brisket
Seasoned salt
Garlic powder
1 package dry onion soup mix
1 cup white wine
2 tablespoons Worcestershire
  sauce

2 tablespoons brown sugar
½ cup water
¼ cup quick-mixing flour
¼ cup cool water

Servings
8-10
Planning
Must make
ahead
Preparing
20 minutes
Roasting
3-4 hours
Storing
Freezes well

Utensil: covered roaster
Do not preheat oven; roast at 300°

First day: Rub brisket on all sides with salt and garlic powder. Coat meat evenly, top and bottom, with soup mix; place in roaster. Combine white wine, Worcestershire sauce and sugar; pour over meat. Add water to pan bottom. Cover and roast 3-4 hours. Remove from oven; drain juices, cover and refrigerate. Cut cooled meat across grain into slices less than ¼-inch thick; cover and refrigerate.

Second day: Skim and discard fat from juices. Combine flour with water and stir into juices. Cook, stirring constantly, over medium heat until mixture thickens (add more flour if needed). Pour gravy over sliced meat. Cover and place in oven until heated through.

Comment: A great company dish. Try serving with wild rice and sauteed mushrooms.

'EL TACKO' POT ROAST MEXICALI

Servings
16
Planning
Must make
day ahead
Preparing
30 minutes
Baking
4-5 hours
Storing
Refrigerate
2-3 days

1 chuck roast (4-5 pounds)
1 cup dry red wine
1 envelope onion soup mix
1 15-ounce can ranch-style
beans, drained
1 15-ounce can kidney beans,
drained
1 15-ounce can garbanzo
beans, drained
1 15-ounce can pinto beans
2 15-ounce cans chili with
beans

2 15-ounce cans tamales,
drained, unwrapped, cut in
1-inch pieces
1 10-ounce can green
enchilada sauce
1 10-ounce can red chili
sauce
Salt and pepper to taste
Shredded Cheddar cheese
Corn or flour tortillas
Chopped green onions,
optional
Salsa, optional

Utensils: large Dutch oven with lid; large casserole
Preheat oven to 325° for meat; 350° for casserole

Place roast in pan, add wine and sprinkle with soup mix. Cover
and bake 3-4 hours at 325° until very tender. Cool and shred
meat into large casserole. Add beans, chili, tamales, sauces, salt
and pepper to taste; mix well. Heat through and refrigerate
overnight. Skim off fat and bake 45 minutes at 350°; remove from
oven to sprinkle generously with cheese, then continue baking 15
minutes or until hot and bubbly. Meanwhile, place tortillas in foil
and heat with casserole last 15 minutes.

*Comment: How to eat? Place a large spoonful on a tortilla, top
with salsa, green onions and more cheese, then roll up and enjoy.*

O appetite, from judgements stand aloof!
A LOVER'S COMPLAINT

HUNGARIAN CABBAGE ROLLS

Servings
10
Preparing
1 hour
Cooking
2 hours
Storing
1-2 days

3 large heads cabbage, cored
3 pounds ground beef
1 large onion, chopped
1½ cups raw white rice
2 teaspoons garlic salt
2 large eggs
1 teaspoon oregano

1 teaspoon salt
½ teaspoon black pepper
1 28-ounce can tomatoes
1 teaspoon sugar
Sour cream
Dill seed
Seedless grapes

Utensil: large stock pot

Dip cored cabbage heads in boiling water and, as leaves loosen, remove 3-4 at a time. Repeat process until all large leaves are separated. Pare down large vein in center of each leaf; set aside. Shred remaining cabbage.

Mix ground beef, onion, rice, garlic salt, eggs, oregano, salt and pepper. At end of each leaf place egg-size amount of meat mixture, roll up and tuck in ends.

Place shredded cabbage in stock pot, reserving small amount for topping, and arrange all rolls on shredded cabbage. Top with reserved cabbage, sprinkled sugar and tomatoes. Add water until pot is ¾ full; bring to boil and simmer 2 hours. (At this point can cool to reheat 1-2 days later.)

For each serving, arrange 2 rolls on shredded cabbage; garnish with sour cream and dill. Tuck a small grape cluster beside the rolls.

Comment: The former Hungarian Baroness sharing this recipe suggests crusty garlic bread and cucumber salad as accompaniments.

LAMB & APRICOT PIE

Servings
8-12
Planning
Can make
ahead
Preparing
1 hour
Baking
10-12
minutes
bottom
crust; 50-60
minutes
whole pie
Storing
Freeze up
to 2 months

4 pie crust sticks, prepared
    according to package
    directions
5-7 pounds leg of lamb,
    boned, fat removed, cut into
    1-inch cubes
8-10 medium mushrooms,
    sliced
½ medium onion, sliced
¼ cup oil

2 16-ounce cans apricot
    halves, drained
1 pound dried apricots
1 tablespoon beef bouillon
    granules
1 teaspoon Worcestershire
    sauce
1-2 tablespoons quick-mixing
    flour
Salt to taste, optional

Utensils: two round deep 9½-inch oven-proof casseroles
Preheat oven to 350°

Line each casserole with one pie crust round; bake 10-12 minutes
until browned. Sauté lamb, mushrooms and onion in oil. Add
canned and dried apricots, bouillon, Worcestershire, flour and salt.
Cook until bubbly and thickened (10-12 minutes). Pour mixture
into casseroles and cover with remaining crusts. Bake 50-60
minutes until top crusts are browned. (May be frozen.)

Comment: Tasty and tangy.

*He is not the flower of courtesy, but I'll warrant him
as gentle as a lamb.*
                                                    ROMEO AND JULIET

LAMB SHANKS WITH MUSTARD & HORSERADISH GRAVY

Servings
2-4
Preparing
30 minutes
Cooking
2 hours

2 tablespoons shortening
4 lamb shanks, fat and fell
  removed
¼ cup prepared mustard
2 tablespoons horseradish
1 teaspoon salt or to taste
⅓ teaspoon paprika
⅓ teaspoon pepper
1 cup water

3-4 cups cooked rice
1 10-ounce package frozen
  peas, cooked

GRAVY
¼ cup water
3 tablespoons flour
Pan juices

Utensils: Dutch oven, deep serving platter
Preheat oven to 225°

Over medium heat melt shortening and brown shanks. In small
bowl mix mustard, horseradish, salt, paprika, pepper and 1 cup
water; pour over shanks. Cover and cook over low heat 2 hours or
until meat is tender. If necessary, add more water. Put cooked rice
and peas in warm deep platter. Place shanks on top and keep in
warm oven while making gravy.

For gravy: Mix water and flour; stir into pan juices. Cook over low
heat, stirring constantly, until slightly thickened. Pour gravy over
shanks and serve.

Comment: The tangy flavor is delightful.

His wit's as thick as Tewkesbury mustard.
                                        II HENRY IV

Servings
4-6
Planning
Make day
ahead
Preparing
15 minutes
Cooking
3-5 minutes
Marinating
Overnight

TERIYAKI STEAK

**2 pounds sirloin, or round
    steak**

MARINADE
½ cup soy sauce
**1-2 teaspoons fresh ginger,
    peeled and grated**
**1 clove garlic, peeled and
    pressed**

2 teaspoons sugar
**Splash vodka or Scotch
    whiskey**
**Orange peel in thin slices,
    optional**

Utensils: wooden skewers, barbecue or broiler

Cut sirloin or round steak in thin strips. Combine soy sauce,
ginger, garlic, sugar, vodka or Scotch and orange peel, if using.
Put steak in plastic bag and add marinade. Refrigerate overnight.
Put steak on wooden skewers and barbecue or broil, 3-5 minutes.

Comment: Fresh ginger is the key ingredient here.

*The air is quick there,
And it pierces and sharpens the stomach.*
                                                    PERICLES

POULTRY

Jeffrey Allan Chandler, Sean Sullivan and G. Wood in *Twelfth Night.*

J. The. Housemen.

JOHN HOUSEMAN

ROAST CHICKEN

Take a Roasting Chicken.

Stuff it with a large size Philadelphia Cream Cheese.

Roast it like you always do.

The cream cheese may be mixed with parsley, rosemary, shallots, celery, etc. chopped up if desired.

It adds greatly to the succulence of the bird.

There's rosemary; that's for remembrance; pray, love, remember; and there is pansies, that's for thoughts.

HAMLET

JOHN HOUSEMAN
Academy Award winner and distinguished actor, director, producer and writer whose work spans decades. Directed "Richard III" for the Globe in 1985.

POULET MARENGO

Servings
4-6
Planning
Best fresh
Preparing
1 hour
Baking
*25-30
minutes*

4 whole chicken breasts,
  skinned, boned, split
Salt and pepper to taste
¼ generous cup butter
3 generous tablespoons
  sherry
½ pound mushrooms, sliced
2 tablespoons flour
1½ cups chicken broth
1 tablespoon tomato paste

1 bay leaf
2 tablespoons chopped fresh
  chives
2 10-ounce packages frozen
  lobster tails prepared
  according to package
  directions, shells removed
  and cut into bite-size pieces
3 ripe tomatoes, peeled,
  cored, quartered

Utensils: large skillet, shallow baking dish, foil cover
Preheat oven to 300°

Season chicken with salt and pepper. Melt ¼ cup butter to foam state and sauté chicken breasts until golden brown. Spoon sherry over chicken. Place chicken in baking dish, cover with foil and bake until tender, 25-30 minutes.

Add mushrooms to skillet and sauté until tender, adding a little more butter and sherry. Blend in flour and chicken broth; simmer, stirring constantly, until thickened. Season with tomato paste, bay leaf, chives, salt and pepper; simmer slowly 15 minutes. Add lobster and tomatoes and simmer additional 5-8 minutes until heated through; remove bay leaf.

To serve, place chicken on large platter and top with sauce, arranging lobster and tomato pieces as garnish.

Comment: The contributor wrote, "The two of us ate the whole thing the first time I made it."

The cook helps to make the gluttony.

II HENRY IV

CHICKEN MARSALA

Servings
4-6
Planning
Serve
immediately
Preparing
30 minutes
Chilling
2 hours
Cooking
30 minutes

3 whole chicken breasts,
   split, skinned and boned
1 egg, beaten
¼ cup milk
½ cup all-purpose flour
¼ teaspoon pepper
3 tablespoons butter
3 tablespoons olive oil
1 small green bell pepper, cut
   in strips

1 small onion, chopped
½ pound fresh mushrooms,
   sliced
2 cloves garlic, minced
1 cup Marsala wine
½ cup chicken broth
1 lemon, cut in wedges

Utensil: large skillet

Flatten chicken with mallet to ¼-inch fillets. Mix egg with milk;
combine flour and pepper. Dip chicken into egg-milk mixture, then
flour to coat all sides. Refrigerate 2 hours. Heat butter and oil in
skillet over medium high heat; brown and cook chicken 1-2
minutes on each side. Remove to platter and place in low oven.

Sauté green pepper, onion, mushrooms and garlic in same skillet
until tender crisp, then remove to platter with chicken. Add wine
and chicken broth to skillet and boil, uncovered, 10 minutes or
until liquid is reduced by half. Return chicken and vegetables to
pan and coat with sauce. Place on serving platter. Serve with
lemon wedges to squeeze over meat.

Comment: Serve with hot buttered noodles.

CHICKEN CACCIATORE

Servings
4-6
Planning
Serve
immediately
Preparing
20 minutes
Baking
1 hour

1 fryer chicken or parts
  (3-3½ pounds)
2 cloves garlic, minced
3 leaves sage or ¼ teaspoon
  ground sage
¼ cup olive or vegetable oil

¼ cup red wine
1 cup chopped tomatoes
1½ cups tomato puree
1 teaspoon salt
1 teaspoon pepper

Utensil: Dutch oven
Preheat oven to 325°

Cut chicken into serving portions. Cook garlic and sage in oil; sauté chicken until light brown. Add wine and simmer, uncovered, until absorbed. Add tomatoes and simmer 15 minutes; then add tomato puree and seasonings. Cover, bake 30 minutes; uncover last 15 minutes.

Comment: Delicious served with antipasto, a spaghetti side dish, garlic bread and Chianti.

MALAYAN PIRATE CHICKEN

Servings
6
Preparing
30 minutes
Cooking
40 minutes

4 pounds chicken pieces
2 tablespoons olive oil
4 cloves garlic, minced
2 bay leaves
½ teaspoon freshly ground
  pepper

¾ teaspoon garlic powder
½ teaspoon ginger
3 cups cider vinegar
2 cups soy sauce

Utensil: heavy deep skillet

Brown chicken pieces in oil and remove from pan. Drain excess oil and brown garlic cloves. Return chicken to pan and add bay leaves, pepper, garlic powder, ginger, vinegar and soy. Cover and simmer 40 minutes or until tender.

Comment: You will sing the pirates' praises when you taste this prize.

Irene Tedrow

LEMON CHICKEN

Recipe for 10 pieces of chicken

⅓ cup grated lemon skin
⅔ cup lemon juice (add water
  to make full cup)

1 teaspoon marjoram
1 teaspoon thyme
1 teaspoon onion salt

Pour over chicken in shallow baking dish and marinate for an hour. Preheat oven to 400°, then put in chicken. Cook for 40 minutes skin side down. Then turn and bake 20 minutes more. Baste occasionally.

Hark, hark! I hear
The strain of strutting chanticleer
Cry, Cock-a-diddle-dow.

THE TEMPEST

IRENE TEDROW, Associate Artist of the Globe
Veteran of Broadway, television and film as well as the original 1935 Globe company. Recipient SD Critics Circle Award in 1985 for "Foxfire" at the Globe.

AROMATIC CHICKEN
WITH PROVENÇAL SAUCE

Servings
4
Planning
Can make
sauce
ahead
Preparing
40 minutes
Cooking
45 minutes
Roasting
1¾-2 hours

1 roasting chicken (4-5
pounds), rinsed and dried

DRESSING
1 bunch Swiss chard or bok
choy, washed, drained
¼ cup olive oil
½ cup pine nuts
1 medium onion, chopped
1 clove garlic, minced or
pressed
Chicken giblets (omit gizzard),
chopped, optional
¾ cup cooked brown or white
rice
¼ cup grated Parmesan
cheese
1 teaspoon rosemary
Salt and pepper to taste

SAUCE
¼ cup olive oil
1 large onion, chopped
4 medium tomatoes, chopped
¼ cup dry vermouth
1 tablespoon chicken
granules
1 clove garlic, minced or
pressed
¾ teaspoon fennel seed
¾ teaspoon rosemary
1 strip orange peel
1 bay leaf
½ teaspoon sugar
Salt and pepper to taste
½ cup ripe pitted olives

Utensils: skillet with cover, medium saucepan, small skewers,
shallow roasting pan with rack
Preheat oven to 325°

For dressing: Separate stems from leaves of chard or bok choy.
Cut stems into ¼-inch slices; coarsely chop leaves. Keep in
separate piles; set aside. Heat oil over medium heat; add pine nuts
and sauté, stirring until golden. Lift out nuts and set aside. Stir in
onions, chard stems and garlic. Cover and cook 4-5 minutes or
until stems are fork tender. Add chicken giblets and cook until
liver loses pink color. Stir in chard leaves, cover and cook 3
minutes or until leaves wilt. Remove from heat and mix in nuts,
rice, cheese, rosemary, salt and pepper.

For sauce: Heat oil over medium heat; add onion and cook until limp. Add tomatoes, vermouth, chicken granules, garlic, fennel, rosemary, orange peel, bay leaf and sugar. Bring to boil and reduce heat; simmer uncovered 45 minutes or until liquid is mostly absorbed. Remove bay leaf and orange peel. Add salt and pepper; stir in olives. (Sauce can be prepared ahead and refrigerated; reheat before serving.)

Stuff chicken cavities with dressing and close with small skewers. Place breast side down on rack; roast 45 minutes. Turn breast side up and continue roasting 1-1¼ hours or until well browned and joints can be moved easily. Remove to platter. Serve with sauce on side.

Comment: Guests always accept seconds.

CHICKEN WITH GARLIC

Servings
6
Planning
Can assemble chicken ahead
Preparing
15 minutes
Baking
1¼ hours

2 tablespoons olive oil
40-60 (correct) garlic cloves, peeled
1 cup chopped celery leaves
½ cup chopped fresh parsley
12 chicken legs or thighs or combination
1 teaspoon white pepper

1 teaspoon tarragon
½ teaspoon allspice
¼ teaspoon cinnamon
1½ cups dry white wine
¼ pound butter, chilled and diced

French bread

Utensils: heavy covered casserole, 6 individual butter pots
Preheat oven to 375°

Put olive oil, garlic, celery leaves and parsley in casserole. Add chicken. Combine pepper, tarragon, allspice and cinnamon; sprinkle over chicken. Pour wine over chicken. Cover tightly and bake 1¼ hours. With slotted spoon remove garlic, celery leaves and parsley; add to butter and mix well. Divide garlic butter into individual pots. (Butter will be soft but not runny; chicken will be juicy but not brown.) Serve with crusty French bread.

Comment: A feast to share with good friends.

HONEY-BAKED CHICKEN

Servings
4-6
Planning
Can make
ahead
Preparing
10 minutes
Baking
1-1¼ hours

2 1½-2 pound broiler/fryer
chickens, cut in serving
pieces
½ cup butter or margarine,
melted

½ cup honey
¼ cup prepared mustard
1 teaspoon salt
1-1½ teaspoons curry powder

Utensil: 9 x 11 inch baking pan, foil-lined for easy clean-up
Preheat oven to 350°

Place chicken in pan, skin side up. Combine butter, honey,
mustard, salt and curry powder; mix well. Pour over chicken and
bake 1-1¼ hours, until chicken is tender and browned; baste every
15 minutes.

*Comment: A delicious, easy dish—serendipity for unexpected
company.*

CAJUN DUCK

Servings
4-6
Preparing
15 minutes
Baking
5 hours

2 4½-5½-pound ducks, split
in half, breast bones
removed
2½ teaspoons garlic powder
2 teaspoons fennel seed
2 teaspoons paprika
1½ teaspoons cayenne
pepper

¾ teaspoon salt
2 teaspoons onion powder
½ teaspoon pepper
⅛ teaspoon white pepper
¾ teaspoon rubbed sage
⅛ teaspoon ginger

Utensils: large roasting pan with rack, mortar or coffee grinder
Preheat oven to 250°

Combine all seasonings; grind and blend in mortar or coffee
grinder. Remove visible fat from ducks and sprinkle seasoning mix
on both sides, rubbing in by hand. Place ducks, breast side up, in
roasting pan on rack and bake 5 hours; drain fat after first hour.

Comment: Serve with rice and a rich Merlot wine.

BEER CHICKEN

Servings
4
Planning
Best served
immediately
Preparing
15 minutes
Baking
½ hour per
pound
chicken

1 large chicken (or 2 small)
Seasoned salt
2 tablespoons margarine,
   melted
1 12-ounce can beer
3-4 tablespoons low-sodium
   soy sauce
1 chicken bouillon cube,
   crumbled

1 large onion, sliced
1 pound carrots, peeled and
   cut in ½-inch slices
5 large potatoes, peeled and
   quartered

Utensil: large roasting pan with lid
Preheat oven to 350°

Season chicken inside and out with salt. Brush outside with
margarine and place in roasting pan. Mix beer, soy sauce and
bouillon cube; pour over chicken. Place vegetables around chicken
and sprinkle with salt. Cover and bake ½ hour for each pound of
chicken, basting occasionally. Uncover last 20 minutes. Add more
beer, if needed.

Comment: The gravy is the greatest.

**There shall be in England seven halfpenny loaves
sold for a penny: the three-hooped pot shall have
ten hoops; and I will make it a felony to drink small
beer.**

II HENRY VI

DUCK À L'ORANGE

Servings
2-4
Planning
Roast duck
ahead; keep
warm
Preparing
30 minutes
Roasting
20-25
minutes per
pound

1 4½-pound Long Island duckling

SAUCE
¼ cup butter
¼ cup orange liqueur
  (Naranja, Cointreau)
¼ cup orange juice
¼ cup powdered sugar

Grated zest 1 orange
Grated zest ½ lemon
1 11-ounce can Mandarin
  oranges, drained

Utensils: roasting pan with rack, chafing dish
Preheat oven to 350°

Roast duckling, 20-25 minutes per pound, pricking skin frequently to let fat escape and ensure crispness. Cut duck into halves or quarters for serving portions, removing back bone and all rib bones.

For sauce: Melt butter in chafing dish and blend in liqueur, orange juice, sugar, zests and Mandarin oranges. Simmer until sauce is syrupy.

When ready to serve, pour ⅔ sauce over hot duck; serve remaining sauce on the side.

Comment: Sweet and succulent.

Beatrice: Will you not eat your word?
Benedick: With no sauce that can be devised to it.
                    MUCH ADO ABOUT NOTHING

HERB CHICKEN

Servings
2-4
Planning
Oven ready
4-5 hours
ahead
Preparing
10 minutes
Baking
1¼-1½
hours

1 fryer chicken (no larger
  than 3 pounds)
3 cloves garlic, minced
3 tablespoons melted butter
¾ teaspoon salt
¼ teaspoon pepper
¼ teaspoon sage

¼ teaspoon thyme
¼ teaspoon marjoram
¼ teaspoon oregano
¼ teaspoon basil
3 bay leaves
White wine or chicken broth,
  if needed

Utensils: roasting pan and rack
Place in 425° oven; do not preheat

Rinse chicken and pat dry. Add spices and garlic to melted butter.
Place 1 tablespoon butter mixture in body cavity. Brush remaining
mixture on chicken. Place chicken, breast up, in pan and roast 45
minutes, then baste. Turn breast down and baste every 15 minutes
while cooking an additional 30-45 minutes. If not enough liquid to
baste, add white wine or chicken broth.

ORANGE-GLAZED
CHICKEN BREASTS

Servings
6-8
Planning
Must
partially
make ahead
Preparing
10 minutes
Marinating
Overnight
Baking
1 hour

6-8 whole chicken breasts,
  skinned, boned and split
1 cup Italian salad dressing

3 ounces frozen orange juice
  concentrate
½ cup orange marmalade

Utensil: large baking dish
Preheat oven to 325°

Marinate chicken in Italian dressing, refrigerating overnight.
Remove from refrigerator 30 minutes before baking; drain and
reserve dressing. Arrange chicken in single layer. Mix reserved
dressing with orange juice and marmalade; brush mixture on
chicken to give thick coating. Bake approximately 1 hour until
tender and glazed, basting frequently.

Servings
4
Planning
*Serve
immediately*
Preparing
45 minutes
Marinating
2 hours
Roasting
1-1¼ hours

FRUITED CORNISH HENS WITH SPINAC & WILD RICE

2 Cornish hens, halved
1 5-ounce package brown and
  wild rice mix
¼ cup diced dried apricots
3 tablespoons apricot jam
½ pound fresh spinach
  leaves, stems removed,
  washed and dried

MARINADE
2 scallions, finely chopped
2 garlic cloves, finely chopped
1 tablespoon safflower oil
2 tablespoons brandy
¼ teaspoon salt
1 teaspoon fresh thyme (or ¼
  teaspoon dried thyme)
1 teaspoon chili powder

DRIED FRUITS
¼ cup golden raisins
¼ cup dark raisins
¼ cup currants
¼ cup sliced dried
  apricots
2 tablespoons sugar
1 tablespoon grated orange
  zest
Water
1 cup unsalted chicken stock
¼ cup fresh lemon juice
4 tablespoons brandy

DRESSING
Reserved liquid from drained
  fruits
1 tablespoon oil
1 tablespoon grainy mustard

Utensil: 9 x 13 inch baking dish
Preheat oven to 350° to roast hens; raise to 400° last 10
minutes

Place hen halves in single layer in baking dish. Pour marinade
over hens, turning to coat. Cover and chill 2 hours. Roast,
uncovered, in marinade 1-1¼ hours until browned. Raise
temperature to 400° last 10 minutes.

For marinade: Whisk together scallions, garlic, oil, brandy, salt,
thyme and chili powder.

For dried fruits: Put golden raisins, dark raisins, currants,
apricots, sugar and orange zest in saucepan. Add water to cover
fruits by ½-inch. Bring to boil, reduce heat and simmer 5 minutes.
Pour in chicken stock, lemon juice and brandy. Simmer until liquid
is reduced by half, about 40 minutes. Strain fruits and reserve
liquid; set both aside.

For dressing: In small bowl whisk together reserved fruit cooking liquid, oil and mustard.

Meanwhile, prepare rice according to package directions, adding diced apricots. Add apricot jam to cooked rice mixture. To serve, toss spinach leaves with half the dressing. Arrange spinach on 4 plates; top with rice and game hen halves. Arrange fruit around hens. Reheat remaining dressing and pour evenly over each portion.

Comment: Gorgeous and gourmet.

MOZZARELLA CHICKEN

4 chicken breasts, boned and skinned (or 8 chicken thighs, boned and skinned)
Salt to taste
Pepper to taste

Garlic powder to taste
4-8 2 x 3-inch slices mozzarella cheese
1 cup finely crushed corn flake crumbs

Utensil: 2-quart casserole with cover, foil-lined and coated with non-stick spray
Preheat oven to 350°

Flatten chicken with mallet to ¼-inch fillets. Season to taste with salt, pepper and garlic powder. Place 1 slice mozzarella on each chicken piece. Roll up and fasten with toothpicks. Roll in crumbs. Place in casserole and bake, covered, 10-15 minutes. Remove cover and continue baking 10-15 minutes or until tender and crisp on top.

Comment: A low fat, low cholesterol entree.

Servings
4
Planning
Serve immediately
Preparing
10 minutes
Baking
20-30 minutes
Storing
Can freeze

ENCHILADAS DE TOMATILLOS Y POLLO

Servings
6
Planning
*Can make 8
hours ahead*
Preparing
30 minutes
Cooking
*40-45
minutes*
Baking
20 minutes

1 bay leaf
2-3 sprigs oregano or thyme
½ teaspoon salt
1 small dried red pepper,
 seeded
3 whole chicken breasts,
 halved

12 flour tortillas
8 ounces sour cream
2 cups grated Monterey Jack
 cheese
Paprika

SAUCE
1½ pounds fresh tomatillos,
 husked, rinsed and
 quartered
1 cup chicken broth (reserved
 from cooking breasts)
1 medium onion, finely
 chopped
3 cloves garlic, mashed
¼ cup chopped cilantro
½-1 teaspoon salt

Utensils: 9 x 13 inch baking dish lightly oiled, large stock pot, blender or food processor, saucepan, foil
Preheat oven to 350°

Place bay leaf, oregano, salt, red pepper and enough water to cover chicken (when added) in pot; bring to full boil. Add chicken immediately, cover quickly and remove from heat. Keep tightly covered 45 minutes (do not open lid during interval). Remove chicken; reserve broth (save 1 cup for sauce, remainder for other uses), removing bay leaf, oregano and red pepper. Cool chicken, then discard skin and bones and slice meat.

For sauce: In saucepan place tomatillos, 1 cup reserved chicken broth, onion and garlic. Bring to boil, cover, reduce heat and cook 10-15 minutes until tender. Let stand, covered, until slightly cooled. Place in blender or food processor with steel blade; add cilantro and salt, then blend or process until smooth.

Soften tortillas by wrapping airtight in foil and heating in 400° oven 10-15 minutes. To assemble enchiladas, put generous amount of sliced chicken down center of each tortilla and roll; place, seam side down, in baking dish. Cover with tomatillo sauce, sour cream and cheese; sprinkle with paprika. Bake 20 minutes until cheese is melted and sauce is bubbly.

Comment: A refreshing new flavor.

MISTRAL CORNISH HENS

Servings
4
Planning
Serve immediately
Preparing
20 minutes
Baking
40-60 minutes
Cooking
30 minutes

4 Cornish hens
Salt and pepper
4 tablespoons unsalted
butter, melted and cooled
4 tablespoons olive oil
4-8 cloves garlic, peeled
½-1 cup Sauvignon Blanc or
other dry white wine

SAUCE
Pan juices (see directions)
1-1½ cups chicken broth
6-12 tablespoons unsalted
butter
Squeeze lemon juice

Utensil: 2½-quart deep casserole
Preheat oven to 450°

Salt and pepper birds inside and out. Combine butter and oil; coat birds with mixture. Place 1-2 cloves garlic inside each and place in casserole; add wine. Bake until skins look reddish, about 20-30 minutes, then turn. Continue baking 30-40 minutes, rotating sides several times; end breast sides up.

Remove birds from casserole and drain, tipping each bird to catch all juices. Set aside and keep warm. Degrease pan juices and reduce liquid to a jelly-like consistency. Add chicken broth gradually and cook until sauce is thickened. Add butter slowly, stirring over medium heat; season with salt and pepper to taste. Smooth and set sauce with lemon juice. Serve sauce over rice or mashed potatoes alongside hens.

Comment: La Jolla Chef Julius Seman developed this intriguing company dish with the buttery overtones.

Epicurean cooks
Sharpen with cloyless sauce his appetite.
                    ANTONY AND CLEOPATRA

POLLO DE COSIO

Servings
8
Planning
*Serve
immediately*
Preparing
30 minutes
Cooking
*20-30
minutes*
Baking
30 minutes
Marinating
2-3 hours

SAUCE
2 pieces bread, lightly
    buttered and toasted
2 tomatoes, skinned and
    seeded
¼ teaspoon ground cloves
½ teaspoon pepper
¼ teaspoon cinnamon
2 tablespoons liquid gravy
    seasoning
1 cup ground pecans
½ teaspoon oil
1 x 1-inch piece canned,
    seeded chipotle* (hot
    pepper)
½ cup sour cream

4 whole chicken breasts,
    boned, skinned, halved
1-2 teaspoons butter
1-2 teaspoons oil
Cooked rice

MARINADE
3 eggs, beaten
½ teaspoon lemon juice
¼ teaspoon salt

**Utensils: food processor or blender, saucepan, skillet, 9 x 13
inch baking pan
Preheat oven to 325°**

For marinade: Combine eggs, lemon juice and salt. Add chicken
breasts and marinate 2-3 hours.

For sauce: In container combine toast, tomatoes, cloves, pepper,
cinnamon, gravy seasoning and pecans. Process until smooth. Heat
oil over medium heat and add pecan mixture; cook 5 minutes to
blend ingredients. Using tongs, add chipotle and cook 5 more
minutes, bringing mixture to slow boil. Remove from heat and
remove chipotle. Add sour cream and stir to combine. (If mixture
is too thick, thin with small amount water.)

Remove chicken from marinade (discard marinade). Heat butter
and oil, add chicken and sauté 5 minutes or until tender (be
careful not to overcook). Drain chicken on paper towels. Place
chicken in baking dish; pour sauce over chicken. Cover dish with
foil; place in oven 20-30 minutes to heat thoroughly (but do not let
mixture bubble). Serve over rice.

*Chipotle probably will be found canned in adobo sauce. Using
tongs (or rubber gloves), remove from can and rinse off sauce
before using.

*Comment: A family's treasured recipe, carried from Spain to
Mexico City, comes to us from south of the border.*

ELEGANT CHAFING DISH CHICKEN

**8 large chicken breast halves
with skin left intact, boned**
**6 cups cooked long grain
white rice (2 cups raw rice)**
½ cup toasted sliced almonds

SAUCE
**4 tablespoons margarine or
unsalted butter**
4 tablespoons flour

2 cups chicken stock
2 cloves garlic, finely minced
**2 teaspoons Worcestershire
sauce**
Salt and pepper to taste
½ cup dry sherry
**24 medium-large mushroom
caps, cleaned**
½ cup heavy cream

Servings
8
Planning
Partially
make sauce
ahead
Preparing
15-20
minutes
Broiling
30 minutes
Cooking
15 minutes

Utensils: broiler pan, chafing dish
Preheat broiler

Broil chicken breast halves 15 minutes per side or until tender but
still moist. Remove skin and discard; set chicken aside.

For sauce: Heat margarine in chafing dish. Add flour and chicken
stock; stir constantly until smooth and thick. Add garlic,
Worcestershire, salt, pepper, sherry and mushroom caps; simmer 5
minutes. (Sauce may be made ahead and refrigerated at this point.
Reheat before proceeding.)

At the table when ready to serve, stir in cream; add chicken
breasts. Heat 4-5 minutes but do not let reach boiling point. Place
each chicken breast on bed of rice. Spoon over sauce with
mushroom caps; sprinkle with almonds.

Comment: This is a gem.

CHICKEN WITH MUSHROOM SAUCE

Servings
4
Planning
Partially
prepare
ahead
Preparing
45 minutes
Baking
45 minutes

2 tablespoons butter or
  margarine
4 chicken breasts, skinned
  and boned
¹/₈ teaspoon salt
Dash of pepper
¼ teaspoon garlic powder
2 10¾-ounce cans cream of
  mushroom soup

1 cup sherry
¹/₈ teaspoon allspice
¼ teaspoon poultry seasoning
¼ cup parsley flakes
½ pound fresh mushrooms,
  sliced

Utensil: 9 x 13 inch baking dish
Preheat broiler; preheat oven to 350°

Place butter in baking dish and melt under broiler. Dip chicken
breasts in butter and arrange in pan, buttered side up. Season
with salt, pepper and garlic powder. Broil until golden brown on
both sides. (Can be refrigerated several hours at this point.) Mix
soup, wine, allspice, poultry seasoning and parsley flakes; heat
just to boiling point. Add sliced mushrooms. Pour sauce over
chicken and bake, uncovered, 45 minutes. Sauce should be golden
brown. Serve over rice.

Comment: The baking aroma is divine.

...the air
Nimbly and sweetly recommends itself
Unto our gentle senses.

MACBETH

KATHERINE HELMOND

CHICKEN-MUSHROOM SUPRÊME

2 whole chickens
3 bay leaves
1 clove garlic
1 tablespoon salt
2 pounds mushrooms, sliced
¾ cup butter or margarine
3 shallots or 5 green onions, sliced

2 tablespoons flour
4 cups dairy sour cream
¼ cup dry sherry
½ teaspoon nutmeg
Salt, pepper
½ pound grated Cheddar cheese

Place chickens in large pot with water to cover. Add bay leaves, garlic and salt. Cook until chicken is tender, about 1½ hours. Remove chicken from water and cool. Skin and bone chicken; cut into bite-size pieces.

Sauté mushrooms in ½ cup butter until lightly browned. Do not overcook. Set mushrooms aside with any remaining liquid.

Sauté shallots in remaining ¼ cup butter until tender. Add flour and cook 1 minute. Add sour cream and blend well. Add mushrooms and liquid from pan, chicken, sherry, nutmeg, salt and pepper to taste. Blend thoroughly. Spoon mixture into casserole. Sprinkle with cheese. Bake at 350° about 20 minutes or until slightly brown and bubbly. Makes 10-12 servings.

Enjoy

KATHERINE HELMOND
Award winning New York actress, recognized nationally for her unique comedy portrayals on televisions's "Soap" and "Who's the Boss?"

CHICKEN FLORENTINE WITH RICE

Servings
4
Planning
Can make
day ahead
Preparing
20 minutes
Broiling
20 minutes
Microwaving
1½
minutes
Baking
20 minutes

5-6 frozen boneless chicken
   breast halves
¾ cup Italian dressing
1 bunch spinach, washed,
   stemmed and drained

BASIC SAUCE
1 cup medium white sauce
   (page 21)
½ teaspoon salt
½ teaspoon pepper
1 teaspoon celery salt
(1 cup cream of celery soup
   can be substituted for basic
   sauce)

1½ cups dry rice and wild
   rice combination
⅛ teaspoon saffron

1 teaspoon salt
Water for cooking rice
½ teaspoon basil
1 clove garlic, minced or ½
   teaspoon garlic powder
¼ cup chopped onion
1 8-ounce can pineapple
   slices, drained and juice
   reserved
2 tablespoons reserved
   pineapple juice
3 tablespoons sherry
½ teaspoon curry powder
¼ cup grated Parmesan
   cheese

GARNISH
Red bell pepper strips,
   optional

Utensils: broiler pan, 7 x 10 inch microwave-proof dish
Microwave oven
Preheat broiler; preheat oven to 325°

Place frozen chicken breasts in broiler pan; pour dressing over
each piece. Broil, skin side up, until well browned. Turn, broil
other side 10 minutes or until cooked through. Set aside and keep
warm.

For basic sauce: To white sauce add salt, pepper and celery salt.
(Or use cream of celery soup.)

Cook rice according to directions, adding saffron and salt to water.
Slice spinach into ½-inch strips and mound in microwave-proof
pan. Cover and microwave on high 1 minute; stir and microwave
30 seconds. Divide basic sauce; reserve. Add basil, garlic and
onions to ½ cup basic sauce; heat to serving temperature and stir
into spinach. Place cooked rice around edges of spinach. Top with
chicken.

Chop 1 pineapple slice and add to reserved ½ cup basic sauce. Add reserved pineapple juice, sherry and curry powder; heat to serving temperature. Pour over chicken; top with remaining pineapple slices and sprinkle with Parmesan. (Can be refrigerated at this point.) Before serving, heat uncovered 20 minutes; garnish.

Comment: A tasty and attractive all-in-one dish presentation.

JOYCIE-A'S CHICKEN PROVINCIAL

Servings
4
Planning
Can
prepare
early in day
Preparing
45 minutes
Baking
1½ hours

1 whole head fresh garlic
1 chicken, quartered or in
  serving pieces
4 potatoes, peeled and
  quartered
3 carrots, sliced diagonally
2 onions, quartered

20 cherry tomatoes
20 mushrooms
1 cup pitted ripe olives,
  drained
1 cup olive oil
1 tablespoon thyme
Salt and pepper to taste

Utensil: roasting pan
Preheat oven to 350°

Break garlic into cloves, peel and cut into slivers. Insert slivers under skin and into chicken meat, poking holes to distribute evenly.

Place chicken in roasting pan; add potatoes, carrots, onions, tomatoes, mushrooms and olives. Pour olive oil over all and sprinkle heavily with thyme until almost green. Bake, uncovered, 1½ hours; baste every 15 minutes. Serve immediately.

Comment: French bread, to soak up the juices, is an absolute must with this recipe which won finalist honors at the Gilroy Garlic Festival.

LOQUAT CHICKEN

Servings
2-4
Planning
*Make
chicken
balls ahead;
make sauce
when ready
to serve*
Preparing
60 minutes
*Deep
frying*
20 minutes

CHICKEN BALLS
2 cups raw chicken meat,
  finely chopped
3 tablespoons green onions,
  finely chopped
10 water chestnuts, finely
  chopped
6 dried black mushrooms,
  soaked 1 hour in hot water,
  stems removed, finely
  chopped
½ teaspoon salt, optional
2 tablespoons dark soy sauce
1 tablespoon rice wine or
  sherry

2 tablespoons cornstarch
2 egg whites, stiffly beaten
2 cups peanut oil for deep
  frying

SAUCE
1 tablespoon peanut oil
1 15-ounce can loquats,
  drained, juice reserved
1 cup loquat juice
½ cup chicken broth
2 tablespoons light soy sauce
2 tablespoons cornstarch

Utensil: wok or deep fryer
Preheat oven to 225°

For chicken balls: Combine chicken, onions, water chestnuts, black mushrooms, salt, dark soy sauce and rice wine. Sprinkle cornstarch over mixture, 1 tablespoon at a time; mix well after each addition. Lightly fold in egg whites. Oil hands and form mixture into apricot-size balls; put on lightly oiled plate. Heat peanut oil and deep fry 5-6 balls at a time 3-4 minutes, turning once. Remove with slotted spoon and put in oven to keep warm. Skim fat and reheat oil after each batch. (Chicken balls can be refrigerated or frozen at this point.)

For sauce: In saucepan heat peanut oil and loquat juice. Combine broth, light soy sauce and cornstarch. When juice boils, slowly add broth mixture, stirring constantly until thickened. When ready to serve, add chicken balls and loquats; stir gently to coat. Serve over rice.

Comment: A gift from China.

CHICKEN DIJON

Servings
6-8
Planning
Can make
ahead
Preparing
20 minutes
Baking
25-30
minutes (45
minutes if
refrigerated)

¼ cup flour
1 teaspoon salt
¼ teaspoon pepper
4 large whole chicken
   breasts, skinned, boned and
   split
2 tablespoons butter
2 tablespoons oil

SAUCE
3 tablespoons butter
3 tablespoons flour
3 tablespoons Dijon mustard
1½ cups milk
¾ cup dry white wine
1 teaspoon salt
¼ teaspoon tarragon

GARNISH, OPTIONAL
Red grapes
Watercress

Utensils: large skillet, saucepan, shallow baking dish
Preheat oven to 350°

Combine flour, salt and pepper; dredge chicken. Melt butter with
oil; sauté chicken until golden (about 5 minutes). Arrange in baking
dish.

For sauce: Melt butter; whisk in flour and mustard. Cook,
whisking constantly, until bubbly. Whisk in milk, wine, salt and
tarragon. Cook 1 minute, stirring constantly, until mixture
thickens and bubbles.

Pour sauce over chicken. (Can be covered and refrigerated
overnight at this point.) Bake 25-30 minutes (45 minutes if
refrigerated.) Arrange chicken on platter, spooning sauce over top.
Garnish with red grapes and watercress, if using.

*Comment: This mustard-flavored chicken is a popular informal
supper entrée. Serve with a dry California Riesling.*

Servings
6
Planning
Can assemble ahead
Preparing
30 minutes
Baking
1 hour 15 minutes

APRICOT-STUFFED CHICKEN BREASTS

6 whole chicken breasts, skinned, boned, but NOT split
6 tablespoons granulated sugar
6 tablespoons brown sugar
Salt to taste
¼ pound butter or margarine, melted
Parsley

24 large dried apricot halves

SAUCE
1 16-ounce can apricot halves, drained, reserving ¼ cup syrup
2 tablespoons granulated sugar
2 tablespoons brown sugar
⅛ teaspoon almond extract

Utensils: blender, 8 x 12 inch baking pan lined with foil
Preheat oven to 300°

Soak dried apricots in water 2 hours; dry with paper towels and set aside.

For sauce: In blender, purée drained canned apricot halves with reserved syrup, both sugars and almond extract.

On inside of each chicken breast, place 4 dried reconstituted apricot halves on one half; sprinkle with 1 tablespoon each of the sugars and 1 tablespoon apricot sauce. Fold other chicken half over filling and secure with skewers or toothpicks. Salt to taste. Arrange in baking dish and drizzle with melted butter and remaining apricot sauce. Bake 1 hour 15 minutes uncovered.

Comment: Outstanding!

BARRY BOSTWICK

NO-COW LO-CAL TURKEY LOAF

1 pound ground turkey
  sausage
1 pound ground turkey meat
½ cup chopped onion
1 medium tomato, seeded and
  diced
⅓ cup chopped green
  bell pepper
½ cup chopped celery

¼ cup chopped fresh parsley
¼ cup chopped fresh dill
½ teaspoon pepper
½ teaspoon onion powder
½ teaspoon garlic salt
½ teaspoon lemon pepper
1 tablespoon soy sauce
1 cup ground Wheat Thin
  crackers

Preheat oven to 350°

In a large bowl combine the two turkey meats. Sauté in butter the onion, green pepper and celery. Add diced tomato and sautéed vegetables to meat. Mix well. Add cracker crumbs and all seasonings. Mix well, again!

Put mixture in oiled meat loaf pan or casserole dish and bake for approximately 45 minutes.

BARRY BOSTWICK
Tony Award winning Broadway star for "The Robber Bridegroom." Numerous television starring roles include portrayals as George Washington. Seen at Globe in "As You Like It" and "Hamlet."

Servings
12
Planning
Make
partially
ahead
Preparing
Day 1: 15
minutes;
Day 2:
1-1¼ hours
Cooking
Day 1: 2
hours
Baking
Day 2: 45
minutes

CHICKEN, HAM & MUSHROOM CASSEROLE

FIRST DAY
2 roasting chickens
  (4-4½ pounds each)
1 14½-ounce can chicken
  broth
2 cups water
1 teaspoon salt
⅛ teaspoon pepper
Chopped celery leaves to
  taste
2 onions, sliced

STOCK
Reserved skin and bones
Reserved chicken broth
2 cups water

SECOND DAY
1½ pounds mushrooms,
  divided
3 tablespoons butter

2 tablespoons minced onions
6 ounces egg noodles
1½ pounds boiled or baked
  ham, cut in 2-inch slivers

SAUCE
⅔ cup butter
2 tablespoons minced onions
¾ cup flour
1 quart light cream
1 quart reserved chicken
  stock, fat removed
¼ teaspoon dry mustard
⅛ teaspoon pepper
2 teaspoons salt, optional

GARNISH
⅓ cup sliced almonds,
  toasted
Reserved sautéed mushroom
  caps

Utensils: large stock pot, skillet, saucepan, 1 large oven-proof casserole or 2 smaller ones
Preheat oven to 350°

First day: Place chickens in pot; add chicken broth, water, salt, pepper, celery leaves and onions. Cover, bring to boil, lower heat and simmer 1 hour or until meat is tender. Remove chicken from broth. Cool; remove meat from bones in large pieces and reserve. Save skin and bones.

For stock: Return skin and bones to broth and add 2 cups water. Cover and cook 1 hour. Strain. Cool and place in refrigerator overnight.

Second day: Reserve a few mushroom caps for garnish. Slice remainder, including stems. Melt butter and sauté mushrooms, including reserved caps. Cook noodles according to directions; drain, rinse in boiling water and set aside.

For sauce: Melt butter and sauté onions; blend in flour. Gradually add cream and reserved chicken stock; cook, stirring constantly, until mixture thickened. Season with mustard, pepper and salt, if using.

Combine reserved chicken with sauce, sliced mushrooms, noodles and ham; pour into casserole. Garnish with almonds and reserved mushroom caps. Bake 45 minutes.

Comment: Guests repeatedly request the recipe for this scrumptious casserole.

CHICKEN SCHNITZEL

Servings
4
Planning
Can assemble ahead
Preparing
30 minutes
Cooking
8-12 minutes

2 whole chicken breasts, skinned, boned and split
½ cup all-purpose flour
2 eggs, beaten

1 cup dry bread crumbs
½ cup butter
½ cup olive oil
Lemon wedges

Utensil: 10-inch skillet

Flatten chicken to ¼-inch thickness with rolling pin or mallet. In separate shallow bowls place flour, eggs and bread crumbs. Coat chicken: dredge lightly in flour (shake off excess), dip into eggs and press bread crumbs firmly into meat. (May be refrigerated at this point.)

When ready to serve, melt butter and oil over medium heat. Add chicken, a portion at a time, and sauté 2-3 minutes on each side until lightly browned. Remove from pan and keep warm until all portions are ready. Serve immediately with lemon wedges to squeeze over meat.

Comment: Superb, yet speedy and simple.

IDAHO PHEASANT

Servings
4
Planning
*Serve
immediately*
Preparing
15 minutes
Baking
1¾ hours

2 pheasants, oven-ready and
  split
Salt, pepper and paprika to
  taste
1 pound bacon, sliced

1 medium onion, thinly sliced
  in rings
½ cup all-purpose flour
1 cup white wine or chicken
  broth

Utensil: roasting pan, aluminum foil cover
Preheat oven to 325°; increase to 350° for final browning

Season pheasants with salt, pepper and paprika. Place in roasting
pan, skin side up. Cover with strips of bacon, then onion rings. Sift
flour lightly over all and add wine. Cover tightly with foil and bake
1 hour. Remove from oven and baste well. Recover and cook
additional 40 minutes, or until fork poked in wing produces clear
liquid. Uncover, increase oven temperature to 350°, and bake until
well browned.

Remove from oven. Discard onion and bacon. Place pheasant on
warm platter. Strain pan juices and make gravy.

Comment: Expensive, but worth it!

Both of you are birds of the selfsame feather.
III HENRY VI

SEAFOOD & FISH

Monique Fowler and Associate Artist Ellis Rabb in *The Tempest*

SEA BASS WITH SWEET BEAN SAUCE

Servings
4
Planning
Serve immediately
Preparing
15 minutes
Cooking
5-10 minutes

4 fillets of sea bass or halibut (about 2 pounds)
2 tablespoons oil
2 tablespoons sweet bean sauce
2 tablespoons low sodium Japanese soy sauce

2 tablespoons sake or dry sherry
¼ teaspoon ground whole black pepper
4 green onions, sliced diagonally

Utensil: wok with steamer rack

Combine bean sauce, soy sauce and sherry. Rub both sides of fillets with oil and spoon bean sauce mixture on fish. Cover bottom of wok with 2 cups water and bring to boil. Put steamer rack in wok and set fish on rack. Place onions and grated pepper on fish. Cover and steam until fillets are tender when pierced with a fork (5-10 minutes). Serve immediately.

Comment: Sweet bean sauce can be found in the oriental section of supermarkets. Steam broccoli with fish and serve with white or fried rice.

LOBSTER OREGANO

Servings
3-4
Planning
Serve immediately
Preparing
10 minutes
Cooking
10 minutes

2 cups diced lobster meat
3 tablespoons butter, divided
½ cup dry white wine
1 teaspoon oregano
Dash salt

2 tablespoons all-purpose flour
1½ cups chicken consommé
Juice of ½ lemon

Sauté lobster in 1 tablespoon butter for 3 minutes. Add wine, oregano and salt. Simmer 5-7 minutes. Remove from heat, but keep warm. In saucepan melt 2 tablespoons butter over low heat. Blend in flour. When smooth, add consommé and lemon juice, stirring constantly until thickened. Pour sauce over lobster and serve in ramekins or shells.

SHRIMP ROCKEFELLER

Servings
6
Planning
Assemble
ahead 4-6
hours
Preparing
40 minutes
Baking
10 minutes

24-28 medium raw shrimp	2 tablespoons margarine
¾ cup sour cream	2 10-ounce packages frozen
6 tablespoons catsup	chopped spinach, cooked,
2 drops hot pepper sauce	drained
½ tablespoon horseradish	Salt and pepper to taste
1 small onion, finely chopped	¾ cup buttered bread crumbs
1 clove garlic, crushed	Lemon garnish, optional

Utensil: 6 seafood shells, buttered
Preheat oven to 450°

Blanch shrimp in boiling water; remove immediately and plunge
into cold water. Peel and devein. Mix sour cream, catsup, hot
pepper sauce and horseradish. Sauté onion and garlic in
margarine until transparent. In bowl combine spinach, onion,
garlic and sour cream mixtures; season with salt and pepper.
Assemble in shells by layering small amount spinach mixture,
shrimp (divide among portions), more spinach and topping with
bread crumbs. Bake; serve with lemon garnish if desired.

Comment: An intriguing presentation.

PRAWNS TOMATILLO

SAUCE
8-10 tomatillos, washed and
  husks removed
1 4-ounce can chopped green
  chiles
½ cup whipping cream
1 egg

2 cups cooked rice
12 large prawns, peeled,
  deveined
4 slices Monterey Jack
  cheese
1 medium red bell pepper, cut
  in strips
1 bunch cilantro, chopped

Servings
4
Planning
Can make
sauce day
ahead
Preparing
1 hour
Baking
15-18
minutes

Utensils: steamer, blender, 4 ramekins or individual baking
dishes
Preheat oven to 475°

For sauce: Steam tomatillos 20 minutes or until soft. Place
tomatillos, chiles, cream and egg in blender; process until smooth.

Fill each baking dish with ½ cup rice, 3 prawns, quarter portion
of sauce and slice of cheese. Top with pepper strips. Bake 15-18
minutes or until prawns turn pink. Garnish with cilantro and serve.

*Comment: Lovely to see, wonderful to eat. Serve with black beans
and a fruit salad.*

He ten times pines that pines beholding food.
                    THE RAPE OF LUCRECE

SHRIMP CRÉOLE

Servings
4
Planning
Can make
sauce
ahead
Preparing
1 hour
Cooking
35 minutes

CRÉOLE SAUCE
2 tablespoons unsalted butter
1 medium onion, chopped
1 green bell pepper, seeded
and chopped
2 celery ribs, chopped
5 cloves garlic, finely chopped
2 teaspoons Créole Seafood
Seasoning (page 135) or to
taste
1 teaspoon paprika,
preferably hot
1/8 teaspoon cayenne pepper
4 bay leaves

1 1/4 cups chicken stock
4 medium tomatoes, peeled,
seeded and diced
1 tablespoon Worcestershire
sauce
1 teaspoon hot pepper sauce
1/2 teaspoon salt
3 green onions, chopped

2 tablespoons oil
1 1/2 pounds medium shrimp,
shelled, deveined
2 teaspoons Créole Seafood
Seasoning (page 135)

Utensils: 2 large skillets

For créole sauce: Heat oil over moderately high heat; add onion, green pepper, celery and garlic. Cook, stirring occasionally, 5 minutes or until softened but not browned. Add Créole Seafood Seasoning, paprika, cayenne pepper, bay leaves and chicken stock. Bring to boil and cook 5 minutes or until slightly reduced and thickened. Stir in tomatoes; cook 10 minutes, stirring occasionally, until thickened. Stir in Worcestershire sauce, hot pepper sauce, salt and green onions; reduce heat to low and simmer 10 minutes.

Heat oil over moderately high heat. Add shrimp and sprinkle with Créole Seafood Seasoning; cook 30 seconds per side or until slightly pink. Pour in hot Créole sauce; stir and cook over moderate heat 2-3 minutes or until shrimp are pink and curled.

Comment: Authentic New Orleans dining.

CRÉOLE SEAFOOD SEASONING

Yield
1¾ cups
Storing
9 months in
airtight
container

⅓ cup salt
¼ cup garlic powder or flakes
¼ cup black peppercorns
2 tablespoons cayenne pepper
2 tablespoons thyme

2 tablespoons oregano
⅓ cup paprika, preferably hot
3 tablespoons onion powder
   or flakes

Utensil: large spice mill or food processor

Combine salt, garlic powder, peppercorns, cayenne pepper, thyme, oregano, paprika and onion powder or flakes. Process 1 minute or until evenly pulverized and blended.

Comment: This will bring back the bayou.

MARINADE FOR FISH

Yield
2-2½ cups
Planning
Can make
ahead

1 cup Italian dressing
Juice of 6-8 limes (¾-1 cup)
¼ cup dry white wine
½-1 onion, sliced
Chopped parsley or cilantro to
   taste

Firm white fish such as
   halibut, sea bass, swordfish

In container with lid combine Italian dressing, lime juice, wine, onion and parsley or cilantro. Shake well to mix. Pour over fish; cover and chill 1-3 hours, turning fish several times.

Comment: You'll reel in the gustatory compliments.

LOBSTER CRÊPES

Servings
4-6 (12 crêpes)
Planning
Can assemble ahead
Preparing
1 hour
Baking
12-15 minutes

CRÊPES
1 cup all-purpose flour
½ cup water
½ cup milk
2 tablespoons butter, melted
2 eggs
¼ teaspoon salt
Oil

1 pound lobster tail, cooked,
  cut into small pieces
½ cup grated Parmesan
  cheese

SAUCE
4 tablespoons butter
1½ cups cream or half-and-
  half
½ teaspoon paprika
3 egg yolks, beaten
½ cup sherry or Madeira
Salt and pepper to taste

Utensils: blender; 6-inch crepe pan; double boiler; baking dish
or ramekins, greased
Preheat oven to 350°

For crêpes: In blender combine flour, water, milk, melted butter,
eggs and salt; blend at low speed until smooth. Let rest in
refrigerator 2 hours. Place crêpe pan over medium heat; brush
lightly with oil. Ladle scant ¼ cup batter into pan and quickly tilt
so batter completely covers surface. Cook until top is set and
underside browned; turn and cook until other side is golden.
Repeat, keeping pan lightly oiled for each crêpe. Cool on paper
towels; stack and store between sheets of waxed paper. (Crêpes
can be baked day ahead and kept refrigerated or frozen.)

For sauce: Melt butter in top of double boiler. Add cream and
paprika and heat over simmering water. Stir a little hot cream
mixture into yolks. Then combine yolks with cream, adding in a
steady stream while beating constantly with wire whisk. Keep
beating until mixture thickens. Add sherry or Madeira and
continue cooking slowly, stirring until sauce again thickens. Season
to taste with salt and pepper.

To assemble, place lobster pieces down middle of each crêpe; spoon small portion cream sauce over lobster. Roll crepe and place, seam side down, in baking dish or ramekins. Spoon remaining sauce over crêpes and sprinkle with Parmesan. (Can be covered and refrigerated several hours at this point.) When ready to serve, bake uncovered 12-15 minutes.

Comment: An easy way to magnify lobster's succulence.

RED SNAPPER EN PAPILLOTE

Servings
6
Planning
Can
assemble
ahead
Preparing
30 minutes
Baking
35-40
minutes

2 pounds red snapper fillets
  cut into 6 pieces
Salt and pepper to taste
½ cup butter, melted
2 tablespoons chopped
  parsley
1 tablespoon lemon juice

1 tablespoon white wine
½ teaspoon dill weed
Butter for greasing
6 thin slices onion
1½ cups thinly sliced carrots
6 slices Swiss cheese

Utensils: parchment paper or heavy duty aluminum foil, cookie sheet
Preheat oven to 400°

Sprinkle fillets on both sides with salt and pepper. Combine butter, parsley, lemon juice, wine and dill weed. Cut 6 pieces of parchment paper or aluminum foil into 12-inch lengths; grease heavily. Place 1 teaspoon butter-parsley mixture on each piece; top with fillet. Separate onion slices into rings and place l slice on each fillet; top each with with ¼ cup carrots. Pour remaining butter-parsley mixture over carrots, dividing evenly. Top each serving with cheese slice. Fold foil over cheese and seal well. (Can be refrigerated several hours at this point.) Place packets on cookie sheet; bake 35-40 minutes.

Comment: Easy to fix, elegant to eat.

SALMON CHABLIS WITH ONIONS AMBROSIAL

Servings
6-8
Planning
Serve
immediately
Preparing
30 minutes
Barbecuing
1-1¼ hours

6-8 pounds whole salmon,
   dressed, rinsed and dried
Juice of 1 lemon

6 whole onions, cleaned
¼ pound butter, softened
⅓ cup seasoned bread
   crumbs

GARNISH
Reserved stuffing
4 mushrooms, sliced
½ lemon, sliced

STUFFING
1 onion, sliced
16 mushrooms, sliced
¼ pound bacon, diced
16-20 cherry tomatoes,
   halved
Soy sauce to taste, optional
⅛ teaspoon herb pepper
½ cup Chablis
½ lemon, sliced

Utensils: sauté pan, greased twine, heavy duty aluminum foil,
barbecue
Preheat barbecue

For stuffing: Sauté onion with mushrooms and bacon until tender.
Add tomatoes, soy sauce and herb pepper; sauté lightly. Cool; add
Chablis.

Rub salmon cavity with lemon juice; fill with ⅔ of stuffing mixture
and lemon slices. Reserve remainder stuffing for garnish. Tie
salmon with twine and wrap securely in foil. Barbecue 1-1¼ hours
or until salmon is flaky but not dry.

Cut 1-inch V-shaped hole in top of each onion. Combine butter and
bread crumbs; fill onions. Wrap onions individually in foil. Place on
barbecue and cook 1 hour or until tender; turn frequently.

When ready to serve, place salmon on very warm platter and quickly bone. Garnish with heated reserved stuffing, mushrooms and lemon slices. Remove foil from onions and place around salmon.

Comment: This original recipe was proclaimed a winner in a contest judged by James Beard.

PRAWNS & PASTA

2 tablespoons low-sodium soy
   sauce
1 cup water
1 pound medium-size
   shrimp, peeled, deveined

½ pound vermicelli,
   spaghettini or linguini,
   cooked and drained
2 tablespoons minced fresh
   parsley

SAUCE
¼ cup butter or margarine
½ cup thinly sliced green
   onions and tops
2 large cloves garlic, minced
1½ teaspoons cornstarch
4 teaspoons lemon juice
Reserved shrimp liquid
¼ cup finely chopped fresh
   basil leaves, packed

Servings
2-4
Planning
Serve
immediately
Preparing
10-15
minutes
Cooking
2 minutes
shrimp; 3
minutes
sauce

Utensils: saucepan, large skillet

Combine soy sauce and water; bring to boil. Add shrimp and cook 2 minutes or until shrimp turns pink. Remove shrimp and keep warm; reserve liquid.

For sauce: Melt butter over medium heat and sauté green onions and garlic 2 minutes. Blend cornstarch and lemon juice; stir into onion mixture. Add reserved shrimp liquid and basil. Bring to boil and simmer 1 minute.

To serve, toss hot pasta with sauce, shrimp and parsley.

Comment: Team with spinach salad and Italian bread for a low calorie feast.

SHRIMP WITH FETA & TOMATO

Servings
6
Planning
Serve
immediately
Preparing
20-30
minutes
Cooking
15-20
minutes

¾ cup olive oil
½ cup finely chopped onions
1-2 cloves garlic, crushed,
 optional
8 medium tomatoes, peeled,
 seeded, drained, coarsely
 chopped
1 cup dry white wine
4 tablespoons finely chopped
 parsley, divided

1 teaspoon oregano
Pepper to taste
3 pounds fresh shrimp,
 peeled, deveined, rinsed
 and dried
5 ounces Feta cheese, cut
 into ¼-inch cubes

Utensil: large heavy skillet

Heat oil over moderate heat. Add onions and garlic, if using; cook 5 minutes until soft and transparent. Stir in tomatoes, wine, 2 tablespoons parsley, oregano and pepper. Bring to boil and continue to cook briskly, uncovered, until mixture thickens to a light purée. Add shrimp; cook 5 minutes or until pink and firm to the touch. Stir in cheese and remaining parsley; adjust seasonings.

Comment: Serve over rice or orzo and listen to the raves.

Polonius: Do you know me, my lord?
Hamlet: Excellent well; you are a fishmonger.
HAMLET

SHRIMP WITH PEPPERS

Servings
4
Planning
Make fresh
Preparing
20 minutes
Cooking
15 minutes

1 green bell pepper
1 red bell pepper
2 tablespoons oil
2 tablespoons butter
1½ pounds large raw shrimp,
   peeled, deveined

2 green onions, chopped
Salt and pepper to taste
¼ cup grated fresh Parmesan
   cheese

Utensil: large skillet

Remove seeds and ribs from peppers and cut into strips ½-inch
wide. Heat oil in skillet and sauté peppers, stirring often, until
tender crisp; remove from skillet. Melt butter in skillet; add shrimp
and sauté 8 minutes or until no longer translucent. Add green
onions, salt, pepper and Parmesan cheese. Return peppers to pan;
stir to mix. Serve over steamed rice.

Comment: Easy and festive.

Servings
4
Planning
Can
partially
make ahead
Preparing
1½ hours
Cooking
45 minutes

CURRY BASE FOR SHRIMP OR LOBSTER

1 cup butter
1 onion, chopped
1 green apple, chopped
8 stalks celery, chopped
12 peppercorns
2 bay leaves
⅓ cup flour
2½-3 teaspoons curry powder
½ teaspoon sugar
¼ teaspoon nutmeg
⅛ teaspoon cinnamon
1¾ cup chicken broth
½ cup coconut milk
¼ cup fresh lime juice
¼ cup whipping cream

2 tablespoons sherry
½ teaspoon Worcestershire sauce

CONDIMENTS
Chutney
Shredded coconut
Chopped peanuts
Crumbled cooked bacon
Sliced green onions
Banana chips
Diced cucumber
Golden raisins
Chopped tomatoes

Utensil: large heavy saucepan

Melt butter; add onion, apple, celery, peppercorns and bay leaves. Cook over medium heat until soft, stirring occasionally. Combine flour, curry powder, sugar, nutmeg and cinnamon. Blend mixture into saucepan; heat until mixture bubbles (a bit more butter may be needed if roux is too thick). Remove from heat; add chicken stock, coconut milk and lime juice, stirring constantly. Return to heat and stir until mixture thickens and comes near a boil. Strain through a fine sieve; discard vegetable pulp. (Can be made 2 days ahead to this point. Can also be doubled, tripled or quadrupled.)

When ready to serve, reheat in heavy saucepan over very low heat, stirring occasionally. Add cream, sherry, Worcestershire and cooked chunks of shrimp or lobster (or chicken breast). Serve with rice and condiments.

Comment: Light and tantalizing, an uncommon curry.

CAMARÓNES TEQUILA

Servings
4
Planning
Serve
immediately
Preparing
30 minutes
Cooking
9-10
minutes
Marinating
1 hour

20-24 large prawns or
  shrimp, shelled, deveined,
  butterflied
2 tablespoons butter
1 yellow bell pepper, sliced in
  thin strips
½ cup gold tequila, warmed
1 tablespoon finely chopped
  parsley

MARINADE
4 tablespoons lemon juice
2 teaspoons Worcestershire
  sauce
¼ teaspoon salt, optional

SAUCE
6 tablespoons butter
½ cup all-purpose flour
½ teaspoon salt
2 cups milk
1½ teaspoons tarragon

Utensils: heavy saucepan or double boiler, large skillet

For marinade: Combine lemon juice, Worcestershire sauce and salt. Add shrimp and marinate 1 hour, turning once.

For sauce: Melt butter over low heat. Blend in flour and salt; add milk. Cook, stirring constantly, until mixture thickens. Remove from heat and stir in tarragon.

Melt butter over medium heat. Sauté pepper strips until crisp-tender; remove to warm plate. Partially drain marinade and discard. Add shrimp and remaining marinade to skillet; sauté 3 minutes, turning once. Pour warmed tequila over shrimp and flame. DO NOT FLAME WITH STOVE FAN ON! Add sauce and simmer over low heat 5 minutes. Serve topped with pepper strips and sprinkled with parsley.

Comment: Flaming creates an intriguing flavor in this south-of-the-border presentation. Gold tequila is an absolute must!

SOLE IN WINE

Servings
4
Planning
Best served
immediately
Preparing
30 minutes
Baking
20 minutes
Broiling
1-2 minutes

4 medium to large sole fillets
Salt and pepper to taste
Paprika to taste
2-3 tablespoons white wine

SAUCE
3 tablespoons butter
½ pound mushroom caps,
  stems removed

2 green onions, chopped
  including green stems
2 tablespoons all-purpose
  flour
1 cup chicken stock
Fish juices
2½ ounces Parmesan cheese,
  grated

Utensils: 8 x 8 inch baking pan coated with non-stick spray,
large skillet
Preheat oven to 350°; preheat broiler

Fold fillets in half and place closely in pan. Sprinkle with salt,
pepper and paprika. Pour wine around sides of fish. Bake 20
minutes or until fish flakes easily with a fork. Immediately remove
from oven.

For sauce: Melt butter; sauté mushroom caps and green onions
until tender. Add flour; cook and stir until absorbed. Add chicken
stock; cook and stir until smooth and slightly thickened. Add any
juices from fish and stir well.

Pour sauce over fish. Sprinkle with Parmesan cheese; broil until
hot and bubbly.

*Comment: The sauce compliments sole's delicacy for this easy
entrée. Serve with seasoned rice.*

Bait the hook well; this fish will bite.
                    MUCH ADO ABOUT NOTHING

DAVID OGDEN STIERS

SCALLOPS IN VERMOUTH

1½-2 pounds scallops,
  rinsed, dried (remove
  valves, if attached)
¾ pound fresh mushrooms,
  sliced
Puréed or powdered garlic or
  garlic granules to taste
Salt and pepper to taste

6 teaspoons butter or butter-
  flavored margarine, divided
6 tablespoons dry vermouth
6 teaspoons grated fresh
  Parmesan cheese
6 teaspoons fresh chopped
  parsley

Divide scallops into 6 portions (if large scallops, cut into bite-size pieces). Place in individual ramekins or shells. Sauté fresh mushrooms, sprinkled with garlic, salt and pepper, in two teaspoons of butter 3-4 minutes. Place equal portions on top of scallops. Dribble 1 tablespoon of vermouth over each portion. Mix Parmesan cheese and parsley. Sprinkle over each portion. Dot with remaining butter. Preheat oven to 450° and bake exactly 12 minutes. Makes 6 servings.

High in flavor, low in calories.

DAVID OGDEN STIERS, Associate Artist of the Globe
Best known to national audiences for his comedy role on "Mash." Appearances on Broadway and in major television dramas. At the Globe portrayed leading classical roles as well as directed.

Servings
12
Planning
Can make
ahead
Preparing
1 hour
Cooking
1 hour

JAMBALAYA

3 pounds hot link sausage,
  cut into ½-inch pieces
2 cups chopped onion
1 cup chopped celery
1 cup chopped green
  bell pepper
½ cup chopped parsley
2 cloves garlic, minced
1 16-ounce can tomatoes,
  coarsely chopped, liquid
  reserved

3½ cups water
½ teaspoon thyme
Salt to taste
2½ cups rice
1½ pounds shrimp, peeled,
  deveined

Utensils: large, heavy skillet; stock pot with cover

Sauté sausage. Add onion, celery and green pepper; cook until
tender. Add parsley and garlic; cook 2 minutes more. Place in
stock pot. Add tomatoes, reserved liquid, water, thyme and salt.
Bring to boil; add rice. Bring back to boil, stir, cover and lower
heat. Cook 30 minutes or until rice is tender and separates easily;
add shrimp last 5 minutes of cooking time. Check after 15-20
minutes to see if more liquid, up to ½ cup, is needed. (Can be
held 1-2 hours until ready to serve; reheat if necessary.)

Comment: A festive entrée for a crowd.

**As merry
As, first, good company, good wine, good welcome,
Can make good people.**
           HENRY VIII

CRAB GIOVANNI

Servings
8-10
Planning
Can make
ahead 1-2
days
Preparing
30 minutes
Baking
45-60
minutes

½ cup butter
2 cups chopped onion
½ pound fresh mushrooms, sliced
2 cloves garlic, minced or mashed
½ pound spaghetti or vermicelli, cooked
2-3 cups crab meat

½ cup sliced stuffed green olives
½ pound sharp Cheddar cheese, grated
½ cup sour cream
1 28-ounce can tomatoes, broken in pieces
1½ teaspoons salt
½ teaspoon basil

Utensils: large skillet; 3-quart casserole, greased
Preheat oven to 350°

Melt butter and sauté onions, mushrooms and garlic until tender. Add spaghetti, crab, olives, cheese, sour cream, tomatoes, salt and basil; stir until well mixed. Pour mixture into casserole (can refrigerate at this point). Bake 45-60 minutes until hot and bubbly.

Comment: Crab with an Italian flair.

Servings
10
Planning
Partially
assemble
ahead
Preparing
2 hours
Baking
1 hour

PAELLA

2 cups raw rice
3 cups water
6 tablespoons extra virgin
olive oil, divided
5 pounds chicken pieces
1 pound smoked sausage, cut
in ¼-inch slices
1 pound cod fillets, cut in
1-inch pieces
5 cups chicken broth, heated,
divided
1 tablespoon salt

1¼ teaspoons dried oregano
1 teaspoon saffron
1½ cups diced green bell
pepper
1 cup chopped onion
3 cloves garlic, minced
3 cups diced fresh tomatoes
1 pound raw shrimp, peeled,
deveined
1 cup frozen green peas
10 clams, steamed in shells
for garnish, optional

**Utensils: large skillet, 5-quart casserole or large roasting or
baking pan
Preheat oven to 325°**

Soak rice in water 30 minutes. In skillet heat 4 tablespoons oil; add chicken, a few pieces at a time, and brown on all sides. Remove chicken and keep warm. Drain rice well. Put remaining oil in skillet and add rice. Cook, stirring, until rice is dry and begins to turn color (it will start to stick to skillet).

Place rice in casserole. Arrange chicken, sausage and fish over rice. Pour 1 cup hot broth into skillet and scrape drippings; pour into casserole. (May be refrigerated several hours at this point.)

Mix remaining hot broth with salt, oregano, saffron, green pepper, onion, garlic and tomatoes; pour into casserole. Bake 40 minutes. Add shrimp and peas; bake additional 20 minutes. Garnish with steamed clams if desired. Serve at once.

Comment: This is a beautiful company rendition of paella, said to have as many versions as there are castles in Spain. Try serving with a green salad, crusty bread, sangria, and flan for dessert.

SCALLOPED OYSTERS

Servings
6
Planning
Make
partially
ahead
Preparing
20 minutes
Baking
40 minutes

2 10-ounce jars shucked
fresh oysters
46 saltines, coarsely
crumbled
½ cup butter or margarine,
melted

¼ cup reserved oyster liquor
2 cups sliced fresh
mushrooms
¾ cup light cream
¼ teaspoon Worcestershire
sauce

Utensil: deep casserole, buttered
Preheat oven to 350°

Drain oysters, reserving liquor; if large, cut into halves or thirds.
Combine one-half crumbs with butter. Combine remainder crumbs
with oysters, oyster liquor, mushrooms, cream and Worcestershire
sauce; place in casserole (can be refrigerated 3-4 hours at this
point). Top with buttered crumbs; bake 40 minutes.

*Comment: The family sharing this traditional holiday dish suggests
doubling the recipe to assure a plenitude.*

Tranio: He...somewhat doth resemble you.
Biondello: As much as an apple doth an oyster.
THE TAMING OF THE SHREW

CALAMARI STEAKS

Servings
4
Planning
Serve
immediately
Preparing
20 minutes
Cooking
10 minutes
Broiling
2-3 minutes

12 medium mushrooms,
  sliced
1 tablespoon butter
4 calamari (squid) steaks
1 large clove garlic, crushed
¼ cup virgin olive oil
Parmesan cheese, grated, for
  topping
Chopped parsley or cilantro
  for garnish

SAUCE
1 tablespoon butter
1 teaspoon flour
1 cup cream, heated
½ teaspoon oregano
2 tablespoons dry white wine

BREADING
3 egg yolks, lightly beaten
1 cup bread crumbs

Utensils: large skillet, shallow 9- or 10-inch oven-proof
casserole
Preheat broiler

Sauté mushrooms lightly in butter; remove and set aside.

For sauce: In same skillet melt butter, add flour and stir until well
blended. Slowly add cream and stir until thickened. Add oregano
and wine. Set aside and keep warm.

For breading: Dip steaks in egg yolks, then bread crumbs.

Sauté garlic lightly in olive oil; add steaks and cook until lightly
browned (about 2-3 minutes per side). Place in casserole, top with
mushrooms and cover with sauce. Sprinkle with Parmesan. Place
under broiler until lightly browned. Garnish with parsley to serve.

Comment: A Mediterranean taste treat.

MESQUITE-GRILLED 'ORANGE' SNAPPER

Servings
3-4
Preparing
15 minutes
Marinating
30-45 minutes
Barbecuing
8 minutes

2 pounds red snapper fillets

SAUCE
4 tablespoons butter, melted
Zest 1 orange
Juice ½ orange
**1 teaspoon Worcestershire
    sauce**

1 large garlic clove, crushed
½ teaspoon tarragon
¼ teaspoon black pepper

Utensil: barbecue grill with mesquite charcoal
Preheat grill until coals are white hot

For sauce: Melt butter and add orange zest, juice, Worcestershire, garlic, tarragon and pepper. Heat to mingle flavors but do not boil.

Marinate fish in sauce 30-45 minutes. To barbecue, place fish on grill set close to coals; grill 4 minutes per side, basting with leftover sauce.

Comment: A grand flavor fillip—sauce goes equally well with seabass or orange roughy.

'Twas merry when you wager'd on your angling; when your diver
Did hang a salt-fish on his hook, which he
With fervency drew up.
ANTONY AND CLEOPATRA

BROILED SALMON IMPÉRIAL

Servings
6
Planning
Serve
immediately
Preparing
30 minutes
Broiling
11 minutes

6 1-inch thick salmon fillets
2 tablespoons butter, melted
2 tablespoons lemon juice
2 teaspoons anchovy paste
1 clove garlic, crushed
1 teaspoon dry mustard

½ teaspoon paprika

1 cup Hollandaise sauce
   (recipe follows)
2 tablespoons caviar

Utensil: broiler pan, greased
Preheat broiler

Place salmon on pan. Combine butter, lemon juice, anchovy paste, garlic, dry mustard and paprika. Brush salmon on one side with mixture; broil 6 minutes at 5-inch distance from heat. Turn and brush other side with mixture; broil 5 minutes or until fish flakes easily. Combine Hollandaise and caviar; serve over salmon or on the side.

Comment: A royal presentation for a magnificent fish.

HOLLANDAISE SAUCE

3 egg yolks
2 tablespoons lemon juice
¼ teaspoon salt

½ cup butter, heated to
   bubbly stage

Utensil: blender

Place egg yolks, lemon juice and salt in blender; cover and turn on high speed 2-3 seconds to blend. Remove lid, turn to high and in a gradual stream pour butter into blender. Serve warm.

SALMON SORREL SUPRÊME

Servings
6
Preparing
15 minutes
Cooking
45-50
minutes

3 pounds fresh salmon fillet,
   cut into very thin slices
½ cup oil

SAUCE
1 cup dry white wine
1 cup dry vermouth
1 cup strong fish stock
   (page 154)

6 tablespoons chopped
   shallots
2 cups cream
Salt and pepper to taste
¼ pound sorrel (main stem
   removed), cooked in salted
   water, drained

Utensils: saucepan, skillet and fine sieve

For sauce: In saucepan place white wine, vermouth, fish stock
and shallots; reduce over medium heat until mixture thickens
(about 30 minutes). Strain through fine sieve and return to
saucepan. Add cream and reduce, over high heat, whisking until
mixture thickens (about 15 minutes). Season to taste with salt and
pepper; add sorrel. Set aside and keep warm.

Season salmon slices with salt and pepper. Heat oil in skillet and
sauté a few seconds on each side. Do not overcook. Place salmon
slices on warmed plates; cover with sorrel sauce or serve on side.

Comment: Sorrel's unique sour flavor complements the salmon's
succulence.

How many things by season seasoned are
To their right praise and true perfection!
                THE MERCHANT OF VENICE

STRONG FISH STOCK

1 quart water
2 pounds white fish
  (preferably sole) backbones
2 large onions, thinly sliced
2 sprigs parsley
2 tablespoons thinly sliced
  mushrooms
1 tablespoon lemon juice

1 teaspoon salt
1 tablespoon dried thyme
1 tablespoon bay leaf
1 tablespoon sage
½ teaspoon coriander
½ teaspoon mace
1½ tablespoons pepper

Utensil: stock pot

Add fish backbones to cold water. When water starts to boil, add onions, parsley, mushrooms, lemon juice and salt. Return to boil, skim stock and add spices. Reduce heat and boil gently 30 minutes. Strain through cloth and cool. Freeze leftover stock for later use.

Third Fisherman: Master, I marvel how the fishes live in the sea.
First Fisherman: Why, as men do a-land; the great ones eat up the little ones.

PERICLES

BAKED TROUT PARMA

Servings
4
Planning
Can
assemble
ahead
Preparing
15 minutes
Baking
40 minutes

BREADING
½ cup grated Parmesan
  cheese
½ cup cracker crumbs
2 tablespoons chopped green
  onion

4 medium-size trout,
  cleaned, heads removed

Salt and pepper to taste,
  divided
Lemon juice to taste
⅓ cup cream
4 thick tomato slices
2 tablespoons butter
¼ cup dry white wine

Utensil: shallow baking pan
Preheat oven to 375°

For breading: Combine Parmesan cheese, cracker crumbs and onion; mix well.

Salt and pepper trout cavities; sprinkle with lemon juice. Dip fish in cream, then roll in breading mixture and place in pan. Place tomato slice on each fish; season with salt and pepper. Dot with butter; spoon wine over fish. Bake 40 minutes or until tender.

Comment: An ideal way to enhance trout's delicacy.

Parolles: I love not many words.
Lord: No more than a fish loves water.
                    ALL'S WELL THAT ENDS WELL

MAGGIE'S MARVY FISH STUFF

Servings
12
Planning
Must make
sauce day
ahead
Preparing
30 minutes
Baking
45-60
minutes

DAY AHEAD SAUCE
1 cup undiluted evaporated
  milk
1½ cups whole milk
1 cup consommé
½ cup butter
¾ cup flour
1 tablespoon lemon juice
1 tablespoon Worcestershire
  sauce
4 tablespoons catsup
1 tablespoon horseradish
1 large clove garlic, minced
1 teaspoon prepared mustard

½ teaspoon salt
1 tablespoon soy sauce
¼ teaspoon cayenne
4 tablespoons chopped fresh
  parsley
½ cup sherry
2 pounds boneless white fish,
  cut into chunks

1 pound cooked lobster meat,
  cut into chunks
1 pound peeled, deveined and
  cooked shrimp

Utensils: saucepan, large skillet, casserole
Preheat oven to 350°

For sauce: Combine evaporated milk, whole milk and consommé;
stir and heat, but not to boiling point. In skillet melt butter, add
flour and stir until smooth. Gradually add milk mixture, stirring
constantly, and cook until thickened. Add lemon juice,
Worcestershire sauce, catsup, horseradish, garlic, mustard, salt,
soy sauce, cayenne and parsley. Stir well. Add sherry and fish
chunks; simmer 8-10 minutes. Remove from heat, place in covered
casserole and refrigerate overnight to allow flavors to absorb.

Next day: Remove sauce from refrigerator and let reach room
temperature, 1-2 hours. When ready to bake, stir in lobster and
shrimp, reserving some for garnish after baking. Place, uncovered,
in oven and bake 45-60 minutes or until mixture just reaches
bubbly stage. Do not overcook. Remove from oven and garnish top
with reserved lobster and shrimp.

(Note: This never-fail recipe multiplies well. Serve with converted
white rice, fresh green beans, salad and sourdough bread. For
wine, a California Chardonnay.)

Comment: "It's to die for!"

ABULÓN CON ALMENDRAS

Servings
4
Planning
Serve
immediately
Preparing
5 minutes
Cooking
2 minutes
per steak

½ cup butter or margarine
¾ cup sliced almonds
4 abalone steaks (about 1
  pound total), pounded
Flour for coating
¼ teaspoon salt

⅛ teaspoon pepper
1 tablespoon lemon or lime
  juice
Lemon wedges for garnish,
  optional

Utensil: large skillet

Melt butter over medium heat; add almonds, stir and sauté until
butter froths and nuts turn light brown. Remove pan from heat
and set almonds aside. In shallow pan combine flour, salt and
pepper; coat steaks with mixture and shake off excess. Return
buttered pan to medium heat, stir in lemon juice and heat until
butter begins to froth. Add steaks and brown quickly, 1 minute per
side. Remove steaks to heated platter. Return almonds to pan with
lemon butter and stir to heat. Pour almonds over abalone and
serve with lemon wedge garnish.

*Comment: Sea divers wait for low tide along the San Diego coast
to gather abalone, the shellfish prized by connoisseurs.*

**The imperious seas breed monsters, for the dish
Poor tributory rivers as sweet fish.**
                                   CYMBELINE

SHELLFISH CASSEROLE

Servings
4-6
Planning
Must make
ahead
Preparing
25 minutes
Resting
12-24 hours
Baking
1 hour

7 slices white bread, crusts
  removed
1 8-ounce package sliced Old
  English cheese
1 6-7-ounce can crab, drained
1 6-7-ounce package frozen
  shrimp

¼ cup butter, melted
3 eggs, beaten
1½ cups milk
1 tablespoon dry mustard
½ teaspoon salt

Utensil: 2-quart casserole, buttered
Preheat oven to 325°

Break bread into quarter-size pieces; cut cheese into bite-size
pieces. Line casserole bottom with ⅓ bread, ⅓ cheese, ⅓ crab
and ⅓ shrimp (separated but not defrosted); repeat layering
process twice. Pour melted butter over mixture. Combine eggs,
milk, mustard and salt; pour over mixture in casserole. Cover and
place in refrigerator overnight. Bake 1 hour uncovered.

Comment: Party perfect.

A cup of wine that's brisk and fine,
And drink unto the leman mine;
*   And a merry heart lives long-a.*

II HENRY IV

CHEESE, EGGS & BRUNCH

Larry Drake in *Greater Tuna*

GREEN CHILI CASSEROLE

Servings
6
Planning
Can make
day ahead
Preparing
30 minutes
Baking
45 minutes

1 4-ounce can whole green
  chiles
½ pound Cheddar cheese,
  grated
1 12-ounce can evaporated
  milk
2 eggs

1 tablespoon all-purpose flour
½ pound Monterey Jack
  cheese, grated
1 8-ounce can tomato sauce,
  optional
Pimiento

Utensil: 9 x 9 inch casserole, greased
Preheat oven to 400°

Split chiles and remove seeds; lay half in casserole. Sprinkle with
Cheddar and top with remaining chiles. Combine milk, eggs and
flour; pour over chiles. (Can be refrigerated 24 hours at this point.)
Bake 30 minutes. Top with Jack cheese (and tomato sauce, if
used) and bake 15 minutes more. Garnish with pimiento.

MARY'S EGGS ITALIANO

Servings
6-8
Planning
Can
assemble
day ahead
Preparing
30 minutes
Baking
45-60
minutes

12 ounces Italian sweet
  sausage
6 slices white bread, crusts
  removed, cubed
4 ounces mushrooms, sliced

1 cup grated Cheddar cheese
6 eggs
2 cups milk
1 teaspoon salt
1 teaspoon dry mustard

Utensil: 9 x 13 inch baking dish, greased
Preheat oven to 350°

Brown sausage; drain on paper towels and cut into bite-size
pieces. In dish layer bread, sausage, mushrooms and cheese. Beat
eggs and add milk, salt and mustard. Pour egg mixture over
layered ingredients. Bake 45-60 minutes or until eggs are set.

Comment: Delicious with fresh fruit and bran muffins.

CASTILLO HUEVOS ESPECIALES

Servings
8
Planning
Can make
ahead 1
day
Preparing
45 minutes
Baking
25 minutes

EGGS
8 hard-cooked eggs
4 tablespoons margarine,
  softened
1 teaspoon minced parsley
2 tablespoons grated onion
6 tablespoons minced ham

TOPPING
½ cup grated mild Cheddar
  cheese

SAUCE
3 tablespoons margarine
6 tablespoons flour
1 beef bouillon cube
1 cup hot water
Salt and pepper to taste
Paprika to taste
¾ cup half-and-half
Dash of curry powder

Utensil: 6 x 10 inch baking dish, greased
Preheat oven to 325°

Peel and halve eggs. Blend mashed yolks with softened margarine, parsley, onion and ham; stuff egg whites generously. Arrange in baking dish.

For sauce: Melt margarine; blend in flour. Dissolve beef bouillon cube in hot water; slowly add bouillon to flour mixture. Season with salt, pepper and paprika. Add half-and-half and dash of curry. Cook over low heat, stirring frequently, until thick and smooth. Be careful not to scorch.

When ready to bake, pour sauce over eggs; sprinkle cheese over top. Bake 25 minutes until hot and bubbly. (Eggs and sauce may be prepared day ahead, but keep separate until ready to bake.)

Comment: Delicious. Serve over toasted English muffins.

They say we are almost as like as eggs.
                                    THE WINTER'S TALE

BREAKFAST BURRITOS

Servings
2-4
Planning
Can
assemble
ahead
Preparing
15 minutes
Cooking
5-6 minutes

6 hard-cooked eggs, finely
   chopped
¾ cup grated Monterey Jack
   cheese
1 4-ounce can chopped green
   chiles
3 tablespoons mayonnaise
Salt and pepper to taste
6 flour tortillas (8-inch
   diameter)

2-3 tablespoons or more
   margarine

GARNISHES, OPTIONAL
Salsa
Guacamole
Sour cream

Utensils: aluminum foil, skillet
Preheat oven to 400°

Combine eggs, cheese, chiles, mayonnaise, salt and pepper; mix
well. Soften tortillas by wrapping tightly in foil and heating in oven
10-15 minutes.

To make burritos, divide egg-cheese mixture evenly and heap on
softened tortillas. Roll tortillas and tuck in ends. Melt margarine
and sauté until light brown on each side. Serve with garnishes if
desired.

Comment: A handy snack or a hearty breakfast.

Now can I break my fast, dine, sup and sleep,
Upon the very naked name of love.
                    THE TWO GENTLEMEN OF VERONA

SPINACH SOUFFLÉ

Servings
6-8
Planning
Can ready
for baking
3-4 hours
ahead
Preparing
20 minutes
Baking
1 hour

2 10-ounce packages frozen
  chopped spinach, thawed,
  well drained
6 eggs, beaten
½ cup butter, melted
2 cups all-purpose flour
¾ teaspoon salt
¼ teaspoon pepper

¼ teaspoon nutmeg
Juice of 1 lemon
½ pound Monterey Jack
  cheese, grated
½ pound American cheese,
  grated
2 pounds cottage cheese,
  any style

Utensil; 2½-quart round casserole or 9 x 13 inch baking dish,
greased
Preheat oven to 350°

In large bowl mix spinach and eggs. One at a time add butter,
flour, salt, pepper, nutmeg and lemon juice, stirring well after each
addition. Fold in 3 cheeses. Spoon into baking dish. Bake 1 hour
or until center is set.

Comment: A perfect light supper.

Let's to supper, come, And drown consideration.
                    ANTONY AND CLEOPATRA

CRAB QUICHE

Servings
4-6
Planning
Can
assemble
ahead
Preparing
15 minutes
Baking
40-45
minutes

Prepared 9-inch pie shell
  (page 229)
½ cup mayonnaise
2 tablespoons flour
2 eggs, beaten
½ cup milk

1 7½-ounce can flaked crab,
  drained and flaked
8 ounces Swiss cheese, cubed
⅓ cup sliced green onions
  including tops

Utensils: 9-inch pie pan, heavy duty foil
Preheat oven to 350°

Combine mayonnaise, flour, eggs and milk. Add crab, cheese and
onions; mix well. Pour into pie shell; place in oven on sheet of
heavy duty foil. Bake 40-45 minutes.

*Comment: Beautiful for brunch, lovely for lunch and super for
supper. Serve with a green salad and fruit.*

She's as like this as a crab's like an apple.
                                        KING LEAR

BLINTZ SOUFFLÉ

Servings
2-4
Planning
Serve
immediately
Preparing
15-20
minutes
Baking
45 minutes

4 eggs, beaten
1½ cups sour cream
½ teaspoon salt
¼ cup sugar
1 teaspoon vanilla
2 tablespoons orange juice

Pinch cinnamon
½ cup butter, melted
1 15-ounce package frozen
    cheese blintzes (6 crêpes)
Fresh fruit for topping,
    optional

Utensil: 3-quart casserole, greased
Preheat oven to 350°

Combine eggs, sour cream, salt, sugar, vanilla, orange juice and cinnamon. Stir in butter. Arrange blintzes evenly in casserole; add egg mixture. Bake 45 minutes and serve immediately. Top with fresh strawberries or other fruit, if using.

Comment: Perfect for a brunch. You can vary this light and easy soufflé by using fruit-filled blintzes such as blueberry, cherry or apple.

'Tis as like you as cherry is to cherry.
HENRY VIII

CRAB QUICHE MADEIRA

Servings
6
Planning
Serve
immediately
Preparing
30 minutes
Baking
30 minutes

Pastry for 9-inch pie shell
  (page 229)
2-4 tablespoons chopped
  green onions
2 teaspoons butter
1 7½-ounce can crab meat,
  drained and flaked

2 tablespoons Madeira
Salt and pepper to taste
3 eggs, beaten
1 tablespoon tomato paste
1 cup heavy cream
¼-½ cup grated Gruyère
  cheese

Utensil: 9-inch pie pan
Preheat oven to 400°

Sauté onions in butter until just transparent. Stir in crab, add
Madeira and just bring to simmer. In bowl mix eggs, salt, pepper,
tomato paste and cream. Add crab mixture to eggs; mix lightly.
Place in pie shell and sprinkle cheese over top. Bake 30 minutes.

Comment: A class act.

*Iago: Come, come, good wine is a good familiar
creature, if it be well used: exclaim no more against
it.*
                                          OTHELLO

CATALINA QUESO

Servings
4-6
Planning
Can reheat
Preparing
10 minutes
Baking
35-45 minutes

½ cup butter, melted
½ pound cheese (Jarlsberg, Cheddar or Monterey Jack), grated
1 pint cottage cheese
6 eggs, beaten
1 cup milk

1 cup all-purpose flour
1 4-ounce can diced green chiles
1 cup diced ham or bacon, optional
2-3 sliced green onions including tops, optional

Utensil: 9 x 13 inch baking dish
Preheat oven to 375°

Put butter in baking dish; melt in hot oven. In large bowl combine grated cheese, cottage cheese, eggs, milk, flour, chiles, ham and green onions, if using. Carefully remove hot baking dish from oven. Pour ½ butter into cheese mixture; stir well. Pour mixture into baking dish; bake 35-45 minutes or until top is golden brown.

Comment: A quiche-like entrée that also can be cut into "fingers" and served as an appetizer.

Our stomachs will make what's homely savoury.
CYMBELINE

CRÊPES POLLO DE MEXICANA

Servings
6-8
Planning
Can
assemble
ahead
Preparing
30 minutes
Baking
1 hour

10 flour tortillas (8-inch
  diameter)
½ cup or more melted butter
1 pound Tillamook or
  Monterey Jack cheese,
  shredded, divided
1 8-ounce carton sour cream
1 4-ounce can chopped green
  chiles

½ cup chopped dehydrated
  onion, softened in water
  and drained
1 6-ounce can chopped black
  olives
4 cups cooked, cubed chicken
  breasts (3 breasts skinned,
  boned)
Summer savory to taste

Utensil: 9 x 13 inch baking dish
Preheat oven to 350°

Soften tortillas by dipping both sides in hot melted butter. Reserve
1 cup shredded cheese for topping. Divide and layer down center
of each tortilla: sour cream, shredded cheese, chiles, onion, olives,
chicken and savory. Fold each tortilla over stuffing; place seam
side down in baking dish. Top filled pan with drizzled melted
butter and reserved cheese; sprinkle with summer savory. Cover
and bake 1 hour. (Note: The contributor claims that dehydrated
onions are a "must.")

*Comment: Our tester's husband said, "The best Mexican dish I've
had, in or out!"*

**Fair ladies, you drop manna in the way of starved
people.**
                                THE MERCHANT OF VENICE

SPANOKAPITTA À LA GLOBE

Yield
15 portions
Planning
Can
assemble
24 hours
ahead
Preparing
40 minutes
Baking
35 minutes

½ pound filo dough (9-12
sheets)
½ cup butter, melted

FILLING
2 tablespoons butter
4 green onions, chopped
2 10-ounce packages frozen
spinach, thawed, well drained
1 3-ounce package cream
cheese

8 ounces Ricotta cheese
8 ounces Feta cheese,
crumbled
3 eggs, beaten
3 tablespoons all-purpose
flour
¾ teaspoon nutmeg
½ teaspoon pepper

Utensil: 9 x 13 inch baking pan
Preheat oven to 375°

For filling: Melt 2 tablespoons butter in large skillet and sauté
onions until soft; add drained spinach and stir until mixture is dry.
Remove from heat and cool slightly. In large bowl, using electric
mixer, combine cream cheese, Ricotta, Feta, eggs, flour, nutmeg
and pepper. Add spinach mixture and blend well.

Cut filo roll in half crosswise. (Keep filo covered with plastic wrap
while preparing recipe as it dries out quickly.) Using pastry brush,
coat bottom of baking dish with melted butter. Line pan with sheet
of filo and brush lightly with butter. Cover first sheet with second
and again brush with butter. Proceed in same fashion until you
have used half the sheets.

Spread cheese and spinach mixture evenly over filo layers; cover
with sheet of filo, brushing with butter. Continue layering and
buttering until all filo is used. Brush top well with butter. Score
into approximately 2½ x 3 inch serving portions (score smaller
portions if planning to use as appetizers). Bake 35 minutes or until
golden brown. (If made ahead, cover with plastic wrap and
refrigerate until ready to bake.)

Comment: Rich and fragrant.

CRAB BENEDICT

Servings
4
Planning
Can make
crab
mixture day
ahead
Preparing
15 minutes
Cooking
30 minutes

¼ cup chopped yellow bell
  pepper
¼ cup chopped red bell
  pepper or pimiento
¼ cup chopped green onions
3 tablespoons oil
1 cup medium white sauce
  (see below)
½ pound crab meat
Dash hot pepper sauce
Salt and pepper to taste
4 English muffins, split,
  toasted

8 eggs, poached
1 cup grated Cheddar cheese
Sliced green onions or
  pimiento for garnish,
  optional

MEDIUM WHITE SAUCE
2 tablespoons butter, melted
2 tablespoons flour
1 cup milk

Utensils: saucepan, skillet
Preheat broiler

For white sauce: Melt butter in saucepan; add flour and mix well.
Add milk; cook and stir until thickens.

Heat oil in skillet and sauté peppers and onion 10 minutes. Add
white sauce, crab, hot pepper, salt and pepper; cook over low heat
until heated through. When ready to serve, spoon crab mixture
onto English muffins; top with eggs and sprinkle with cheese. Broil
briefly until cheese melts. Garnish with sliced green onions or
pimiento, if desired.

Comment: A delicate crab version of an old favorite.

I will bestow a breakfast to make you friends.
                                              HENRY V

CHEESE-NOODLE PUDDING

Servings
8-10
Planning
Can make
ahead
Preparing
20-30
minutes
Baking
1-1¼ hours

3 8-ounce packages hoop (or
   Ricotta) cheese, room
   temperature
½ cup butter or margarine,
   softened
¾ cup sugar
Dash salt, optional

1 teaspoon vanilla
1 8-ounce carton sour cream
3 eggs
4 ounces medium or wide
   noodles, cooked and
   drained
Fresh strawberries, optional

Utensils: electric mixer, 9 x 9 inch oven-proof pan
Preheat oven to 325°

In large bowl combine cheese, butter, sugar, salt, vanilla, sour
cream and eggs; beat well. Add noodles and pour into baking dish.
Bake 1-1¼ hours or until set and lightly browned. Cut into slices
or squares; serve warm or at room temperature with fresh
strawberries, if using. (Can be refrigerated overnight; warm before
serving.)

Comment: A treasured family recipe—ideal for a brunch.

Prince: Shall we be merry?
Poins: As merry as crickets, my lad.

          I HENRY IV

CRÊPES LA PAZ

Servings
6
Planning
Can
assemble
ahead
Preparing
10 minutes
Baking
45 minutes

CHEESE SAUCE
½ cup butter
½ cup flour
1 quart milk
1 pound soft processed
cheese with jalapeño
peppers, grated
2 teaspoons Dijon-style
mustard
½ teaspoon salt
White pepper to taste

12 flour tortillas (8-inch
diameter)
12 thin slices ham
1 pound Monterey Jack
cheese, cut into 12 sticks
1 4-ounce can whole green
chiles, cut into 12 strips
Paprika

Utensils: saucepan; 9 x 13 inch baking pan, greased
Preheat oven to 350°

For cheese sauce: Melt butter and blend in flour; cook gently 5-7
minutes over low heat until brown. Add milk slowly, blending well.
Add cheese, mustard, salt and pepper. Cook, stirring until smooth.

To assemble: On each tortilla place 1 slice ham, 1 stick cheese
(at edge) and 1 strip chile (on cheese). Roll tortilla and place in
baking pan, seam side down. Cover with cheese sauce and sprinkle
with paprika. (Can be refrigerated overnight at this point.) Bake
45 minutes.

*Comment: For a beach picnic, prepare in a sturdy pan to reheat
over barbecue.*

*Who wanteth food, and will not say he wants it,
Or can conceal his hunger till he famish?*
                                        PERICLES

HOT CHICKEN (OR TUNA) SALAD SANDWICHES

Servings
6
Planning
Can make
filling day
ahead
Preparing
30 minutes
Baking
10-15
minutes

6 small French rolls

FILLING
1 cup sliced mushrooms
1 tablespoon butter
2 cooked chicken breasts, skinned, boned, cubed (or 2 6½-ounce cans albacore white tuna, drained and flaked)
1 cup mayonnaise

1 teaspoon lemon juice
1 cup finely chopped celery
½ of 10¾-ounce can cream of mushroom soup
1 cup shredded sharp Cheddar cheese
2 teaspoons minced onion
1 teaspoon sherry wine vinegar
Salt and pepper to taste
½ cup toasted sliced almonds

Utensils: sauté pan, cookie sheet coated with non-stick spray
Preheat oven to 350°

Cut tops off rolls and reserve; scoop out centers with fork.

For filling: Sauté mushrooms in butter until browned; drain well. Mix mushrooms, chicken, mayonnaise, lemon juice, celery, soup, cheese, onion, wine vinegar, salt and pepper. (Filling may be made ahead and refrigerated overnight at this point.) When ready to bake, bring mixture to room temperature. Add almonds and mix well.

Generously stuff filling into rolls; replace tops. Place on sheet and bake 10-15 minutes or until filling is hot and bubbly.

Comment: A super supper sandwich.

STUFFED FRENCH BREAD

Servings
12
Planning
Make fresh
Preparing
20 minutes
Baking
30 minutes

1 long loaf French bread (about 1 pound)	¼ cup grated Parmesan cheese
½ cup butter	1 cup grated Cheddar cheese
6 cloves garlic, pressed	1 4-ounce can artichoke
2 tablespoons sesame seeds	hearts, drained
1½ cups sour cream	
2 tablespoons parsley	GARNISH
2 teaspoons lemon pepper	6 ounces sliced ripe olives
2 cups cubed Monterey Jack cheese	Beefsteak tomatoes, sliced

Utensils: cookie sheet, large frying pan
Preheat oven to 350°

Split loaf lengthwise and tear out bread in chunks; place bread shells on cookie sheet. In large frying pan melt butter and add garlic, sesame seeds and bread chunks; sauté until bread chunks are toasted. In medium bowl combine sour cream, parsley, lemon pepper, Jack, Parmesan and Cheddar cheeses. Chop artichoke hearts and add to bread mixture. Combine bread and cheese mixtures and spoon into the two bread halves. Bake 30 minutes. To serve, garnish tops with chopped olives and sliced tomatoes; cut into 1½-inch slices.

Comment: Superb for a Sunday supper.

I'll rhyme you so eight years together, dinners and suppers and sleeping-hours excepted: it is the right butter-women's rank to market.
AS YOU LIKE IT

RICH CAKE WAFFLES

Yield
4-6 waffles
Planning
Serve
immediately
Preparing
15 minutes
Baking
4-5 minutes

⅓ cup shortening
⅔ cup sugar
2 eggs, separated
1¼-1½ cups milk, divided

1 teaspoon vanilla
1¾ cup flour
½ teaspoon salt
2 teaspoons baking powder

Utensil: waffle iron
Preheat according to manufacturer's directions

Cream shortening and sugar until light and fluffy. Beat egg yolks with 2 tablespoons milk; add to shortening. Add remaining milk and vanilla. Mix batter well.

Sift together flour, salt and baking powder; add to batter. Beat egg whites until stiff; fold into batter. Pour batter onto ⅔ waffle iron surface; close lid and bake about 4 minutes or until steam stops emerging. Do not raise cover during baking. When done, raise cover and loosen waffle with fork. Serve hot.

Comment: These might be the best waffles yet, light and with a taste reminiscent of ice cream cones.

CORNMEAL PANCAKES

2 eggs
1½ cups buttermilk
1 cup yellow cornmeal
½ cup all-purpose flour

1 teaspoon soda
1 teaspoon baking powder
1 teaspoon salt
3 tablespoons oil

Utensil: griddle, lightly greased
Preheat griddle

Servings
6
Planning
Make batter
8-12 hours
ahead
Preparing
10 minutes
Cooking
2-3 minutes

Beat eggs slightly and mix with buttermilk. Mix together cornmeal, flour, soda, baking powder and salt. Combine dry ingredients with eggs and buttermilk. Add oil and stir lightly. Cook on hot griddle, turning only once.

GINGERBREAD PANCAKES

2½ cups unbleached flour
5 teaspoons baking powder
½ teaspoon salt
1 teaspoon baking soda
1 teaspoon cinnamon
½ teaspoon ginger
¼ cup molasses

2 cups milk
2 eggs, slightly beaten
6 tablespoons butter, melted
1 cup raisins

Lemon Curd, Ye Famous
Tanswell Recipe (page 277)

Utensil: griddle, buttered
Preheat griddle to medium hot

Yield
20
Planning
Best baked
immediately
Preparing
30 minutes
Cooking
5-7 minutes

In large bowl mix and sift flour, baking powder, salt, soda, cinnamon and ginger. Combine molasses and milk and add to eggs; stir in melted butter. Add molasses mixture to flour mixture, stirring only until moistened; stir in raisins. Using ¼ cup batter for each pancake, bake until golden brown, turning once. Serve with Lemon Curd.

Comment: These light and springy pancakes are a special treat, a tradition at Hersey House, Ashland, Oregon.

ICELANDIC PANCAKES (PÖNNAKÖKUR)

Servings
6-8
Planning
Serve hot
or cold
Preparing
20 minutes
Cooking
4 minutes
each

2 eggs, beaten
⅓ cup sugar
½ teaspoon vanilla
½ teaspoon cinnamon
½ teaspoon baking soda
1-2 tablespoons boiling water

½ cup sour cream or
  buttermilk
1½ cup flour
½ teaspoon salt
1 teaspoon baking powder
2 cups milk

Utensil: 7-inch skillet, generously buttered
Preheat skillet

Mix eggs, sugar, vanilla and cinnamon. Dissolve soda in boiling water; let cool. Mix soda with sour cream or buttermilk; add to egg mixture. Sift together flour, salt and baking powder; add to egg mixture. Gradually stir in milk, mixing well.

Butter heated skillet, lift off heat, pour in about ¼ cup batter, tip pan to coat bottom with batter (as when making crêpes) and return to heat. Cook until top is set and underside browned (about 3 minutes). Turn and cook other side until golden (about 1 minute). Repeat until all batter is used. Sprinkle finished pancakes with sugar and roll; serve with fresh berries.

Comment: These crêpe-like pancakes are delicious hot or cold.

Touchstone: No, by mine honour, but I was bid to come for you.
Rosalind: Where learned you that oath, fool?
Touchstone: Of a certain knight that swore by his honour they were good pancakes and swore by his honour the mustard was naught.

AS YOU LIKE IT

PASTA, RICE & SIDES

photo by Robert Burroughs

Monique Fowler, Jeffrey Combs, Associate Artist Sada Thompson, Harold Gould
and Blair Brown in *The Skin of Our Teeth*

CHRISTOPHER REEVE

SUPERMAN PASTA PRIMAVERA

1 jar marinated artichoke
hearts
Olive oil
1 small zucchini, unpeeled
½ green bell pepper
½ red bell pepper
2 cups broccoli flowerets
4 medium plum tomatoes
¼ cup chopped fresh parsley
½ medium onion

2 cloves garlic, pressed
1 teaspoon dried basil
½ teaspoon thyme or oregano
½ cup white wine
Hot pepper sauce
2 eggs beaten
⅔ cup fresh grated Romano
2 tablespoons melted butter
Salt and pepper to taste
1 pound fresh pasta (linguine)

Drain artichoke marinade into skillet. Chop vegetables. Sauté
garlic, onion and bell peppers 2 or 3 minutes, adding olive oil as
needed. Add rest of vegetables, then herbs and wine. Let simmer.

Cook pasta al dente. Add a little hot sauce to eggs, then mix into
vegetables. Drain pasta. Toss with butter and cheese. Add
vegetable mixture. Serve at once. Pass extra cheese if desired.
Serves 6 to 8.

CHRISTOPHER REEVE
After making his professional debut at the Globe, became best known for his "Superman" character on
film. Major starring roles roles in film, on and off-Broadway and distinguished regional theatres.

ASPARAGUS AU GRATIN

Servings
4
Planning
Can
partially
make ahead
Preparing
5 minutes
Cooking
10 minutes
Broiling
2-3 minutes

1½ pounds asparagus
1 cup sour cream
¼ cup mayonnaise

2 tablespoons lemon juice
Freshly grated Parmesan
cheese

Utensil: oven-proof serving dish, buttered

Cook asparagus in boiling water 6-10 minutes until tender; drain. (If not serving immediately, plunge in cold water to stop cooking and retain color.) Combine sour cream, mayonnaise and lemon juice; pour over asparagus. Sprinkle with Parmesan. Broil until lightly browned and bubbly. (If made ahead, reheat asparagus quickly in microwave before adding topping.)

Comment: Wonderfully quick and tasty.

ASPARAGUS STIR

Servings
4
Preparing
15 minutes
Cooking
5 minutes

2 pounds asparagus, washed
2 tablespoons butter, divided
⅓ cup chopped shallots

1½ teaspoons tarragon
¼ teaspoon pepper

Utensils: 10-inch skillet or wok, food processor

Snap off tough ends from asparagus (discard or save for soup). Cut remaining into slices to fit feed tube of food processor (2½-3-inch lengths). With slicing disk (or by hand, if food processor is not available) cut into ⅛-inch pieces lengthwise (as if cutting a log into boards for lumber). Melt 1 tablespoon butter; add shallots and sauté 1 minute or until wilted. Add remaining 1 tablespoon butter, tarragon and pepper; stir to melt. Add asparagus and stir-fry over medium heat until just tender crisp. Serve immediately.

Comment: If you think you don't like asparagus, try this.

TURKISH ARTICHOKES

Servings
4
Planning
*Make
partially
ahead*
Preparing
*20-30
minutes*
Cooking
15 minutes

1 large onion, thinly sliced,
   separated into rings
¼ cup olive oil
1 9-ounce package frozen
   artichoke hearts
½ cup diced carrots
½ cup diced potatoes

½ cup chicken broth or water
1 teaspoon sugar
1 teaspoon dill weed (or 1
   tablespoon fresh dill)
2 tablespoons lemon juice
Salt to taste
½ cup frozen or fresh peas

Utensil: covered skillet

Sauté onions in oil until transparent. Add artichoke hearts, carrots,
potatoes, broth, sugar, dill, lemon juice and salt. Cover and
simmer 10 minutes, stirring as necessary to separate frozen
artichokes. (May be held up to 1 hour at this point.) When ready
to serve, add peas and simmer another 5 minutes or until
vegetables are tender.

ARTICHOKES MEDITERRANEAN

Servings
4
Planning
*Can make
day ahead*
Preparing
15 minutes
Cooking
10 minutes

3 tablespoons olive oil
2 brown onions, thinly sliced,
   separated into rings
1 pound fresh brown
   mushrooms, cleaned, sliced

1 8½-ounce can artichoke
   hearts, drained, quartered
½ teaspoon basil
Salt and pepper to taste

Utensil: 10-inch skillet

Heat oil and sauté onions until lightly browned. Add mushrooms
and, stirring constantly over high heat, cook 3 minutes or until
mushrooms start to brown and liquid is absorbed. Turn off heat.
Pat artichokes dry; add to pan. Season with basil, salt and pepper.
(At this point dish can be chilled overnight or for a few hours.)
When ready to serve, stir well while briefly heating. (Can
microwave.)

GRILLED VEGETABLES

Servings
4
Planning
Must
marinate
ahead
Preparing
15 minutes
Barbecuing
15-18
minutes
Marinating
4-24 hours

2-3 sweet potatoes, yams or
   white potatoes (or mixture),
   peeled and cut into ½-inch
   slices
3-4 small summer squash or
   zucchini, cut lengthwise

(Other choices could include
   mushrooms, bell peppers,
   parboiled carrots, onions)

MARINADE
⅓ cup oil
1 tablespoon basil
½ teaspoon fine herbs
1 teaspoon oregano
½ teaspoon rosemary
¼ teaspoon pepper

Utensil: barbecue
Preheat barbecue to medium

Parboil potatoes 5 minutes and drain; parboil squash 2 minutes
and drain. Plunge briefly into cold water to cool; pat dry. Place
vegetables and marinade in covered shallow bowl or plastic bag;
refrigerate. For best flavor chill overnight, but 4-6 hours minimum.
When ready to grill, drain vegetables and reserve marinade. Place
vegetables directly on grill and cook 15-18 minutes; turn and baste
several times while cooking.

For marinade: Combine oil, basil, fine herbs, oregano, rosemary
and pepper.

Comment: Marvelous!

...Behold, the earth hath roots;
Within this mile break forth a hundred springs;
The oaks bear mast, the briers scarlet hips;
The bounteous housewife, nature, on each bush
Lays her full mess before you. Want! why want?
                                        TIMON OF ATHENS

EGGPLANT TOMATO CASSEROLE

Servings
6
Planning
Can make ahead
Preparing
20-30 minutes
Baking
35-45 minutes

1 large eggplant (about 1½
  pounds), peeled and sliced
Boiling water
½ teaspoon salt
2 eggs, beaten
2 tablespoons margarine,
  melted
Freshly ground pepper to
  taste
2 tablespoons instant minced
  onion

½ teaspoon crushed oregano
½ cup Italian flavored bread
  crumbs
2 large tomatoes, thinly
  sliced
½ cup grated Cheddar cheese
½ cup grated Parmesan
  cheese
Paprika for garnish

Utensils: large saucepan; 8-inch square oven-proof pan, greased
Preheat oven to 350°

Place eggplant slices in 1 inch of boiling salted water; cover tightly
and cook 10 minutes. Drain and mash eggplant. Combine with
eggs, margarine, pepper, onion, oregano and bread crumbs. Place
½ tomato slices in pan and spread evenly with eggplant mixture;
top with remaining tomatoes. Combine Cheddar and Parmesan
cheeses and sprinkle over top. Garnish with paprika. (Can
refrigerate 6-8 hours at this point.) Bake 35-45 minutes.

Comment: Vegetarians love this!

A good digestion to you all.

HENRY VIII

ZUCCHINI PIE

Servings
6-8
Planning
Can make
ahead
Preparing
20 minutes
Baking
45 minutes
Storing
Keep 2-3
days in
refrigerator
or freeze

3 cups coarsely chopped
   zucchini (3-4 medium-size)
1 small onion, chopped
3 tablespoons chopped fresh
   parsley
4 eggs, slightly beaten
1 cup biscuit mix

¼ cup oil
½ teaspoon white pepper
1 cup grated Parmesan and/or
   Romano cheese
½ teaspoon salt, optional
½ teaspoon basil or oregano,
   optional

Utensil: 9 x 13 inch baking pan, greased and lightly floured
Preheat oven to 350°

In large bowl, mix zucchini, onions and parsley. In another bowl, combine eggs, biscuit mix, oil, pepper and cheese; add salt and basil or oregano. Stir vegetable mixture into egg batter and turn into pan. Bake 45 minutes. Cool slightly before serving.

Comment: A food processor makes this a breeze.

LEMON-GLAZED CARROTS

Servings
4-6
Planning
Can cook
carrots
ahead
Preparing
15 minutes
Cooking
10-15
minutes

1-1½ pounds carrots, peeled,
   julienned
¼ cup margarine
1 tablespoon lemon juice

1 tablespoon sugar
1 tablespoon fresh minced
   parsley

Utensil: saucepan

Simmer carrots 10-15 minutes or until tender; drain. Melt margarine; add lemon juice and sugar. Mix well and add carrots. Cook over low heat until warmed through. Sprinkle with parsley and serve.

Comment: Piquant and colorful.

POTATO (YES!) PASTA

1 medium sized potato per person. Peel and dice. Sauté potatoes in olive oil and minced garlic in sauce pan that is not too shallow and can be covered. Before potatoes have browned, add rosemary (fresh if possible). Shortly after (30 seconds), add enough dry vermouth to come halfway up the potatoes. As soon as it's warm, add canned chicken broth to generously cover, freshly ground pepper, and simmer, covered, until potatoes are tender and mixture has thickened slightly.

For pasta, use small shells or arechietti, not spaghetti. When the sauce is near done, boil pasta, drain, mix together, eat from bowls. Great for a winter supper with a green salad.

JOSEPH HARDY, Associate Artist of the Globe
Director of several classical plays for the Globe. Recipient of Broadway's Tony Award for directing "Child's Play."

RATATOUILLE

Servings
6
Planning
Can make
ahead
Preparing
20-30
minutes
Cooking
45 minutes

⅓ cup olive oil
3 cloves garlic, finely chopped
1 medium onion, finely
  chopped
1 medium unpeeled eggplant,
  cut into 1-inch cubes
3 zucchini, sliced
2 green bell peppers, seeded
  and cut in 1-inch squares
4 tomatoes, peeled and
  chopped

2 tablespoons tomato paste,
  optional
1 teaspoon basil
1 teaspoon oregano
1 teaspoon salt, optional
½ teaspoon pepper
1 cup grated Monterey Jack
  or Cheddar cheese, optional

Utensil: large skillet

Heat oil; sauté garlic and onion until tender. Add eggplant; sauté over medium heat until slightly soft. Add zucchini, peppers, tomatoes, tomato paste, basil, oregano, salt and pepper. Simmer uncovered 15-20 minutes or until excess liquid evaporates; stir occasionally. (Can be refrigerated 1-2 days at this point.) When ready to serve, reheat and sprinkle with grated cheese if using.

Comment: Almost better the second day, when flavors have "married."

HOT TOMATO SALAD

Servings
4
Planning
Serve
immediately
Preparing
20 minutes
Broiling
3-5 minutes

4 medium ripe tomatoes
¾ teaspoon dried basil
Salt and pepper to taste
½ cup buttered bread crumbs
4 slices red onion
4 lettuce leaves

SAUCE
½ cup honey or sugar
½ cup water
½ cup lemon juice or cider
    vinegar
¼ teaspoon salt
2 tablespoons cornstarch

Utensils: medium saucepan, small baking dish
Preheat broiler

Core tomatoes and cut to form 6-8 floweret wedges (leave base
uncut); place closely in dish. Sprinkle with basil, salt and pepper;
pour sauce evenly over tops and dust with bread crumbs. Broil
briefly, placing pan 6 inches from heat source, until crumbs are
browned. (Do not overcook as tomatoes should remain firm.) To
serve, arrange onion slices on lettuce leaves and top with
tomatoes; spoon hot sauce from baking pan over each tomato.

For sauce: Combine honey, water, lemon juice, salt and
cornstarch; cook over medium heat, stirring constantly, until
thickened. Continue cooking 5 more minutes.

Comment: Colorful—and a delicious accompaniment to any entrée.

The sauce to meat is ceremony;
Meeting were bare without it.
                        MACBETH

ZUCCHINI CASSEROLE

Servings
4-6
Planning
Can
assemble
ahead
Preparing
10 minutes
Baking
40 minutes

1 medium onion, thinly sliced
2-3 zucchini, thinly sliced
2 tablespoons butter
Seasoned salt to taste

Pepper to taste
2 medium tomatoes, peeled
and sliced
4 ounces mozzarella cheese,
sliced

Utensil: shallow 1-quart baking dish, buttered
Preheat oven to 350°

Spread onion slices evenly in dish; top with zucchini. Sprinkle with salt and pepper; dot with butter. Cover with foil and bake 30 minutes. Remove from oven.

Layer tomatoes over zucchini; top with cheese. Replace foil. Return to oven and turn off heat. Leave in oven long enough to heat tomatoes and melt cheese (about 10 minutes). This recipe may be doubled or tripled.

Comment: A wonderful mélange of colors, textures and tastes.

And if the boy have not a woman's gift
To rain a shower of commanded tears,
An onion will do well for such a shift,
Which in a napkin being close convey'd
Shall in despite enforce a watery eye.
                    THE TAMING OF THE SHREW

HOT CURRIED CABBAGE SLAW

Servings
10
Planning
Can
assemble
ahead
Preparing
30 minutes
Baking
20 minutes

1 10¾ ounce can consommé
1 cup water
1 bay leaf
3 whole cloves
½ teaspoon salt
3 pounds cabbage (1 large
   head), shredded
½ cup fine dry bread crumbs

SAUCE
1 medium onion, chopped
1 clove garlic, crushed
4 tablespoons butter
2 tablespoons flour
1 tablespoon curry powder
1 teaspoon salt
Dash of pepper
1½ cups sour cream
½ cup reserved broth

Utensils: large saucepan, skillet, 1½-quart casserole
Preheat oven to 400°

Combine consommé, water, bay leaf, cloves and salt; simmer
5 minutes. Remove bay leaf and cloves; add cabbage. Cover and
simmer 10 minutes, stirring occasionally. Drain, reserving ½ cup
broth.

For sauce: Sauté onion and garlic in butter 3 minutes; blend in
flour, curry powder, salt and pepper. Stir in sour cream and broth.
Cook over low heat until sauce simmers and thickens.

Combine sauce and cabbage; place in casserole. (Can be
refrigerated up to 8 hours at this point. Bring to room temperature
before baking.) Sprinkle with bread crumbs; bake 20 minutes or
until crumbs are browned.

Comment: A golden dish with a pungent sauce—a wonderful way
with cabbage.

STUFFED CHAYOTES

Servings
4-6
Planning
Can
assemble
ahead
Preparing
45 minutes
Baking
20-30
minutes

2-3 medium chayotes
Salt to taste
1 tablespoon butter or
   margarine
1 clove garlic, minced
1 small onion, chopped

2 small tomatoes, chopped
1 teaspoon mint leaves
2 tablespoons bread crumbs
1 tablespoon chopped fresh
   parsley
¼ cup shredded Parmesan
   cheese

Utensils: large saucepan, skillet, shallow baking pan
Preheat oven to 350°

Wash and scrub chayotes; cut in half lengthwise (through the large flat seed). Drop into boiling salted water, cover and simmer 30-40 minutes or until tender crisp. Remove, drain and cool. Spoon out and reserve pulp (discard seeds); leave ¼-inch thick shell. Chop pulp.

Melt butter; sauté garlic and onion until golden. Remove from heat and add pulp, tomatoes, mint, bread crumbs and parsley. Mound filling into shells and sprinkle with Parmesan. (Can be prepared ahead and refrigerated up to 24 hours at this point.) Place in pan with ¼ inch water; bake uncovered 20-30 minutes or until tops are lightly browned. Serve hot.

Comment: A wonderful side dish that goes particularly well with lamb.

Let it serve for table-talk.
                                            THE MERCHANT OF VENICE

SALSA

Yield
4-6 cups
Planning
Must make ahead
Preparing
30 minutes
Chilling
1 hour

6 large juicy tomatoes
1 medium white onion, finely chopped
1 bunch cilantro, washed and chopped (discard woody stems)

2 cloves garlic, minced
1 teaspoon white vinegar
1 teaspoon crushed oregano
3 green onions, chopped
2-3 jalapeño peppers, seeded, deveined and chopped

Utensil: food processor, optional

Cut tomatoes in half; squeeze juice and seeds into medium bowl and reserve. Chop tomatoes and combine with reserved juice; add white onion, cilantro, garlic, vinegar, oregano, green onions and peppers. Stir well. Chill 1 hour to allow flavors to mellow.

Comment: This is the real stuff!

You and your apron-men; you that stood so much...
Upon...the breath of garlic-eaters!
                                    CORIOLANUS

MOZZARELLA & POTATO PIE

Servings
4-6
Planning
*Can make
ahead*
Preparing
30 minutes
Baking
*20-25
minutes*

2 pounds potatoes, peeled
  (about 5 medium)
¼ cup butter, softened
Salt and white pepper to taste
½ pound mozzarella cheese,
  cut in ¼-inch slices
3 tomatoes, peeled and cut in
  ½-inch slices

1 teaspoon oregano
1 teaspoon basil
½ cup freshly grated
  Parmesan cheese
¼ cup butter, melted

Utensil: 9-inch deep-dish pie pan, buttered and lightly floured
Preheat oven to 425°

Boil potatoes until tender. Drain and mash, stirring in softened butter, salt and pepper. Spread mashed potatoes in pan. Layer half the cheese on potatoes and top with tomato slices. Sprinkle oregano, basil, salt and pepper on tomatoes; top with remaining mozzarella, Parmesan and melted butter. Bake 20-25 minutes.

Comment: This travels well. It's good at home, too!

SWEET & SOUR GREEN BEANS

Servings
6
Planning
Make ahead
1 hour
Preparing
15 minutes
Cooking
10 minutes

2 strips bacon, chopped
1 small onion, diced
1 tablespoon all-purpose flour
⅓ cup sugar
1 teaspoon dry mustard

1 teaspoon salt
¼ teaspoon pepper
¼ cup bean cooking water
2 tablespoons vinegar
2 cups cooked green beans

Sauté bacon and onion until browned. Add flour, sugar, mustard, salt, pepper, water and vinegar. Bring to boil and add cooked beans (if using fresh or frozen, cook only until firm but crisp). Saute to heat thoroughly.

Comment: This delightfully different tasting dish perks up a simple hamburger supper or holds an hour on a buffet table. It also doubles well.

PORT ANGELES WILD RICE CASSEROLE

Servings
10
Planning
Can make ahead
Preparing
30 minutes
Cooking
30 minutes
Baking
30 minutes
Storing
Freezes well

1 cup raw wild rice, washed
and drained
1 pound sausage
1 pound fresh mushrooms,
sliced
2 onions, chopped
¼ cup flour
½ cup cream
2½ cups chicken broth

¼ teaspoon oregano
¼ teaspoon thyme
¼ teaspoon marjoram
2 dashes hot pepper sauce
Salt and pepper, optional
1 10¾-ounce can mushroom
soup, optional
Toasted almonds

Utensil: 10-inch stove-to-oven skillet, with lid
Preheat oven to 350°

Wash rice. Brown sausage; drain (keeping enough drippings for
sauté) and set aside. Sauté mushrooms and onions. Return
sausage to pan and add rice.

In separate bowl, mix flour with cream until smooth; add chicken
broth. Pour cream mixture over sausage mixture. Cover, bring to
boil and then turn to low heat; cook about 30 minutes until
thickened. Season with oregano, thyme, marjoram, hot pepper
sauce, salt and pepper, if using. Remove to oven and bake,
covered, additional 30 minutes. If mixture becomes too dry, add
soup. Sprinkle with toasted almonds before serving.

*Comment: Credit for this great side dish, a perfect foil for
barbecued turkey or chicken, goes to Port Angeles Community
Players in Washington state.*

MOSTACCIOLI

Servings
6
Planning
Serve
immediately
Preparing
1 hour
Cooking
1 hour

½ pound mostaccioli, pennini
  or other tube pasta
1 cup chicken stock
2 cloves garlic, minced
1½ cups whipping cream

½ pound bacon, fried crisp
  and crumbled
1 cup broccoli flowerets,
  blanched
Parmesan cheese to taste

In saucepan over medium heat reduce stock by one-half. Add garlic and cream; continue cooking 20-30 minutes, stirring occasionally. Add bacon and broccoli, stirring until blended. Meanwhile cook pasta in salted water until just tender but firm. Drain but do not rinse. Let sauce rest (to thicken) a few minutes before serving. Toss sauce with pasta and generously sprinkle with cheese.

PASTA WITH CLAM SAUCE

Servings
4-6
Planning
Serve
immediately
Preparing
20 minutes
Cooking
20 minutes

4 cloves garlic, minced
¼ cup butter or margarine
¼ cup olive oil
1¼ cups chicken broth
¼ cup chopped parsley
1 10-ounce can whole baby
  clams, undrained

1 pound pasta (linguini, thin
  spaghetti, etc.)
Parmesan or Romano cheese,
  grated

Sauté garlic in oil and butter until golden. Add chicken broth and parsley. Bring to a boil, reduce heat to low and simmer 10 minutes. Add clams with liquid and simmer 2 minutes more, stirring gently. Meanwhile, cook pasta in boiling water until just tender but firm. Drain, turn onto warm platter and top with sauce. Serve with grated cheese.

BRIAN BEDFORD

SPAGHETTI CARBONARA AL BEDFORD

1 medium sized onion
½ pound boiled ham ¼-inch
thick
Stick of butter
Small package of frozen tiny
peas

Small container of heavy
cream
Grated fresh Parmesan
2 tablespoons of vegetable oil
Spaghetti

In a frying pan sauté the chopped onion in the vegetable oil until just cooked but not brown. Dice the ham and add to onions. Cook at low heat for about 15 minutes. Add stick of butter and when it has melted, add the peas. Simmer for 15 minutes, stirring occasionally and breaking up the frozen peas.

Meanwhile, cook enough spaghetti al dente for 4 people, drain and return to the boiling pan along with ⅔ of the carton of heavy cream. Stir the cream and spaghetti mixture, pour into a heated serving dish and top with the ham and pea sauce. Sprinkle generously with Parmesan cheese.

Serve with a green salad, warm French bread and a full bodied red wine.

BRIAN BEDFORD
One of the most distinguished directors in English-speaking theatre, has received Broadway's Tony as best actor. Directed and starred in numerous classical dramas. At Globe performed title character in "Richard II" and directed "Much Ado About Nothing."

WALICIA'S PASTA VERDE

Servings
6-8
Planning
Can
assemble
ahead
Preparing
10-15
minutes
Baking
20 minutes

1 12-ounce package green
  spinach noodles, cooked
  and drained
1 12-ounce can white corn,
  drained
1 large green bell pepper,
  seeded

1 8-ounce package cream
  cheese, softened
1 cup half-and-half
Salt and pepper to taste
1½ cups grated fresh
  Parmesan cheese, divided

Utensil: food processor or blender, 8 x 12 inch low-sided
baking dish
Preheat oven to 350°

Combine noodles and corn. In covered container chop green
pepper; remove and set aside. Add cream cheese, half-and-half,
salt and pepper; blend well. Combine cheese, pepper and noodle
mixtures; add ½ cup Parmesan cheese and mix well. Pour in
baking dish and top with remaining Parmesan. Bake 20 minutes.

*Comment: A Tijuana favorite. Serve with broiled chicken and a
pico de gallo salad.*

**To make our appetites more keen, With eager
compounds we our palate urge.**

SONNET CXVIII

SALADS

Associate Artist Jonathan McMurtry at lunch

EMERALD SURPRISE—
IT'S CRAB!—SALAD

Servings
6
Planning
Make
dressing
day ahead
Preparing
1 hour
Chilling
2-4 hours

DRESSING
1 cup sour cream
Salt and pepper to taste
Dash of cayenne
Candied ginger to taste, optional
Dill weed to taste

GARNISHES
½-¾ cup cashew nuts
Fresh grapes

1 10-ounce package petite or baby peas, thawed
½ cup chopped green onions
1 cup chopped celery (use center stalks)
1 cup chopped fresh jicama
12 ounces crab meat
1 cup sliced cucumber
½ cup crisp bacon crumbled
Sesame seeds to taste
Butter lettuce leaves

For dressing: Combine sour cream, salt, pepper, cayenne, candied ginger and dill weed. Chill overnight to blend flavors.

In large bowl combine peas, onions, celery, jicama, crab and cucumber. Chill 2-4 hours. When ready to serve, combine with dressing, bacon and sesame seeds. Arrange butter lettuce leaves on serving plates, and divide salad into portions. Garnish with cashews and grapes.

Comment: THE luncheon salad. Serve with deviled egg halves, cherry tomatoes and lemon wedges.

Come and crush a cup of wine.
                    ROMEO AND JULIET

SWEET & SOUR SALAD

Servings
12
Planning
Make dressing 1-2 days ahead
Preparing
30 minutes

DRESSING
1 egg, beaten
1 tablespoon dry mustard
1 tablespoon salt
¼ teaspoon pepper
½ teaspoon paprika
¾ cup apple cider vinegar
¼ cup oil
1 14-ounce can sweetened
   condensed milk

3 heads romaine lettuce,
   washed, dried, torn
½ pound bacon, cooked,
   crumbled
2 Bermuda onions, thinly
   sliced

Utensil: electric mixer or blender

For dressing: Mix egg with mustard, salt, pepper and paprika. Alternately add vinegar and oil. Slowly add milk, beating well after each addition. Chill.

In large bowl combine lettuce, bacon and onions; toss with dressing or serve dressing on side.

Comment: Outstanding accompaniment to barbecued chicken, turkey or pork chops.

CREAMY ITALIAN DRESSING

Servings
20
Planning
Must make ahead
Preparing
10 minutes
Chilling
Overnight

8 ounces mayonnaise
8 ounces Italian oil and light
   vinegar salad dressing
6 garlic cloves, crushed

Combine mayonnaise, Italian dressing and garlic; chill overnight.

Comment: Marvelous over green salad with cilantro.

MOUSSE VERDE DE MARIBEL

1 pound cooked crab meat,
  flaked

MOUSSE
6 ripe avocados, pitted,
  skinned
½ cup plain yogurt
2 8-ounce packages cream
  cheese
1 medium onion, chopped
1 cup chopped fresh spinach
½ cup chopped parsley
1 cup chopped watercress

¼ cup lemon juice
2 medium zucchini, chopped
3 garlic cloves, chopped
1 cup oil
¼ teaspoon salt
¼ teaspoon pepper
4 envelopes (4 tablespoons)
  unflavored gelatin
¾ cup cold water

GARNISH
Cherry tomatoes
Red leaf lettuce

Servings
4-6 as
entrée,
10-12 as
side dish
Planning
Must make
ahead
Preparing
35-40
minutes
Chilling
3-4 hours

Utensils: blender or food processor, double boiler, 3-quart
ring mold coated with non-stick spray, platter

For mousse: Process in two batches. In container combine
avocados, yogurt, cream cheese, onion, spinach, parsley,
watercress, lemon juice, zucchini, garlic, oil, salt and pepper;
process until smooth.

Sprinkle gelatin over cold water; dissolve over boiling water. Add
gelatin to mousse mixture; combine well. Pour into mold and chill
3-4 hours or until thoroughly set. To serve, unmold on platter;
place crab in center. Garnish with cherry tomatoes and lettuce.

*Comment: It's rich, delicious and comes from south of the border.
You'll wow your guests by serving either as a luncheon entrée or,
omitting the crab, as a side dish.*

CRUNCHY PEA SALAD

Servings
6-8
Planning
Make ahead
4 hours
Preparing
1 hour
Chilling
1 hour
minimum

1 10-ounce package frozen
  peas
1 8-ounce can water
  chestnuts, drained and
  sliced
4 stalks celery, sliced
5 green onions, sliced
4 tablespoons mayonnaise

1 head lettuce, washed, dried
  and torn
¼ pound bacon, cooked and
  crumbled
Salt and pepper to taste

MARINADE
2 tablespoons oil
2 tablespoons wine vinegar
1 tablespoon soy sauce
1 teaspoon sugar

1 teaspoon paprika
1 teaspoon dry mustard
½ teaspoon salt
1 clove garlic, pressed

First prepare marinade by mixing together oil, vinegar, soy sauce, sugar, paprika, mustard, salt and garlic.

Place peas in colander and hold under running hot water to thaw; drain well. Combine peas, water chestnuts, celery and green onions; pour marinade over vegetables. Chill at least 1 hour. To serve, drain marinade from vegetables; toss vegetables with mayonnaise, lettuce and bacon. Salt and pepper to taste.

Comment: This flavorful, surprisingly different salad will give your buffet a new dimension.

CALIFORNIA CHINESE SALAD

Servings
4-6
Planning
Must make
ahead
Preparing
20-30
minutes
Chilling
½-1 hour

2 tomatoes, sectioned
½ English (hothouse)
  cucumber, sliced
2 green onions, sliced
  diagonally
1 rib celery, sliced
1 small avocado, cut in
  crescents
1 teaspoon minced fresh
  ginger root, optional
Salad greens

DRESSING
3 tablespoons rice wine
  vinegar
3 tablespoons light soy sauce
1 tablespoon sugar
2 tablespoons sesame oil

Utensils: cruet, large bowl

For dressing: Combine vinegar, soy sauce, sugar and oil; mix well.

Combine tomatoes, cucumber, onions, celery, avocado and ginger root, if using. Add dressing and chill ½-1 hour. Serve on bed of greens.

Comment: An enticing Far Eastern flavor for California vegetables.

Adam was a gardener.
                    II HENRY VI

MAYAN SALAD (PICO DE GALLO)

Servings
6-8
Planning
Can make
ahead
Preparing
1 hour

1 large head romaine lettuce
1 large head red leaf lettuce
1½ cups jicama, cut in
    julienne strips
1 medium red onion, sliced in
    rounds
1 grapefruit, seeded and
    sectioned
2 oranges, seeded and
    sectioned
½ pound cherry tomatoes,
    halved
1 large avocado

DRESSING
3 tablespoons cider vinegar
2 tablespoons fresh lime juice
6 tablespoons oil
1 clove garlic, mashed
1 teaspoon black pepper
⅛ teaspoon cayenne pepper

Utensils: large platter, blender

Wash romaine and red leaf lettuce; tear into bite-size pieces.

Prepare salad in layer fashion. Starting with lettuce, add jicama,
onion, grapefruit, oranges and tomatoes. Cover and chill 1-2 hours.
When ready to serve, peel and slice avocado and add to salad.
Pour dressing over salad.

For dressing: In blender combine vinegar, lime juice, oil, garlic,
black and cayenne peppers; process.

Comment: The ideal salad with Mexican entrées.

THE ORIGINAL RECIPE FOR CAESAR SALAD

Servings
4
Planning
Ready
lettuce
ahead
Preparing
30 minutes

1 clove garlic, peeled and sliced
½ cup olive oil
2 medium heads romaine lettuce
½ teaspoon freshly ground pepper
½ teaspoon salt
2 coddled eggs (raw eggs boiled 1 minute)

8-10 drops Worcestershire sauce
4 tablespoons lemon juice
6-8 tablespoons freshly grated Parmesan cheese
½ cup croutons
8 anchovy fillets, optional

Utensil: large salad bowl

Steep garlic in oil 24 hours or longer. Discard garlic when ready to use.

Wash romaine; tear into 2-inch lengths or use whole inner leaves. (Discard coarse outer leaves.) Dry and chill to crisp.

Place lettuce in bowl. Pour garlic-flavored oil over lettuce and sprinkle with pepper and salt. Toss gently 2-3 times. Break coddled eggs into small bowl, add Worcestershire and lemon juice; blend. Pour egg mixture over salad; toss 2-3 times. Sprinkle with Parmesan; add croutons. Toss once. Serve immediately on chilled dinner plates; garnish with anchovies if using.

Comment: The world famous salad from Caesar's Restaurant in Tijuana.

Now in the names of all the gods at once,
Upon what meat doth this our Caesar feed,
That he is grown so great?
                                                  JULIUS CAESAR

BEAN SPROUT SALAD

Servings
6-8
Planning
Partially
make ahead
Preparing
15 minutes
Chilling
3-4 hours
for dressing

SALAD
1 pound bean sprouts
1 cup thinly sliced celery
2 tablespoons minced green
   onions
1 cup slivered almonds,
   toasted
½ cup sliced water chestnuts
Crisp lettuce for bedding

DRESSING
1 cup mayonnaise
¼ cup soy sauce
2 teaspoons curry powder
2 teaspoons powdered ginger
2 teaspoons lemon juice

Utensil: salad bowl

For salad: Combine bean sprouts, celery, green onion, almonds and water chestnuts.

For dressing: Mix mayonnaise, soy sauce, curry powder, ginger and lemon juice thoroughly. Chill several hours to blend flavors.

When ready to serve, toss salad with dressing; drain slightly and place on bed of lettuce.

Comment: A refreshing contrast of flavors and textures.

My salad days,
When I was green in judgement: cold in blood.
ANTONY AND CLEOPATRA

COLD & TANGY VEGETABLE SALAD

Servings
6-8
Planning
Must make
ahead
Preparing
15 minutes
Storing
2-3 days
Chilling
4-24 hours

1 cup chopped green bell pepper
1 cup chopped celery
½ cup sliced green onions
2 tablespoons chopped
  pimiento
1 17-ounce can whole corn,
  drained
1 17-ounce can green peas,
  drained
1 16-ounce can sliced green
  beans, drained

DRESSING
½-⅔ cup apple cider vinegar
⅓ cup oil
½-¾ cup sugar
½ teaspoon salt
½ teaspoon ground pepper

In large bowl combine pepper, celery, onions, pimiento, corn, peas
and green beans. Whisk together vinegar, oil, sugar, salt and
pepper; stir mixture into vegetables. Cover and marinate 4-24
hours, stirring 2-3 times.

*Comment: Colorful, simple and ideal barbecue fare. Serve in
lettuce cups.*

Our corn's to reap, for yet our tithe's to sow.
MEASURE FOR MEASURE

MARY BETTY'S POTATO SALAD

Servings
8-10
Planning
Must make
ahead
Preparing
20 minutes
Cooking
30-45
minutes
Chilling
6-8 hours
minimum

6-8 medium white thin-
  skinned potatoes
½ cup olive oil
2 tablespoons red wine
  vinegar
1 teaspoon salt
1½ tablespoons prepared
  mustard
½ teaspoon freshly ground
  pepper

1 bunch chives, finely
  chopped
Chopped parsley to taste
Mayonnaise to bind
Celery and chopped black
  olives, optional
Paprika for garnish, optional
Sliced hard-cooked eggs for
  garnish, optional

Boil potatoes in salted water until just tender and pierceable.
Remove from heat, drain and plunge into cold water. Peel and cut
into slices or chunks. In large bowl mix oil, vinegar, salt, mustard,
pepper, chives and parsley. Add potatoes and toss to coat. Cover
and chill 6-8 hours minimum. When ready to serve, add enough
mayonnaise to bind; add celery and olives, if using. Garnish with
paprika and egg slices, if using.

Comment: If you like olive oil, this is the salad for you!

**Here's the challenge, read it: I warrant there's
vinegar and pepper in't.**
                                    TWELFTH NIGHT

CRISPY CELERY & CORN SALAD

Servings
4-6
Planning
Can make
day ahead
Preparing
15 minutes

1 16-ounce can whole kernel corn, well-drained
¾ cup chopped celery
¼ cup chopped green (or red) bell pepper
¼ cup chopped parsley
¼ cup chopped green onions
½ teaspoon salt or to taste

Pepper to taste
1 hard-cooked egg, chopped, optional
⅓ cup mayonnaise (or part yogurt or sour cream)
1 2¼-ounce can sliced ripe olives, drained
Pimiento strips for garnish

Utensil: salad bowl

Combine corn, celery, green pepper, parsley, green onions, salt, pepper, egg if using, mayonnaise and olives. Mix well and chill. Garnish with pimiento strips.

HOT GERMAN POTATO SALAD

Servings
4-6
Planning
Can make
2-3 days
ahead
Preparing
30 minutes
Cooking
30 minutes

½ pound bacon
⅓ cup reserved bacon drippings
⅓-½ cup apple cider vinegar
1 egg, slightly beaten
1 teaspoon sugar

1 teaspoon salt
¼ teaspoon pepper
5 cups cooked diced white thin-skinned potatoes
½ cup chopped green onion

Utensil: skillet

Cook bacon in skillet until crisp; remove, crumble and set aside. Reserve ⅓ cup bacon drippings; add vinegar, egg, sugar, salt and pepper. Cook and stir until thickened. Add potatoes, onion and bacon. Stir and heat thoroughly. Serve immediately, or refrigerate 2-3 days and reheat in 325° oven.

Comment: A perfect mate for bratwurst, knockwurst or Polish sausage.

CRUNCHY RICE SALAD

Servings
6
Planning
Can make
day ahead
Preparing
30-35
minutes
Chilling
4-24 hours

3 cups cold cooked rice
3 cups cooked small shrimp
1 cup thinly sliced celery
1 cup chopped green bell
  pepper
1½-2 cups frozen peas,
  defrosted
1 8-ounce can water
  chestnuts, drained, sliced
Salt and pepper to taste

GARNISHES
½ cup sliced almonds,
  toasted
Parsley sprigs

CREAMY DRESSING
1 cup mayonnaise
1 teaspoon grated lemon peel
¼ cup lemon juice
1 tablespoon prepared
  mustard
1 tablespoon prepared
  horseradish
¼ teaspoon garlic powder
½ cup thinly sliced green
  onions
¼ cup chopped parsley
1 2-ounce jar sliced
  pimientos, drained

Gently combine rice, shrimp, celery, green pepper, peas and water chestnuts. Add creamy dressing and blend well; add salt and pepper to taste. Cover and chill. When ready to serve, garnish with almonds and parsley.

For creamy dressing: Combine mayonnaise, lemon peel, lemon juice, mustard, horseradish and garlic powder; blend well. Stir in green onions, parsley and pimientos.

Comment: The ultimate luncheon salad.

GENA ROWLANDS CASSAVETES

GREEK SALAD

6 medium tomatoes
1 large cucumber
3 large stalks celery
1 large red onion
¼ cup fresh chopped parsley
1 bunch watercress
2 tablespoons chopped basil
1 tablespoon chopped mint

5 tablespoons olive oil
5 tablespoons fresh lemon
 juice
Salt and fresh cracked pepper
 to taste
¾-1 pound Feta cheese,
 crumbled

1. Peel tomatoes and cut in small wedges.

2. Chop onion, celery, watercress, cucumbers and add to tomatoes.
Toss well.

3. Mix oil, lemon juice, mint, salt and pepper.

4. Mix together. Add Feta cheese.

5. Garnish with basil and chill 15 minutes before serving.

GENA ROWLANDS CASSAVETES
Award winning film actress, has created numerous major dramatic roles in her career.

CHINESE CHICKEN SALAD

Servings
6-8
Planning
Prepare
dressing
ahead;
assemble
when ready
to serve
Preparing
1 hour

4 whole chicken breasts,
  cooked, skinned, shredded
1 head lettuce, thinly sliced
1 small package won tin skins,
  sliced in $1/8$-inch strips and
  deep fried
1 tablespoon white sesame
  seeds
1 4-ounce package sliced
  almonds, toasted
2 green onions, sliced

DRESSING
1 teaspoon soy sauce
$1/2$ teaspoon cornstarch
6 tablespoons sugar
$1/4$ cup vinegar
$1/4$ cup catsup
$1/4$ cup water

Utensil: large salad bowl

Layer large salad bowl with shredded chicken, lettuce and won ton strips. Sprinkle with sesame seeds and almonds; garnish with onions. Serve with dressing on side.

For dressing: Combine soy sauce, cornstarch, sugar, vinegar, catsup and water. Cook until clear. Cool.

Comment: A light crunchy chicken salad with a zesty dressing.

**The best of happiness,
Honour and fortunes keep with you!**
TIMON OF ATHENS

CHICKEN TORTILLA SALAD

Servings
8
Planning
Can make
partially
ahead
Preparing
1 hour

4 cups cooked, cubed chicken
Salt and pepper to taste
2 cups real mayonnaise,
  divided
1 pint salsa, divided
1 head lettuce, shredded
1 large onion, minced
1 pound Cheddar cheese,
  grated, divided

½ pound Monterey Jack
  cheese, grated, divided
2 large tomatoes, chopped,
  divided
1 15½-ounce bag fresh
  tortilla chips or strips
1 2¼-ounce can sliced olives

Season chicken with salt and pepper. In large bowl combine 1 cup mayonnaise and ½ cup salsa. Add lettuce, onion, ¾ pound Cheddar, ⅜ pound Monterey Jack, 1½ tomatoes and chicken. Toss mixture.

When ready to serve, arrange chips on large plate and place salad in center. Cover with remaining cheeses, tomato and olives. Mix remaining mayonnaise and salsa in blender to desired consistency; serve on side. (If made ahead, do not mix chicken with ingredients until ready to serve.)

Comment: A luncheon feast with zip.

SPINACH CHICKEN SALAD WITH POPPY SEED DRESSING

Servings
10
Planning
*Can
partially
make ahead*
Preparing
30 minutes

3 bunches fresh spinach
1 red or white onion, sliced
5 cups cooked, cubed chicken
1 8-ounce can water
  chestnuts, drained and
  sliced

1 11-ounce can mandarin
  oranges, drained
1 15¼-ounce can pineapple
  chunks, drained
½ cup sliced, toasted
  almonds

Poppy Seed Dressing (recipe follows)

Wash spinach thoroughly, remove stems, tear into bite-size pieces and spin or pat dry. Slice onion into thin slices and separate into rings. (Can be prepared day ahead to this point.)

In large bowl combine spinach, cubed chicken, onions, water chestnuts, mandarin oranges and pineapple; toss with approximately 1 cup Poppy Seed Dressing. Serve with additional dressing and almonds on the side.

Comment: A fine luncheon salad to serve with hot rolls and a dessert.

Yield
4 cups
Planning
*Can make
week ahead*
Storing
Refrigerate

POPPY SEED DRESSING

1 cup sugar
2 teaspoons dry mustard
2 teaspoons salt
⅔ cup rice wine vinegar
3 tablespoons finely chopped
  onion

1 tablespoon sesame oil
1 cup olive oil
1 cup salad oil
3 tablespoons poppy seeds

Utensil: blender

Put sugar, mustard, salt, vinegar and onion into blender and blend well. Add sesame oil, olive oil and salad oil slowly and blend until thick. Add poppy seeds and blend a few more seconds.

ORANGE CHICKEN SALAD

Servings
4-6
Planning
Make ahead
partially
Preparing
30 minutes
Marinating
Up to 4
hours

3-4 cups cut-up cooked
chicken breasts (large
chunks)
1 bunch green onions,
chopped
1½ cups cubed fresh
pineapple
1½ cups orange sections (if
canned, drain)

1½ cups chopped celery
1½ cups seedless green
grapes
½ cup slivered almonds
Mayonnaise to coat
Lettuce leaves

MARINADE
4 tablespoons oil
4 tablespoons undiluted
frozen orange juice
concentrate, thawed

4 tablespoons vinegar
½ teaspoon salt
½ teaspoon marjoram

Place chicken in plastic bag. Mix together oil, orange juice
concentrate (do not add water), vinegar, salt and marjoram; add to
chicken. Refrigerate no longer than 4 hours before using (to let
chicken keep its firm consistency). When ready to serve, drain
chicken slightly and put in large bowl. Add pineapple, onions,
oranges, celery, grapes and almonds; toss with enough mayonnaise
to bind (about ½ cup). Serve at once on crisp lettuce leaves.

*Comment: The orange flavor is a surprise in this fresh chicken
salad.*

*Lafeu: 'Twas a good lady: we may pick a thousand
salads ere we light on such another herb.
Clown: Indeed, sir, she was the sweet-marjoram of
the salad, or rather, the herb of grace.*
                    ALL'S WELL THAT ENDS WELL

TROPIC FRUIT SALAD

Servings
4
Planning
Serve
immediately
Preparing
20 minutes

2 bananas, peeled and sliced
1 avocado, pitted, peeled and
  sliced, optional
1 kiwi, peeled and sliced
1 papaya, peeled, seeded and
  sliced
2 apples, cored and grated

1 cup grapes
1 cup berries
Juice of 2 oranges
1-2 tablespoons honey
1 tablespoon brandy or rum,
  optional

In large bowl combine fruit with orange juice, honey and brandy or
rum.

*Comment: Versatile is the word for this fruit medley. Try it for a
pancake breakfast. For lunch, add cottage cheese. For dinner turn
it into a light dessert by adding brandy or rum to serve alone—or
as a topping for ice cream or cake.*

SWEET FRUIT DRESSING

Yield
1½ cups
Planning
Must make
ahead
Preparing
15 minutes
Storing
1 month

½ cup sugar
1 teaspoon salt
1 teaspoon dry mustard
1 teaspoon celery seed

1 teaspoon paprika
1 cup oil
¼ cup vinegar
¼ cup finely chopped onion

Utensil: 2-cup covered container

Combine sugar, salt, mustard, celery seed and paprika. Using fork
and beating well, alternately add oil and vinegar. When thoroughly
mixed, add onion. Place in container and chill 24 hours for best
flavor. Keeps up to 1 month refrigerated.

Comment: A fine topping for any citrus or mixed fruit salad.

LOUIS DRESSING FOR SEAFOOD

Yield
3 cups
Planning
*Can make 2
days ahead*
Preparing
15 minutes

½ cup real mayonnaise
½ cup bottled chili sauce
1 tablespoon prepared
    horseradish
1 tablespoon lemon juice
½ teaspoon dry mustard

½ teaspoon paprika
½ teaspoon salt
1 pint sour cream
Black pepper and cayenne to
    taste

Utensil: blender, optional

In blender (or bowl) combine mayonnaise, chili sauce, horseradish,
lemon juice, dry mustard, paprika, salt, sour cream, black pepper
and cayenne. Mix well.

Comment: A zippy dressing for shrimp, lobster or crab.

LEMON FRENCH DRESSING

Yield
1⅓ cups
Planning
*Must make
ahead*
Preparing
*5-10
minutes*
Storing
1 month

⅓ cup lemon juice
1 cup oil (not olive)
1 teaspoon Dijon mustard
¼ teaspoon dried salad herbs
1 teaspoon white vinegar

1 tablespoon sugar
1 teaspoon salt
1 large clove garlic, mashed
Freshly ground pepper

Mix lemon juice, oil, mustard, herbs, vinegar, sugar, salt, garlic
and pepper in glass or ceramic container. Shake well. Allow to
stand unrefrigerated for 24 hours. Taste and adjust for herbs;
refrigerate.

When ready to serve, bring to room temperature and shake well.
(When doubling recipe, use a generous ½ teaspoon herbs.)

POPPY SEED DRESSING FOR FRESH FRUIT SALAD

Yield
3 cups
Planning
Make ahead
Preparing
5 minutes
Storing
1 week

1 cup honey
1 ¼ teaspoon salt
½ cup vinegar
1 ⅓ cups oil
1 tablespoon grated onion

1 ¼ teaspoons dry mustard
2 teaspoons poppy seeds

Fresh fruit in season

Combine honey, salt and vinegar in a quart jar; add oil, onion, mustard and poppy seeds. Shake to mix well; refrigerate. When ready to serve, shake well and spoon over salad.

Prepare salad with seasonal fresh fruits such as melons, peaches, apples, strawberries, oranges, pears and avocados; garnish with kiwi fruit. Before combining squeeze lemon juice over apples, pears and avocados. Serve on a bed of Boston lettuce.

Comment: Jonathan McMurtry's recipe for the perfect salad to accompany his Braised Viennese Pork Roast (page 89).

AVOCADO ASPIC SALAD

Servings
8-10
Planning
Must make
ahead
Preparing
20 minutes

3 cups tomato juice
1 clove garlic or ½ teaspoon garlic powder
1 6-ounce package lemon-flavored gelatin

1 tablespoon white wine vinegar
4 ice cubes
1-1½ cups chopped celery
2 avocados, peeled and cubed

Utensil: 8-cup mold, prepared with non-stick spray

Heat tomato juice with garlic. Add gelatin, stirring to dissolve. Add vinegar and ice cubes; stir until cooled and remove garlic. Fold in celery and avocado. Place in mold and chill until firm.

Comment: Tangy, crisp and colorful.

AVOCADO SHRIMP SALAD

Servings
8
Planning
Make ahead
Preparing
30 minutes
Chilling
4-24 hours
Marinating
2-4 hours

1 pound cooked and cleaned
  medium or large shrimp
1 cup French dressing
  (see below)
2 tablespoons unflavored
  gelatin
1 cup cold water

2 cups boiling water
4 cups mashed avocado pulp
  (about 4 medium)
¼ cup lemon juice
Salt to taste
Dash hot pepper sauce

Utensil: 3-quart ring mold

Marinate shrimp in French dressing 2-4 hours. Soften gelatin in
cold water; dissolve in boiling water. Pour small amount of gelatin
in bottom of ring mold; drain shrimp and arrange in bottom of
mold. Refrigerate until set (about 1 hour).

Add avocado, lemon juice, salt and hot pepper sauce to balance of
gelatin mixture. Pour over shrimp and refrigerate until well set.
Unmold to serve.

*Comment: Tastes as splendid as it looks. A perfect candidate for a
buffet dinner.*

FRENCH DRESSING

Yield
1 cup
Planning
Can make
ahead
Preparing
5 minutes
Storing
1 month

½ cup oil
Scant ½ cup vinegar
1 teaspoon salt
½ teaspoon pepper

1 teaspoon sugar
2 teaspoons prepared Dijon
  mustard
2 tablespoons port wine

In cruet mix oil, vinegar, salt, pepper, sugar, mustard and port
wine; shake vigorously.

BLUEBERRY SALAD

Servings
12-15
Planning
*Must make
ahead*
Preparing
20 minutes
Chilling
10 hours
Storing
*Up to 3
days*

LAYER 1
1 cup boiling water
1 3-ounce package raspberry
  gelatin
1 cup cold water

1 teaspoon vanilla
1 8-ounce package cream
  cheese, softened
½ cup coarsely chopped
  walnuts

LAYER 2
1 envelope (1 tablespoon)
  unflavored gelatin
½ cup cold water
1 cup light (coffee) cream
1 cup sugar

LAYER 3
1 cup boiling water
1 3-ounce package raspberry
  gelatin
1 16-ounce can blueberries
  with juice

Utensil: 9 x 13 inch glass pan

Layer 1: Add 1 cup boiling water to 1 package raspberry gelatin; stir until dissolved. Add 1 cup cold water. Pour into pan and chill 2 hours or until set.

Layer 2: Sprinkle unflavored gelatin on cold water to soften. Combine cream and sugar; heat almost to boiling point. Add softened gelatin and stir until thoroughly dissolved. Add vanilla and cream cheese; stir to smooth consistency. Mix in walnuts. Pour over first layer (after it has firmed). Cover and chill 4 hours or until set.

Layer 3: Add 1 cup boiling water to 1 box raspberry gelatin; stir until dissolved. Add blueberries with juice; stir to combine thoroughly. Pour over second layer (after it has set). Cover and chill at least 4 hours or until set.

Comment: Red, white and blue—perfect for the Fourth of July!

CRANBERRY HOLIDAY SALAD

Servings
12
Planning
Make day ahead
Preparing
15 minutes
Chilling
Overnight

2 6-ounce packages raspberry gelatin
2 cups hot water
2 16-ounce cans whole cranberry sauce
1 20-ounce can crushed pineapple, undrained
1⅓ cups port wine or fruit juice
1 cup chopped pecans or walnuts
1 11-ounce can mandarin oranges, drained, optional

CREAM CHEESE FROSTING (optional)
1 3-ounce package cream cheese, softened
1 cup sour cream

Utensil: 9 x 13 inch pan

Dissolve gelatin in hot water; pour in pan. Stir in cranberry sauce, pineapple, wine (or fruit juice), nuts and oranges, if using. Chill until firm. Cut into squares and serve on lettuce leaves.

For frosting: Blend cream cheese and sour cream until smooth; spread on firmly-set gelatin. Chill 30 minutes.

Comment: Serve with turkey, chicken or ham.

Here, with a cup that's stored unto the brim.
                                        PERICLES

AVOCADO MOUSSE À LA YORSTON

Servings
8-10
Planning
Make ahead
4-6 hours
(no longer)
Preparing
20 minutes
Chilling
4-6 hours

4 large avocados, peeled,
  seeded
¾ cup mayonnaise
1 onion, grated
1-4 chiles (jalapeño or
  serrano), seeded and
  minced

Lemon juice to taste
Salt and pepper to taste
¼ cup finely chopped cilantro
  leaves
½ cup water
1½ tablespoons unflavored
  gelatin

Utensil: ring mold

Mash and sieve avocado; combine with mayonnaise, onion, chiles, lemon juice, salt, pepper and cilantro. Heat water, add gelatin and stir until dissolved. Cool slightly and stir into avocado mixture; adjust seasonings if desired. Rinse ring mold with cold water and add mixture. Cover and chill 4-6 hours (no longer or mixture will darken). Unmold to serve.

Comment: Tastes like a rich guacamole. Serve small portions on butter lettuce with sliced tomatoes.

COLD WILD RICE SALAD

Servings
10-12
Planning
*Can make
ahead*
Preparing
20 minutes
Chilling
2-4 hours

1⅔ cups white and wild rice
  mixture, cooked al dente
2 6-ounce jars marinated
  artichoke hearts, drained,
  sliced
1 10-ounce package frozen
  peas, thawed

1½ pints cherry tomatoes,
  sliced in half
2 bunches green onions,
  sliced (include some green
  tops)
8 ounces Italian salad
  dressing prepared with
  olive oil

Combine rice with artichoke hearts, peas, tomatoes and onions. Gently toss with dressing; chill.

Comment: Easy and very good.

SALADE NIÇOISE

Servings
6-8
Planning
Must
partially
assemble
ahead
Preparing
45 minutes
Chilling
4-8 hours

24 Greek or black olives,
   pitted, halved
2 cups fresh green beans, cut
   into 1½-inch pieces,
   blanched
2 10-ounce cans water-
   packed tuna, drained, flaked
1 bunch green onions,
   chopped
4 hard-cooked eggs, sliced
Salt and pepper to taste
1 pound small shell pasta,
   cooked, drained

DRESSING
½ cup plus 2 tablespoons
   lemon juice
6 tablespoons olive oil
2 tablespoons Dijon mustard
1 tablespoon minced fresh
   oregano

For dressing: Combine lemon juice, olive oil, mustard and oregano.

Add olives and beans to dressing; chill several hours. Then add tuna, onions, eggs, salt and pepper; refrigerate several more hours. When ready to serve, add prepared pasta and toss gently.

Comment: This is excellent.

ANTIPASTO SALAD FOR A CROWD

Servings
50
Planning
Must
partially
make ahead
Preparing
1 hour
Marinating
24 hours

DRESSING
3 cups Italian oil and vinegar
  salad dressing
½ cup olive oil
¼ cup balsamic vinegar

SALAD
2 15¼-ounce cans kidney
  beans, drained
2 15¼-ounce cans garbanzo
  beans, drained
2 15-ounce jars giardinara,
  drained
1 7½-ounce jar cocktail
  onions, drained
2 15-ounce jars pepperoncini,
  drained, larger pieces
  halved

2 6-ounce (drained weight)
  cans black olives, drained
1 14½-ounce jar green salad
  olives, drained
1 pound Mozzarella or
  Provolone cheese (or
  combination), diced
¼ pound Parmesan cheese,
  finely grated
2 pounds Italian dry salami,
  thinly sliced or cubed
½ pound pepperoni, thinly
  sliced
8-10 heads mixed lettuce,
  washed and torn into bite-
  size pieces

Utensils: large covered bowl, large salad bowl

For dressing: Mix Italian salad dressing, olive oil and balsamic vinegar; set aside.

For salad: Combine kidney and garbanzo beans, giardinara, cocktail onions, pepperoncini, black and green olives, cheese, salami and pepperoni. Add dressing and marinate overnight.

When ready to serve, toss lettuce with bean mixture.

Comment: A crowd pleaser. Serve as a luncheon main course with garlic bread.

PIES & PASTRIES

Linda Candace Hart and Deborah Van Valkenburgh in *Pump Boys and Dinettes*

OLD-FASHIONED CREAM PIE

Servings
6-8
Planning
Can make
ahead
Preparing
30 minutes
Baking
45 minutes

Pastry for 9-inch single-crust
  pie (see below)

FILLING

1¼ scant cups sugar	1 cup boiling water
½ scant cup all-purpose flour	1 teaspoon vanilla or rum
2 tablespoons butter	flavoring
1 cup heavy cream	Nutmeg for topping
¼ teaspoon salt	

Utensil: 9-inch pie pan
Preheat oven to 400°, lower to 325°

Line pan with pastry. In large bowl, using electric mixer, combine
sugar, flour, butter, cream and salt; blend well. Add boiling water
and vanilla; beat well. Pour into unbaked pie shell; sprinkle with
nutmeg. Bake 10 minutes at 400°; lower to 325° and bake
additional 35-40 minutes. Cool to serve.

Comment: A different tasting pie, rich, but not too sweet.

BASIC PIE CRUST

Yield
Makes 1
double-crust
or 2 single-
crust pie
shells

1 cup flour
Dash of salt
½ cup shortening
¼ cup cold water

Place flour in bowl and add salt. Using a fork or pastry blender,
work shortening into flour until mixture becomes crumbly. Add
water and blend, using a light touch, until dough just holds
together. Wrap in waxed paper or plastic wrap and chill at least 1
hour or even overnight. When ready to use, divide dough in half.
Roll out on floured board to desired size.

Comment: This makes a thin, light and flaky crust.

ANGEL PIE

Servings
6
Planning
*Can make
ahead*
Preparing
40 minutes
Baking
*55-60
minutes*
Chilling
6-8 hours

MERINGUE CRUST
4 egg whites
¼ teaspoon cream of tartar
⅛ teaspoon salt
1 cup sugar

FILLING
4 egg yolks
¼ cup fresh lemon juice
**2 tablespoons grated lemon
  rind**
½ cup sugar
1 cup heavy cream, divided

Utensils: 9-inch pie pan, greased; double boiler
Preheat oven to 300°

For crust: Combine egg whites with cream of tartar and salt; beat until soft peaks form. Add sugar gradually, 2 tablespoons at a time, and beat constantly until egg whites are stiff and glossy. Pour into pan and form a nest-like shell with sides ½ inch above edge. Bake 55-60 minutes. Cool.

For filling: Beat egg yolks until thick and lemon colored; add lemon juice, rind and sugar. Cook in double boiler over hot water, stirring constantly, until mixture thickens. Cool to room temperature. Whip ½ cup cream and fold into mixture; pour into meringue shell. Chill 6-8 hours.

When ready to serve, whip remaining cream and garnish pie.

Comment: Light and heavenly.

A dish for the gods.
ANTONY AND CLEOPATRA

HEATHER'S TEMPTATION PIE

Servings
10-12
Planning
*Can make
day ahead*
Preparing
1 hour
Baking
*8-10
minutes*
Chilling
5-6 hours

CRUST
1½ cups all-purpose flour
¾ cup butter, room
temperature
2 tablespoons powdered
sugar
¾ cup chopped macadamia
nuts (or pecans or walnuts)

CREAM CHEESE FILLING
1½ cups powdered sugar
2 8-ounce packages cream
cheese, softened
1 8-ounce package whipped
topping

**CHOCOLATE PUDDING
FILLING**
1 3½-ounce package
chocolate pudding and pie
mix
1 5⅛-ounce package
chocolate pudding and pie
mix
4 cups milk

TOPPING
1 8-ounce package whipped
topping
Chopped macadamia nuts

Utensil: 9 x 13 inch baking dish
Preheat oven to 425°

For crust: Mix flour and powdered sugar; cut in butter until
crumbly. Add nuts. Press into baking dish. Bake 8-10 minutes.
Cool.

For cream cheese filling: Beat cream cheese with powdered
sugar; add whipped topping and mix well. Pour over crust.

For chocolate filling: Cook chocolate pudding according to
package directions but use only 4 cups milk. Cool. Pour over
cheese layer.

For topping: Spread whipped topping over chocolate layer and
sprinkle with chopped macadamias. Chill 5-6 hours before serving.

Comment: You won't be able to resist this temptation.

DOROTHEA'S CHEESE PIE

Servings
8
Planning
Make ahead
Preparing
45 minutes
Baking
30 minutes
Chilling
5 hours
minimum

CRUST
1½ cups graham cracker
  crumbs (12-14 crackers)
⅓ cup brown sugar
⅓ cup butter, melted
½ teaspoon cinnamon

TOPPING
1 cup sour cream
1 teaspoon vanilla
3½ tablespoons sugar

FILLING
12 ounces cream cheese,
  softened
2-3 eggs, beaten
¾ cup sugar
½ teaspoon fresh lemon juice
2 teaspoons vanilla

Utensil: 9-inch pie pan
Preheat oven to 350°

For crust: Combine crumbs, brown sugar, butter and cinnamon. Press firmly on bottom and sides of pan; chill.

For filling: Combine cream cheese, eggs, sugar, lemon juice and vanilla; beat until light and fluffy. Pour into crust and bake 20 minutes. Remove from oven and cool 5 minutes.

For topping: Combine sour cream, vanilla, and sugar; spread over baked filling. Return to oven and bake 10 minutes. Chill at least 5 hours.

Comment: A family favorite.

All yet seems well; and if it end so meet,
The bitter past, more welcome is the sweet.
ALL'S WELL THAT ENDS WELL

BUTTERMILK PIE

1 unbaked 8-inch pie crust,
 chilled
1¼ cups granulated sugar
3 tablespoons all-purpose
 flour
4 eggs, lightly beaten
1 stick unsalted butter,
 melted and cooled

1 cup buttermilk
1 tablespoon fresh lemon
 juice
1 teaspoon vanilla extract
Grated nutmeg to taste

Preheat oven to 425°. Combine sugar and flour in large bowl. Add beaten eggs and mix well. Stir in butter and buttermilk. Add in lemon juice (lemon rind of 1 lemon may also be added), vanilla and nutmeg. Pour into pie shell. Place in center of oven for 15 minutes; lower heat to 350° and continue baking for 40 minutes until filling is set. Serve at room temperature.

DOWN HOME BASIC PIE CRUST

2½ cups all-purpose flour
1 cup or 2 sticks cold
 unsalted butter, cut into
 small pieces

1 teaspoon salt
1 teaspoon sugar
¼ cup ice water

Sift together flour, salt and sugar. Using knives, cut butter chunks into flour mixture until blended. Separate into two balls and chill for 15-30 minutes. Remove ball of dough from refrigerator and place in pie pan. Using palms of hands, press dough until flat. Use thumbs to push dough up sides of pan. Decorate edge of crust in favorite way. Makes two 8- to 10-inch single crust pies or one double crust.

I make my pie crusts the old-fashioned way, without a rolling pin. I think it makes the crust more tender and flaky.

LINDA HART
Actress and singer, appeared at Globe in "Pump Boys and Dinettes." Performed with Bette Midler on Broadway and featured in "Anything Goes."

COUNTRY APPLE PIE

Servings
8
Planning
Can make
ahead
Preparing
1-1½ hours
Baking
50 minutes

DOUBLE-CRUST PASTRY
1 ¼ cups all-purpose flour
½ cup cake flour
2 tablespoons sugar
½ teaspoon salt
⅓ cup vegetable shortening
⅓ cup butter or margarine
¼ cup cold milk
Sugar for topping

FILLING
8 tart apples, peeled, cored, sliced
1 tablespoon lemon juice
1 cup sugar
3 tablespoons all-purpose flour
1 teaspoon cinnamon
⅛ teaspoon nutmeg
⅛ teaspoon salt
2 tablespoons butter

Utensils: food processor, optional; 9 or 10-inch pie pan
Preheat oven to 400°

For crust: In food processor or by hand (using a fork or pastry cutter) mix all-purpose and cake flours, sugar, salt, shortening and butter until mixture resembles corn meal. Stir in milk just until dough begins to clump. Chill 1 hour. Halve dough and roll out each piece on floured board. Put 1 crust in bottom of pie pan; reserve other for topping.

In large bowl combine apples, lemon juice, 1 cup sugar, flour, cinnamon, nutmeg and salt. Pour mixture into pie pan and dot with butter. Place remaining crust over apples; crimp edges. Cut slits in top and sprinkle with sugar. Bake 50 minutes or until golden brown.

Comment: An exceptionally tasty crust for a favorite apple pie.

How like Eve's apple doth thy beauty grow,
If thy sweet virtue answer not thy show!
                                          SONNET XCIII

TEXAS PECAN PIE

Servings
8
Planning
Can make
ahead
Preparing
15 minutes
Baking
40-45 minutes

3 eggs, lightly beaten
¾ cup dark corn syrup
¾ cup sugar
¼ teaspoon salt
2½ teaspoons vanilla
1 cup pecan halves

3 tablespoons butter or
margarine, melted

Pastry for 9-inch single-crust
pie (page 229)

Utensil: 9-inch pie pan
Preheat oven to 375°

Combine eggs and corn syrup; mix well. Stir in sugar, salt and vanilla; mix thoroughly. Let stand about 5 minutes. Spread pecans evenly over bottom of pie shell. Stir butter into syrup mixture; pour over pecans (pecans will rise to top). Bake 40-45 minutes or until center is firm.

SUBLIME KEY LIME PIE

Servings
6-8
Planning
Must make
ahead
Preparing
30 minutes
Baking
15 minutes
Freezing
4 hours
minimum

1 14-ounce can sweetened
condensed milk
4 egg yolks
½ cup lime juice
Few drops green food
coloring

2 egg whites, beaten stiff
½ pint heavy cream, whipped

1 9-inch graham cracker
crust (page 232)

Utensil: 9-inch pie pan
Preheat oven to 350°

Combine milk, egg yolks and lime juice; beat until smooth. Stir in food coloring. Fold egg whites into mixture; pour into crust. Bake 15 minutes or until firm but not browned. Cool, cover with plastic wrap and freeze. When ready to serve, top with whipped cream.

Comment: Smooth and luscious.

PUMPKIN PIE

Yield
3 pies
Planning
Can make
ahead
Preparing
15 minutes
Baking
40 minutes

2 cups sugar
1 heaping tablespoon
  cornstarch
1 teaspoon nutmeg
2 teaspoons cinnamon
½ teaspoon allspice
½ teaspoon ginger
2 teaspoons salt

5 eggs, well beaten
4 cups cooked or canned
  pumpkin
1 quart milk*

Pastry for three 9-inch single-
  crust pies (page 229)

Utensils: three 9-inch pie pans
Preheat oven to 425°, lower to 325°

Combine sugar, cornstarch, nutmeg, cinnamon, allspice, ginger and
salt. Add eggs and mix well. Stir in pumpkin and milk. Pour
mixture evenly into 3 pie pans. Bake at 425° for 15 minutes; then
reduce heat to 325° and continue baking 25 minutes or until
filling is set.

*For a richer pie, use 1 12-ounce can evaporated milk plus fresh
milk to equal 1 quart.

Comment: The crowning glory to a Thanksgiving dinner.

He's of the colour of the nutmeg.

HENRY V

Bob Morgan

ROBERT MORGAN

RHUBARB CUSTARD PIE

Here's a knockout:

1. Dice 4 cups rhubarb. Place in 9-inch unbaked pie shell (always best if your own pastry shell; supermarket frozen is OK).

2. Mix and pour over rhubarb:
   1½ cup sugar
   3 eggs
   ¼ cup flour
   Dash salt
   Dash nutmeg—very important—use fresh grated if possible

3. Make lattice top crust; glaze with butter and sprinkle with cinnamon sugar if so desired. OK without.

4. Bake at 375° for 30-45 minutes.

Terrific served with a hardy V.S.O.P Cognac, Ben & Jerry's vanilla ice cream on side. XOXO

ROBERT MORGAN, Associate Artist of the Globe
Designer of scenery and costumes for multiple Globe and Broadway productions as well as major resident theatres throughout the United States.

LEMON CREAM CHEESE PIE

Servings
10
Planning
Can make
1-2 days
ahead
Preparing
30 minutes
Baking
35-40
minutes
Chilling
5 hours

GRAHAM CRACKER CRUST
1½ cups graham cracker
  crumbs (22 squares,
  crushed)
¼ cup sugar
½ cup melted butter

TOPPING
1 cup sour cream
3½ tablespoons sugar
1 teaspoon vanilla

FILLING
12 ounces cream cheese,
  softened
2 eggs, beaten
1-2 tablespoons fresh lemon
  juice
1 tablespoon grated fresh
  lemon rind
¾ cup sugar
2 teaspoons vanilla

Utensil: 9-inch pie pan
Preheat oven to 350°

For crust: Combine crumbs, sugar and butter. Mix well and press firmly in pan.

For filling: Beat cream cheese until smooth. Add eggs, lemon juice, lemon rind, sugar and vanilla; beat until light. Pour into graham cracker crust and bake 25-30 minutes. Remove from oven and cool 5 minutes.

For topping: Blend sour cream, sugar and vanilla. Pour over filling. Return to oven and bake additional 10 minutes. Chill at least 5 hours.

Comment: Easy to make, easier to eat.

No man's pie is freed From his ambitious finger.
HENRY VIII

WATERMELON PIE

Servings
8-10
Planning
*Make ahead
to serve
same day*
Preparing
2 hours
Chilling
3-4 hours

FILLING
4 cups watermelon, seeded
  (to make 2½ cups slush)
2 envelopes (2 tablespoons)
  unflavored gelatin
⅔ cup sugar, divided
⅛ teaspoon salt
2½-3 tablespoons fresh
  lemon juice
2 egg whites
1 cup heavy cream, whipped

CRUST
16 graham crackers, crushed
2 tablespoons sugar
4 tablespoons butter, melted

GARNISH
Fresh watermelon balls
Mint sprigs

Utensils: 10-inch pie pan, blender
Preheat oven to 350° for crust

For crust: Combine cracker crumbs, sugar and butter; press into
pan. Bake 10-12 minutes. Cool.

For filling: Place watermelon in container; process to make 2½
cups slush. Place 1 cup slush over low heat, sprinkle with gelatin
and stir 5 minutes or until dissolved. Remove from heat and stir in
⅓ cup sugar and salt. Add remaining 1½ cups watermelon slush
and lemon juice. Chill, stirring occasionally, until completely
thickened. Beat egg whites until soft peaks form. Continue beating,
gradually adding remaining ⅓ cup sugar, until very stiff and
glossy. Fold egg whites and whipped cream, alternately, into
watermelon mixture. Pour into prepared crust; chill.

When ready to serve, garnish with mint sprigs and watermelon
balls.

Comment: Very delicate. Wonderful for a hot summer night.

GRANDMOTHER KNUTSON'S LEMON PIE

Servings
6–8
Planning
Can make day ahead
Preparing
30 minutes
Baking
12 minutes

3 eggs, separated
1 egg white
1 cup sugar, divided
1 lemon, juiced, rind grated

1 8-inch baked pie crust
(page 229)

Utensils: electric mixer, 8-inch pie pan, double boiler
Preheat oven to 325°

Beat egg yolks. Slowly blend in ½ cup sugar, lemon juice and rind. Cook in double boiler over simmering water, stirring with whisk until thickened. Beat egg whites until stiff; slowly stir in remaining sugar and beat again until soft peaks form. Fold ½ egg white mixture into yolk mixture; pour into pie crust. Spread remaining egg whites across top and seal to edge of crust. Bake 12 minutes. Chill until ready to serve.

Comment: Beautiful in its simplicity.

O, knowst thou not his looks are my soul's food?
Pity the dearth that I have pined in,
By longing for that food so long a time.
                    THE TWO GENTLEMEN OF VERONA

ALMOND TART

Servings
6-8
Planning
Can make
ahead
Preparing
30 minutes
Baking
For crust,
10 minutes;
for filling
25-30
minutes

CRUST
1 cup flour
1 tablespoon sugar
½ cup unsalted butter, room
  temperature
1 tablespoon cold water
½ teaspoon vanilla
Several drops almond extract

FILLING
1 cup sliced almonds
¾ cup sugar
¾ cup heavy cream
¼ teaspoon salt
1 teaspoon or more Amaretto
Several drops almond extract

Utensils: 9-inch tart shell
Preheat oven to 400° for crust; 375° for filling

For crust: In large bowl mix flour and sugar; cut in butter until crumbly. Work in water, vanilla and almond extract until dough forms ball. Press into tart shell; chill 1 hour. Bake 10 minutes in 400° oven.

For filling: Combine almonds, sugar, cream, salt, Amaretto and almond extract; mix well. Let stand 20 minutes. Pour into shell and bake 25-30 minutes at 375°.

Comment: Elegant, absolutely delicious—and relatively easy.

Nathaniel: Sir, he hath never fed of the dainties that are bred in a book:...
                    LOVE'S LABOUR'S LOST

Servings
8-12
Planning
Must make
ahead
Preparing
40-50
minutes
Baking
20-25
minutes
Chilling
2 hours or
longer

SUPER DELICIOUS STRAWBERRY PIE

FILLINGS
½ pound butter, softened
1 8-ounce package cream
  cheese, softened
2 cups powdered sugar
½ cup chopped walnuts

1 6-ounce package strawberry
  gelatin
2 10-ounce packages frozen
  strawberries, drained (or 1½
  boxes fresh strawberries,
  sliced)
1 cup boiling water

CRUST
½ pound butter or margarine,
  softened
2 tablespoons sugar
1½ cups all-purpose flour

TOPPING
1 pint heavy cream, whipped
½ cup chopped walnuts

Utensil: 9 x 11 inch pan
Preheat oven to 350°

For crust: Mix butter, sugar and flour; spread in pan and bake
20-25 minutes. Set aside to cool.

For fillings: (1) Blend butter, cream cheese and powdered sugar;
spread on cooled crust. Cover cheese mixture with ½ cup chopped
walnuts. (2) Pour boiling water over gelatin; stir to dissolve. Add
strawberries and cool to a syrupy texture. Spread thickened
gelatin mixture over walnuts. Chill at least 2 hours.

For topping: Spread whipped cream over gelatin mixture and
sprinkle with walnuts. Serve at once.

Comment: It is....Super Delicious!

KATHERINE McGRATH

FRESH STRAWBERRY PIE

CRUST
2 cups all-purpose flour
1 cup shortening
1 teaspoon salt
2 tablespoons cold water

Sift flour, cut in shortening. Combine salt and cold water and add to flour mixture, stirring quickly until soft dough is formed. Roll on floured board to ¼-inch thickness and fit into 10-inch pan. Bake in 425° hot oven for 15 minutes or until golden brown.

FILLING
1 cup crushed fresh strawberries
1 cup sugar
1 tablespoon cornstarch
Fresh strawberries (enough to fill shell), washed and hulled
Soft cream cheese for bottom of shell
Whipped cream

Mix crushed berries with sugar and cornstarch. Boil until mixture becomes translucent and syrupy. Spread cream cheese over bottom of pie shell and top with whole fresh berries. Pour hot syrup over fresh berries and chill. Serve with whipped cream.

Comment: My grandmother's recipe.

KATHERINE McGRATH, Associate Artist of the Globe
Has performed leading roles, ranging from high tragedy to high comedy, on all three Globe stages in contemporary and classical productions.

BRANDIED MINCEMEAT PIES

Yield
5 pies
Planning
Must make
mincemeat
ahead
Preparing
1 hour
Baking
45 minutes
Storing
Up to 60
days

Pastry for 5 double-crust pies
(see Basic Pie Crust, page
229)

FILLING FOR 5 PIES
1 pound currants
1 pound golden raisins
1 pound apples, cored, peeled
and diced
1 pound dried figs, chopped
1 pound pitted dates,
chopped
1 pound pecan meats,
chopped

1 pound walnut meats,
chopped
1 pound kidney suet, ground
1 pound brown sugar
½ tablespoon nutmeg
½ tablespoon ground cloves
1 tablespoon cinnamon
2 cups brandy
2 cups ale

HARD SAUCE
½ cup butter, softened
1½ cups powdered sugar
3-4 tablespoons brandy

Utensils: 1½ gallon plastic bowl with lid, 10-inch pie pans,
electric mixer
Preheat oven to 450°, lower to 350°

For filling: Combine currants, raisins, apples, figs, dates, pecans,
walnuts, suet, sugar, nutmeg, cloves, cinnamon, brandy and ale;
mix well. Cover and store in refrigerator 7-60 days, stirring every
day.

For each pie: Fill each prepared crust with ⅕ mincemeat
mixture. Center top crust over filling. Flute edges and make
several slits in top. Put in 450° oven for 10 minutes, then reduce
temperature to 350° and bake 35 minutes. Serve warm with hard
sauce.

For hard sauce: In small bowl beat butter until light and fluffy;
gradually add sugar and brandy. Mix until creamy.

Comment: You'll like this better than your mother's recipe.

FIRE & ICE PIE

VANILLA WAFER CRUST
(recipe follows)

FILLING
½ cup diced mixed candied
  fruit
2 tablespoons rum
1 quart vanilla ice cream,
  softened

FLAMING FRUIT SAUCE
½ cup apricot preserves
½ cup diced mixed candied
  fruit
¼ cup light corn syrup
4 tablespoons rum, divided

Servings
8
Planning
Must
partially
make ahead
Preparing
45 minutes
Cooking
5 minutes
Baking
5 minutes
Freezing
3-4 hours

Filling: Moisten candied fruit with 2 tablespoons rum; stir into ice cream. Spoon ice cream mixture into prepared Vanilla Wafer Crust and freeze until firm, 3-4 hours.

Sauce: In small saucepan combine apricot preserves, candied fruit, corn syrup and 2 tablespoons rum; warm over low heat. When ready to serve, cut pie into wedges. Add remaining rum to sauce; ignite and ladle flaming sauce over each serving.

VANILLA WAFER CRUST
¾ cup finely crushed vanilla
  wafer crumbs
½ cup wheat germ
2 tablespoons sugar

½ teaspoon nutmeg
¼ cup butter or margarine,
  melted

Utensil: 9-inch pie pan
Preheat oven to 350°

Combine crumbs, wheat germ, sugar, nutmeg and butter. Press firmly on bottom and sides of pan. Bake 5 minutes. Cool.

Comment: A grand finale to a festive dinner.

STRAWBERRY CHEESECAKE

Servings
8
Planning
Must make
ahead
Preparing
15-30
minutes
Baking
30 minutes
Chilling
5 hours

CRUST
1½ cups graham cracker
   crumbs (18-20 crackers)
3 tablespoons sugar
⅓ cup butter, melted

FILLING
⅔ cup sugar
2 8-ounce packages cream
   cheese, softened
2 eggs
2 tablespoons lemon juice

Utensil: 9-inch pie pan
Preheat oven to 350°

TOPPING
1 cup sour cream
1 10-ounce package frozen
   strawberries, drained
   (or 1½ boxes fresh
   strawberries, sliced)
2 tablespoons lemon juice
½ cup sugar or to taste

For crust: Combine butter and sugar; add crackers. Press into pan. Chill before filling.

Filling: Cream sugar and cheese. Add eggs and lemon juice. Pour into prepared crust and bake 20 minutes. Cool 5 minutes.

Topping: Combine sour cream, strawberries, lemon juice and sugar, to taste. Pour on top of cooked filling and bake additional 10 minutes. Chill 5 hours.

The strawberry grows underneath the nettle
And wholesome berries thrive and ripen best
Neighbour'd by fruit of baser quality.
                                    HENRY V

MINIATURE CHEESECAKES

FILLING
1 8-ounce package
  Philadelphia cream cheese
2 eggs slightly beaten

1 teaspoon vanilla
¼ to ½ cup sugar to taste

For filling: Mix together until smoothly blended.

CRUST
1 cup graham cracker crumbs
¼ stick butter or margarine
About ¼ cup sugar

For crust: Mix together with a fork until it holds together.

TOPPING
Cherry or blueberry fruit topping

Fill miniature muffin tin with minature muffin cups.

Put 1 teaspoon of graham cracker mixture into each cup. Fill cup with 2 teaspoons of cheesecake mixture.

Bake at 375° for 10-12 minutes or until toothpick comes out clean. Cool.

Immediately prior to serving, top with cherry or blueberry fruit topping.

Makes about 3 dozen.

Cheesecakes may be frozen *without* topping.

MICHAEL BYERS
Globe debut at age 17. His triple theatrical talents—acting, singing and dancing—have earned plaudits for numerous Globe roles and credits on Broadway, television, film and concert.

APPLE TART

Servings
6-8
Planning
*Best freshly
baked*
Preparing
30 minutes
Baking
1 hour

1 9-inch prepared single pie
  crust (page 229)
6 large green apples, peeled
  and cored
2 tablespoons flour

¾ cup sugar
½ teaspoon cinnamon
¼ cup heavy cream
2 tablespoons butter

Utensil: 9-inch pie pan
Preheat oven to 400°

Thinly slice 2 apples and place in pie shell. Mix flour, sugar and
cinnamon; sprinkle half over apples. Halve remaining apples
crosswise and space evenly across top; sprinkle with remaining
sugar mixture. Pour cream over and around apples. Dot with
butter. Bake at 400° for 1 hour. Apples should hold their shape.
Serve warm.

RAISIN PIE

Servings
8
Planning
*Can make
ahead*
Preparing
30 minutes
Baking
45 minutes

1 9-inch prepared double pie
  crust (page 229)
1½ cups raisins
2 cups hot water
2 tablespoons all-purpose
  flour

3 tablespoons sugar
1 tablespoon butter
2 tablespoons lemon juice

Utensil: 9-inch pie pan
Preheat oven to 400°, lower to 375°

Line pan with pastry. Boil raisins and water 15 minutes. Add flour
and sugar; stir until thick. Add butter and lemon juice. Put mixture
in unbaked pie crust, cover with top crust and slash to vent. Bake
15 minutes at 400°; lower oven to 375° and bake additional 30
minutes.

Comment: A classic from the San Joaquin Valley.

CAKES & COOKIES

Shuko Akune, Takayo Fischer, Lily Mariye and Diana Tanaka in *TEA*

GLAMOROUS CHOCOLATE-RASPBERRY RUM CAKE

Servings
12
Planning
Must make ahead
Preparing
30-45 minutes
Baking
25-30 minutes
Freezing
1 hour
Chilling
1-2 hours

1 18¼-ounce package
   chocolate fudge cake mix
½ cup chopped walnuts or
   pecans
¼ cup light or dark rum,
   divided
½ cup raspberry jam, divided

FROSTING
12 ounces chocolate chips
1 cup sour cream
Dash of salt
¼ cup chopped walnuts or
   pecans

Utensils: three 8-inch cake pans, greased
Preheat oven to 350°

Mix cake according to package directions and pour into pans.
Sprinkle nuts over raw cake batter; bake according to directions
(about 25-30 minutes). When cake tests done, remove from oven
and cool in pans on wire racks. Remove layers from pans and
place in individual plastic bags; freeze. (Freezing makes layers
easier to handle. This can be done days ahead, but layers should
freeze at least 1 hour.)

For frosting: Melt chocolate chips; cool 5 minutes. Add sour
cream and salt; blend thoroughly.

To assemble cake: Place 1 layer, flat side up, on serving plate;
sprinkle with ⅛ cup rum. Spread with frosting, ¼ cup jam and
then more frosting. Repeat with second layer. Place third layer on
top with rounded side up; frost top and sides. Sprinkle with nuts.
Chill until 30 minutes before serving.

Comment: Positively superb!

'Tis an ill cook that cannot lick his own fingers.
                     ROMEO AND JULIET

TURTLE CAKE

Servings
12-16
Planning
Can make
2-3 days
ahead
Preparing
20-30
minutes
Baking
40 minutes
Storing
Refrigerate

1 package chocolate cake mix
   (without pudding)
16 ounces caramels
1 14-ounce can sweetened
   condensed milk

16 ounces chocolate chips
1 cup pecans, whole or pieces
1 cup additional pecans,
   optional

Utensil: 9 x 13 inch pan, well greased
Preheat oven to 350°

Prepare cake mix as directed; pour ½ batter into pan. Bake 20
minutes and remove from oven. In meantime, heat caramels with
milk, stirring well, until melted. Pour mixture over baked half of
cake; sprinkle with chocolate chips and 1 cup pecans. Top with
remainder of batter and sprinkle with additional pecans, if using.
Bake 20 minutes. Cool cake thoroughly before cutting.

*Comment: You can't fail with this recipe for a rich and irresistible
cake.*

*Torches are made to light, jewels to wear,
Dainties to taste, fresh beauty for the use,
Herbs for their smell, and sappy plants to bear;
Things growing to themselves are growth's abuse.*
                                    VENUS AND ADONIS

CARROT CAKE

Servings
24
Planning
Can make
ahead
Preparing
1 hour
Baking
25-30
minutes

2 cups all-purpose flour,
  sifted
2 teaspoons cinnamon
2 teaspoons soda
1 teaspoon baking powder
1 teaspoon salt
½ cup oil
2 cups sugar
4 eggs
1 teaspoon vanilla
1 20-ounce can crushed
  pineapple, drained and
  divided

3 cups grated carrots (about
  3-4 large)
1 cup chopped walnuts or
  pecans

CREAM CHEESE FROSTING
6 ounces cream cheese,
  softened
½ cup butter or margarine,
  softened
1 pound powdered sugar
⅓ cup reserved crushed
  pineapple

Utensil: 9 x 13 inch cake pan, greased and floured
Preheat oven to 375° for metal, 350° for glass pan

Combine flour, cinnamon, soda, baking powder and salt. In large
bowl thoroughly mix oil, sugar and eggs. Add flour mixture to oil
mixture; beat well and stir in vanilla. Reserve ⅓ cup pineapple for
frosting. Add remaining pineapple, carrots and nuts to cake batter.
Pour into pan and bake 25-30 minutes. Frost when completely
cooled.

For frosting: Blend cream cheese and butter. Slowly add
powdered sugar, beating until smooth. Add reserved pineapple.

Comment: Moist and wonderful.

**Do you look for ale and cakes here, you rude
rascals?**

                                        HENRY VIII

AWESOME CHOCOLATE SHEET CAKE

Servings
24-32
Planning
Can make
ahead
Preparing
45 minutes
Baking
20 minutes

1 cup margarine (not butter)
4 tablespoons cocoa
1 cup water
2 cups sugar
2 cups all-purpose flour
1 teaspoon baking soda
¼ teaspoon salt
½ cup buttermilk
2 eggs
1 teaspoon vanilla

CHOCOLATE ICING
½ cup margarine
4 tablespoons cocoa
6 tablespoons buttermilk
1 pound powdered sugar
1 teaspoon vanilla
1½ cup chopped nuts,
    optional

Utensil: 11 x 16 inch sheet cake or 10 x 15 inch jelly roll
pan, greased
Preheat oven to 350°

Heat margarine, cocoa and water to boiling point; remove from
heat and cool. In large bowl sift together sugar, flour, baking soda
and salt. Pour cocoa mixture into dry mixture; combine well. Add
buttermilk, eggs and vanilla; beat well and pour into pan. (Batter
will be thin.) Bake 20 minutes. Spread icing on warm cake. Cool
thoroughly before slicing.

For icing: Melt margarine with cocoa and buttermilk; bring to boil.
Add powdered sugar, vanilla and nuts if using; mix well.

Comment: Chocoholics watch out—this is addictive!

AMANDA McBROOM

YOU WANT A DISH?!?!?!?! I'LL GIVE YOU A DISH. MY DEATH DEFYING, THIGH DESTROYING BLACK RUSSIAN CAKE RECIPE. LOOK OUT!

1 package Duncan Hines
  yellow cake mix
1 package instant chocolate
  pudding
1 cup salad oil
4 eggs
¼ cup vodka
¼ cup Kahlua
½ cup water

Mix together. Bake at 325° for 45-55 minutes. Preferable to make the cake in a bundt pan.

FROSTING

1 cup powdered sugar
1-3 tablespoons Kahlúa
A little water

Mix together and pour over the cake.

CHEERS!

Servings
6-8
Planning
Can make
ahead
Preparing
30 minutes
Baking
25-35
minutes
Storing
Can freeze

SPICY BANANA CAKE

½ cup shortening
1 cup sugar
2 eggs
¼ cup milk
1 tablespoon lemon juice
1½ cups mashed ripe
  bananas (3-4 bananas)

1 teaspoon salt
2½ teaspoons baking powder
1 teaspoon baking soda
1 teaspoon cinnamon
1 teaspoon nutmeg
2 cups cake flour

Utensil: 9 x 13 inch cake pan, greased and floured
Preheat oven to 375°

Cream shortening with sugar until fluffy; then beat in eggs, one at a time. Combine milk, lemon juice and bananas. Combine salt, baking powder, soda, cinnamon, nutmeg and flour. Add flour and banana mixtures to shortening mixture, alternately, until well combined. Pour into pan and bake 25-35 minutes until toothpick inserted in center comes out clean.

Comment: This is good fresh from the oven topped with whipped cream, or frosted with butter cream and stored well wrapped for several days. Unfrosted or with butter cream frosting, it will keep 6 weeks in the freezer.

Though other things grow fair against the sun,
Yet fruits that blossom first will first be ripe.
                                        OTHELLO

RAISIN CAKE

2 cups dark raisins
2 cups water
2 teaspoons baking soda
1 cup oil
2 cups sugar
4 eggs

3 cups sifted all-purpose flour
2 teaspoons baking powder
2 teaspoons allspice
2 teaspoons cinnamon
½ cup chopped walnuts

Utensil: bundt pan, greased
Preheat oven to 350°

Servings
10-12
Planning
Can make
ahead 3-4
days
Preparing
20 minutes
Baking
55-60
minutes

In saucepan combine raisins and water; bring to boil. Remove
from heat and add baking soda. Set aside and cool 2 hours.

In large bowl combine oil and sugar; beat with electric mixer. Add
eggs, one at a time, beating thoroughly after each addition. In
another large bowl sift flour, baking powder, allspice and
cinnamon. Alternately add flour mixture and raisin mixture to
batter, blending well after each addition. Add nuts and stir well.
Spoon into pan and bake 55-60 minutes. Allow to cool before
removing from pan.

Comment: Moist and wonderful.

**The heathen philosopher, when he had a desire to
eat a grape, would open his lips when he put it into
his mouth; meaning thereby that grapes were made
to eat and lips to open.**
                                        AS YOU LIKE IT

EUROPEAN ALMOND CAKE

Yield
16 squares
Planning
Serve
immediately
Preparing
30 minutes
Baking
30-40
minutes

1 cup butter, softened
⅓ cup honey
⅓ cup sugar
1 egg, separated

½ cup almond paste
1 teaspoon almond extract
2 cups sifted all-purpose flour
¼ cup sliced almonds

Utensil: 8 x 8 inch pan, ungreased
Preheat oven to 350°

Combine butter, honey and sugar in a large bowl; using electric mixer on medium speed, beat until fluffy. Add egg yolk, almond paste and extract; beat until smooth. Add flour and beat at low speed just until well combined. Spoon mixture into pan. Beat egg white until frothy and brush over top of dough. Cover with sliced almonds. Bake 30-40 minutes or until golden brown. Cool completely on wire rack. Cut into squares and serve immediately.

Comment: This is a dessert that goes equally well with coffee or champagne and is a family Christmas tradition.

POUND CAKE

Servings
16
Planning
Can make
ahead
Preparing
30 minutes
Baking
1½ hours

1 cup butter, softened
3 cups sugar
6 eggs, separated
¼ teaspoon baking soda

3 cups sifted all-purpose flour
1 cup sour cream
1½ teaspoons vanilla

Utensil: tube pan or angel food cake pan, greased and floured
Preheat oven to 300°

Cream butter and sugar. Add egg yolks to mixture, one at a time, and beat well after each addition. Add soda to flour. Alternately, add flour and sour cream to butter mixture until thoroughly blended. Beat egg whites until stiff and fold in vanilla; lightly combine with batter. Pour into pan and bake 1½ hours. Turn cake out of pan immediately after removing from oven.

CREAM CHEESE POUND CAKE

1 cup butter, softened
1 8-ounce package cream
   cheese, softened
3 cups sugar

6 eggs
3 cups sifted cake flour
2 teaspoons vanilla, or
   almond, extract

Utensil: bundt or tube pan, greased and floured
DO NOT PREHEAT OVEN

In large bowl combine butter and cream cheese, beating with
electric mixer until fluffy. Gradually add sugar, beating and
scraping bowl. Add eggs, one at a time, beating well after each
addition. Add flour and extract, mixing well. Pour batter into pan
and place in a cold oven on the middle rack position. Set oven
temperature to 325° and bake 1 hour 20 minutes, or until it tests
done. Cool in pan 15 minutes before removing.

*Comment: An exceptional pound cake that becomes fantastic
served with fresh peach ice cream or strawberries and whipped
cream.*

Servings
16
Planning
*Can make
several
days ahead*
Preparing
30 minutes
Baking
*1 hour 20
minutes*
Storing
Freezes well

ALMOND SOUFFLÉ CAKE

4 large eggs, separated
5 tablespoons sugar
1 tablespoon grated lemon
   rind

1 teaspoon vanilla
1 cup finely ground almonds
Whipped topping
Strawberries

Utensil: 9-inch spring-form pan, lightly greased
Preheat oven to 300°

Beat egg whites until stiff but not dry. Blend yolks, sugar, lemon
rind and vanilla; add almonds. Slowly fold egg whites into egg yolk
mixture. Pour into pan; bake 50 minutes. Cool before removing
from pan. Before serving, spread with whipped topping and fresh
strawberries.

Servings
8
Planning
*Can make
day ahead*
Preparing
20 minutes
Baking
50 minutes

HOLIDAY SURPRISE FRUITCAKE

Yield
300 1-inch cakes
Planning
Must do ahead
Preparing
1 hour
Baking
3 hours
Chilling
4-6 weeks
Dipping
1½-2 hours
Storing
Up to 2 months

2½ cups sifted all-purpose
 flour
1½ teaspoons baking powder
1 teaspoon cinnamon
½ teaspoon freshly ground
 nutmeg
½ teaspoon ginger
½ teaspoon allspice
½ teaspoon cloves
1 cup unsalted butter,
 softened
1 cup light brown sugar,
 firmly packed
6 eggs
½ cup apricot nectar
½ cup heavy cream
1 tablespoon lemon juice

1½ pounds dried apricots,
 sliced
1 pound pecan halves
½ pound pitted dates,
 chopped
½ pound white raisins
¼ cup fresh orange peel zest,
 julienned
½ cup brandy
¼ cup Grand Marnier

TOPPING
Grand Marnier to taste
2 pounds premium quality
 French or Belgian semi-
 sweet chocolate

Utensils: two 9½ x 5 inch loaf pans, buttered and floured;
aluminum foil; plastic wrap; double boiler
Preheat oven to 250°

Combine flour, baking powder, cinnamon, nutmeg, ginger, allspice
and cloves. Cream butter with brown sugar until light and fluffy.
Add eggs, 1 at a time, beating well after each addition. Add ½
flour mixture to creamed mixture. Combine apricot nectar, cream
and lemon juice; add to batter. Dredge apricots, pecans, dates,
raisins and orange zest with remaining flour mixture; fold into
batter. Spoon batter into pans. Bake 3 hours or until cake tester
inserted in center comes out clean. Cool pans on wire racks.
Combine brandy and Grand Marnier; sprinkle evenly over cakes.
Remove from pans and wrap tightly, first in aluminum foil and
then plastic. Chill 4-6 weeks before topping with chocolate coating.

For topping: Melt chocolate in double boiler. Slice fruitcakes into
1-inch cubes and sprinkle with Grand Marnier to taste. Coat cubes
by dipping, 1 at a time, in melted chocolate. Cool on waxed paper.
Keep refrigerated up to 2 months.

*Comment: A delightful holiday treat that's a cross between cake
and candy.*

ORANGE WEDDING CAKE

1 scant teaspoon soda
1 cup milk
½ cup butter
1 cup sugar
2 eggs, separated
Grated rind of 1 orange
2 cups all-purpose flour
2 teaspoons baking powder

¼ teaspoon salt
¾ cup raisins
1 cup chopped nuts

TOPPING
1 cup orange juice
¾ cup sugar

Servings
12
Planning
*Can make
day ahead*
Preparing
30 minutes
Baking
1 hour

Utensil: 8-inch square or 6 x 10 inch oblong pan, lightly greased and floured
Preheat oven to 350°

For topping: Mix orange juice and ¾ cup sugar until dissolved; set aside.

Add soda to milk; allow to sour. In large bowl cream butter with 1 cup sugar; add egg yolks and orange rind. Sift together flour, baking powder and salt. To creamed mixture add soured milk and flour mixture. Beat egg whites until stiff; fold into cake mixture. Gently fold in nuts and raisins. Bake 1 hour or until cake tests done. Remove from oven and pour orange juice mixture over hot cake.

Comment: Fragrant and scrumptious.

If music be the food of love, play on...
                                    TWELFTH NIGHT

PECAN PIE COOKIE BARS

Yield
20-24 bars
Planning
Can make
ahead
Preparing
20 minutes
Baking
40 minutes

FILLING
4 eggs, beaten
½ cup brown sugar
1½ cups dark corn syrup
1 teaspoon vanilla
⅓ cup all-purpose flour
½ teaspoon salt
1½ cups chopped pecans

CRUST
½ cup margarine, softened
⅔ cup brown sugar
2 cups all-purpose flour
1 teaspoon baking powder

Utensil: 9 x 13 inch pan, greased
Preheat oven to 350°

For crust: Blend margarine with brown sugar; add flour and baking powder, mixing until crumbly. Pat into pan and bake 15 minutes. Remove from oven.

For filling: Mix eggs, brown sugar, corn syrup, vanilla, flour and salt. Pour over baked crust and top with pecans. Return to oven for 25 minutes. When partly cooled, cut into bars.

Comment: These "little pies" are delectable treats.

Measure for measure must be answered.
III HENRY VI

SAN FRANCISCO FUDGE FOGGIES

1 pound bittersweet
   chocolate, finely chopped
⅓ cup strong brewed coffee
1 cup unsalted butter, cut in
   tablespoons
4 large eggs, room
   temperature

1½ cups sugar
½ cup all-purpose flour
2 cups walnuts, coarsely
   chopped

Yield
32
Planning
Must make
ahead
Preparing
20 minutes
Baking
28-30
minutes
Storing
Refrigerate

Utensil: 9 x 13 inch baking pan; line pan with double thickness foil extending 2 inches beyond edges and butter thoroughly. Position rack in center of oven and preheat to 375°.

In top of double boiler, set over hot but not simmering water, melt chocolate, coffee and butter; stir frequently until smooth. Remove pan from heat and cool mixture, stirring occasionally, for 10 minutes.

In large bowl, using electric mixer on high speed, beat eggs 30 seconds or until foamy. Gradually add sugar and continue beating 2 minutes, or until mixture is light and fluffy. Using low speed, gradually add chocolate mixture until just blended. With wooden spoon, stir in flour and then walnuts; be careful not to overbeat.

Transfer batter to prepared pan. Bake 28-30 minutes or until just set around edges (center will remain moist). Place pan on wire rack and cool 30 minutes. Cover pan tightly with foil and refrigerate overnight (or a minimum 6 hours). Remove foil cover and run sharp knife around edges. Using two ends of foil as handles, lift mixture onto a plate and peel off foil. Invert onto smooth surface and cut into 16 portions.

Comment: Foggies are heavenly and sinfully rich.

COOKIES-WHILE-YOU-SLEEP

Yield
50-60
cookies
Planning
Must make
ahead
Preparing
30 minutes
Baking
Overnight

2 egg whites
⅛ teaspoon salt
¼ teaspoon cream of tartar
⅔ cup sugar
1 teaspoon vanilla

¼ teaspoon almond extract
¾ cup coarsely chopped
  pecans
½ cup chocolate bits

Utensil: two 12 x 16 inch cookie sheets, foil-lined
Preheat oven to 350°

With electric mixer beat egg whites until frothy; add salt and
cream of tartar, and continue beating. When almost stiff, add
sugar gradually and continue beating until very stiff peaks form.
Add vanilla and almond extracts; fold in nuts and chocolate bits.
Drop by teaspoon into small kisses on cookie sheets. Place in
oven, turn off heat and leave overnight. Do not peek.

BUTTER COOKIES

Yield
96
Planning
Can make
ahead
Preparing
30 minutes
Baking
12 minutes

1 cup butter
1 cup oil
1 cup sugar
1 cup powdered sugar
1 teaspoon vanilla
2 eggs, lightly beaten

4 cups all-purpose flour
1 teaspoon baking soda
1 teaspoon cream of tartar
1 teaspoon salt
Sugar for topping

Utensil: cookie sheets, greased
Preheat oven to 375°

Cream butter, oil, both sugars, vanilla and eggs until light and
fluffy. Sift together flour, soda, cream of tartar and salt; stir into
creamed mixture. Chill 1 hour. Shape dough into walnut-size balls
and roll in sugar. Place on cookie sheets and flatten with bottom
of glass dipped in sugar. Bake 12 minutes.

HOLLY'S FABULOUS COOKIES

¼ cup unsifted all-purpose
  flour
¼ teaspoon double-acting
  baking powder
¼ teaspoon cinnamon
⅛ teaspoon salt
8 ounces German sweet
  chocolate

1 tablespoon butter
1 8-ounce package chocolate
  chips
2 eggs
¾ cup sugar
½ teaspoon vanilla
¾ cup (2½ ounces) walnuts,
  finely chopped

Utensils: cookie sheets covered with aluminum foil
Preheat oven to 350°

Sift together flour, baking powder, cinnamon and salt. Set aside.

Break up chocolate and place in top of small double boiler over
hot water. Add butter and place over moderate heat; cover and
cook 'til melted. Stir 'til smooth. Set aside to cool.

In small bowl beat eggs at high speed a minute or two 'til light in
color. Gradually add sugar and continue to beat 4 or 5 minutes
until mixture forms a ribbon when beater is raised. Beat in vanilla.

Add cooked cooled chocolate; beat on low speed until smooth. Add
sifted ingredients and beat only 'til blended. Stir in nuts and chips.

Use a nice soup spoon to ladle the dough on the cookie sheets,
about 6 big cookies per sheet. Bake about 12 minutes. They
should be only semi-firm to touch when done.

Yum!

BETH HOWLAND
Featured in the Globe's "The Torch Bearers" and nationally recognized for her starring role in
television's "Alice" series.

LEMON LOVE NOTES

Yield
12-16
squares

Planning
Can make
day ahead

Preparing
20 minutes

Baking
37-40
minutes

CRUST
½ cup butter or margarine,
  melted

¼ cup powdered sugar
1 cup all-purpose flour

FILLING
1 cup granulated sugar
2 tablespoons all-purpose
  flour
½ teaspoon baking powder
2 eggs, beaten until foamy

2 tablespoons lemon juice
2 teaspoons grated lemon
  peel
Powdered sugar, optional

Utensil: 8 x 8 inch baking pan, ungreased
Preheat oven to 350°

For crust: Mix butter, powdered sugar and flour. Press into pan; bake 12-15 minutes, or until lightly browned. Cool.

For filling: Combine sugar, flour and baking powder; add eggs, lemon juice and peel. Pour onto crust and bake 25 minutes. Sprinkle powdered sugar on top, if desired. Cool and cut into squares.

SWEDISH LEMON SQUARES

Prepare as for Lemon Love Notes. Omit grated lemon peel and add ½ cup coconut.

Comment: Tart, lemony, great with vanilla ice cream.

KITA'S OATMEAL CAKE BARS

Yield
12-15 bars
Planning
Can make
ahead
Preparing
30 minutes
Baking
30-40
minutes

1 cup quick-cooking oats
1 cup boiling water
½ cup butter or margarine
2 eggs
½ cup sugar
½ cup brown sugar
1 teaspoon vanilla
½ cup all-purpose flour
½ cup whole-wheat flour
1 teaspoon baking powder
1 teaspoon baking soda
1 teaspoon cinnamon
½ teaspoon salt

½ cup raisins or currants
½ cup chopped dates

TOPPING
½ cup brown sugar
½ cup shredded coconut
   (or ½ cup chopped walnuts
   or pecans)
4 tablespoons butter or
   margarine, softened
1 teaspoon vanilla
1 tablespoon cream

Utensil: 9 x 13 inch pan, greased
Preheat oven to 350°; broiler to brown topping

Put oats in medium bowl and cover with boiling water; add
margarine and mix until melted. When cool add eggs, sugar and
brown sugar; beat well. Fold in vanilla.

In sifter combine all-purpose and whole-wheat flours, baking
powder, baking soda, cinnamon and salt. Sift directly into egg and
sugar mixture and combine; fold in raisins and dates. Pour into
pan and bake 30-40 minutes.

For topping: In saucepan combine brown sugar, coconut (or
walnuts), butter, vanilla and cream; bring to boil.

Remove oatmeal mixture from oven and, while still hot, spread
topping evenly over surface. Then, watching closely, broil until
lightly browned. Cool; cut into bars or squares. Keeps well in
covered container.

Comment: A fine autumn dessert.

HELEN'S WHAT?

Yield
24-32
squares
Planning
Best served
same day
Preparing
30 minutes
Baking
20 minutes

2 cups all-purpose flour
½ teaspoon salt
1 teaspoon baking soda
1 cup butter, softened
½ cup sugar
½ cup light brown sugar, packed
1 tablespoon water
1 teaspoon vanilla

2 egg yolks
1 12-ounce package chocolate chips, divided
1 cup chopped nuts

MERINGUE
2 egg whites
1 cup light brown sugar, packed

Utensil: 10 x 15 inch pan, greased
Preheat oven to 375°

Sift together flour, salt and baking soda. Cream butter, both sugars, water and vanilla until light and fluffy. Beat in egg yolks. Gradually add flour mixture, beating well after each addition. Spoon batter into pan. Sprinkle with ½ chocolate chips and press into batter. Spread meringue over raw batter and seal to edge of crust. Sprinkle with remaining chocolate chips and chopped nuts. Bake 20 minutes. Cool and cut into squares.

For meringue: Beat egg whites until slightly stiff but not dry; gradually add brown sugar and beat until stiff.

Comment: What? It's a deluxe chocolate chip cookie bar!

His words are a very fantastical banquet, just so many strange dishes.
                                    MUCH ADO ABOUT NOTHING

CHINESE CHEWS

Yield
36 squares
Planning
*Can make
ahead*
Preparing
20 minutes
Baking
*20-30
minutes*

1½ cups flour
2 cups chopped dates
2 cups chopped pecans
1 cup chopped candied
  cherries
2 cups sugar

4 eggs, well beaten
1 teaspoon vanilla
Pinch salt
Powdered sugar for topping,
  sifted

Utensil: 10½ x 15½ inch jelly-roll pan, buttered and floured
Preheat oven to 350°

Sift flour; stir in dates, pecans and cherries. Cream sugar, eggs, vanilla and salt. Combine egg mixture with flour mixture. Place in pan and bake 20-30 minutes. While still warm, cut into squares (tops will crack). Cool, remove from pan and sift powdered sugar over top.

Comment: These won't last long.

CHOCOLATE RAISIN COOKIES

Yield
24 medium
Planning
*Can make
ahead*
Preparing
10 minutes
Baking
10 minutes

½ cup melted butter or
  margarine
2 1-ounce squares
  unsweetened chocolate
1 cup lightly packed brown
  sugar

1 egg
½ cup milk
½ teaspoon baking soda
1½ cups all-purpose flour
¾ cup raisins (or nuts)

Utensil: cookie sheet, greased
Preheat oven to 375°

In saucepan melt butter and chocolate together over low heat. Remove from heat and beat in sugar and egg; add milk, soda, flour and raisins, stirring well. Drop by spoonfuls onto greased cookie sheet. Bake about 10 minutes, watching carefully that cookies do not burn.

MAGIC PEANUT BUTTER COOKIES

Yield
18-24
Planning
*Can make
ahead*
Preparing
15 minutes
Baking
*8-10
minutes*
Storing
*Several
days*

1 cup crunchy peanut butter
1 cup sugar

1 large egg
1 teaspoon vanilla

Utensil: cookie sheet, ungreased
Preheat oven to 350°

Combine peanut butter, sugar, egg and vanilla in mixing bowl until creamy. With teaspoon, drop mixture on cookie sheet; lightly press flat with fork. Bake 8-10 minutes. Remove from oven and let cool on cookie sheet.

Comment: Super fast and super delicious!

MEXICAN WEDDING CAKES

Yield
3½ dozen
Planning
*Can make
day ahead*
Preparing
15 minutes
Baking
*10-12
minutes per
sheet*

6 tablespoons powdered
   sugar
1 cup butter, softened
2 cups all-purpose flour

2 teaspoons vanilla
2 cups ground walnuts
Sifted powdered sugar for
   rolling cookies

Utensil: cookie sheet, greased
Preheat oven to 325°

Cream sugar and butter. Add flour, vanilla and nuts; mix thoroughly. Roll into small balls about the size of a quarter. Place on cookie sheet and press each ball with fork (first one way and then at right angle) to desired thickness. Bake 10-12 minutes. Remove from sheet and roll warm cakes in a generous amount of powdered sugar.

Comment: Don't wait for a wedding to enjoy these melt-in-the-mouth morsels.

DESSERTS

Associate Artist Irene Tedrow and Don Sparks in *Foxfire*

RASPBERRY SOUFFLÉ

Servings
8
Planning
Can make
sauce
ahead
Preparing
30-40
minutes
Baking
25 minutes

½ cup packaged cheesecake
filling mix
4 ounces cream cheese,
softened
¼ cup sour cream
2 ounces raspberry liqueur
(Chambord)
1 10-ounce package frozen
raspberries, puréed to
equal ½ cup
3 egg yolks

6 egg whites
Pinch cream of tartar
½ cup sugar
Fresh raspberries for garnish

COLD SABAYON SAUCE
4 egg yolks
¾ cup powdered sugar
¾ cup raspberry liqueur
(Chambord)

Utensils: food processor; electric mixer; 2½-quart soufflé
mold or 8 individual molds, buttered and sugared; double
boiler; whisk
Preheat oven to 400°

In food processor combine cheesecake mix, cream cheese, sour
cream, liqueur and raspberry purée. Process until well mixed,
6-8 seconds. Transfer to moderately large bowl.

In small bowl beat 3 egg yolks until lemon-colored; stir into
raspberry mixture. (Can be refrigerated 1-2 hours at this point.)

In medium bowl beat 6 egg whites until stiff. Add cream of tartar
and sugar; beat until firm peaks form. Gently fold into raspberry
mixture. Pour into soufflé mold (or molds). Bake 25 minutes;
remove from oven. Punch hole in top (or tops) and ladle generous
portion sauce (at room temperature) over and into soufflé. Garnish
with fresh raspberries.

For sauce: Place 4 egg yolks, powdered sugar and liqueur in
upper part of double boiler over, not in, boiling water. With whisk,
beat until very thick. Set double boiler top in pan of cracked ice
and beat until cold. (Sauce can be stored in refrigerator several
days.)

*Comment: Light and airy, this soufflé has an intense complex
flavor and a lovely lavender color.*

Servings
6
Planning
Must make
ahead
Preparing
30-40
minutes
Chilling
Overnight

COEUR À LA CRÈME WITH RASPBERRY OR STRAWBERRY SAUCE

FILLING
1 8-ounce package cream
   cheese, softened
⅔ cup sifted powdered sugar
1¼ cups heavy cream
1 teaspoon vanilla
1 teaspoon lemon juice
1 teaspoon Framboise
   (raspberry brandy) or
   Kirsch (cherry brandy)

SAUCE
2 pints raspberries or
   strawberries, hulled,
   washed
½ cup sugar
1 tablespoon Framboise or
   Kirsch
1 teaspoon lemon juice

OPTIONAL GARNISH
6 whole raspberries or
   strawberries

Utensils: 6 coeur à la crème molds (½ cup) or one 3-cup closely woven basket; food processor or electric mixer; cotton cheesecloth; shallow baking pan; fine sieve

For filling: Using processor or mixer, beat cream cheese until smooth; add sugar, a few tablespoons at a time, and continue processing or mixing (scrape sides of bowl with spatula occasionally). In chilled bowl whip cream until stiff; gently fold half the whipped cream into cream cheese mixture. Add vanilla, lemon juice and Framboise (or Kirsch); gently fold in remaining whipped cream. Line molds or mold with a double thickness of dampened cotton cheesecloth. Fill with mixture; fold cheesecloth over tops and place in a shallow baking pan. Chill overnight.

(Note: Coeur à la crème molds have tiny holes in their bottoms to allow liquids to drain from cheese. You can substitute a small, tightly woven basket, but do not use a solid mold as liquid must drain overnight.)

For sauce: In blender or food processor purée berries, sugar, Framboise (or Kirsch) and lemon juice. Strain through fine sieve, pressing solids with spoon to extract liquid.

To assemble and serve: Unfold cheesecloth and invert molds onto individual dessert plates or one larger plate. Spoon sauce around each heart. Garnish each serving with a berry, optional.

Comment: A delicate, light and refreshing dessert.

QUICK RICH MOUSSE

½ cup sugar
⅓ cup water
1½ cups heavy cream, whipped
4 ounces unsweetened chocolate, in pieces

¼ cup rum or Kahlúa
4 eggs, separated
Whipped cream, mint sprigs or white chocolate shavings for garnish, optional

Utensil: food processor

Servings
6-8
Planning
Must make ahead
Preparing
20-25 minutes
Chilling
2-24 hours

In saucepan boil sugar and water 3 minutes to make syrup. With plastic blade in workbowl of food processor, add cream and process uninterrupted until a thick cream forms (about 1 minute). Empty cream into large bowl. Without washing workbowl, insert metal blade and add chocolate pieces. Process 15-20 seconds, turning on and off; scrape bowl at least once during pulverizing process. Continue processing while adding hot syrup, rum and egg yolks; fold into whipped cream. Beat egg whites until stiff and fold into chocolate mixture. Spoon into individual serving dishes. Chill. Before serving, garnish with a dollop of sweetened whipped cream, a sprig of mint or white chocolate shavings.

Comment: A taste wow!

VIENNESE STRAWBERRY TORTE

Servings
10
Planning
*Can make
ahead 1-2
days*
Preparing
30 minutes
Baking
40 minutes

CRUST
1⅓ cups all-purpose flour
1⅓ teaspoons baking powder
½ cup shortening, softened
½ cup sugar
4 egg yolks
5 tablespoons milk
½ teaspoon almond extract

MERINGUE
4 egg whites
⅛ teaspoon cream of tartar
1 cup sugar

TOPPING
Fresh strawberries
Whipped topping or sour
    cream

**Utensils: two 8-inch cake pans lined with waxed paper, oiled
Preheat oven to 250°, raise to 350°**

Sift together flour and baking powder; set aside. Blend shortening
and ½ cup sugar until fluffy; add egg yolks, one at a time,
beating briskly after each addition. Add flour mixture to
shortening mixture alternately with milk; stir in almond extract.
Spread mixture in two pans, keeping mixture higher on sides than
in middle.

Beat egg whites until stiff; add cream of tartar, beating well.
Slowly beat in remaining sugar. Spread meringue over torte layers
leaving ½- to 1-inch space from edge. Bake 20 minutes at 250°
then raise to 350° for 20 minutes more. Cool and serve with fresh
strawberries and either whipped topping or sour cream. (Note:
Does not freeze. Can be made 1-2 days ahead; keep in airtight
container to prevent meringue from weeping.)

Comment: An elegant dessert.

 277

BERTRAM TANSWELL

LEMON CURD, YE FAMOUS TANSWELL RECIPE

4 large eggs
4 large lemons
1½ cups sugar
3 tablespoons cornstarch
½ cup butter or margarine
(All at room temperature)

Grate the lemons, set rind aside. Beat the eggs and juice the lemons (you'll need 1 cup plus 2 tablespoons juice). Sift cornstarch with sugar in heavy pan, then alternately add the juice and the beaten eggs, constantly stirring. Place over medium heat and stir, stir, stir until thickens and comes to a full boil. Lower heat and add the rind and boil gently for 3-4 minutes. Remove from heat and blend in the butter. When cool enough, place in sterilized jars and when cold, refrigerate.

In case people don't know what to do with lemon curd, it is delicious as a frosting and filling in sponge cake or pound cake, filling for cookies or an ingredient in Trifle.

Trifle, in English cookery, is a dessert consisting of custard and usually containing cake soaked in wine or liqueur, and jam and fruit or the like.

Good sooth, she is
The queen of curds and cream.

THE WINTER'S TALE

BERTRAM TANSWELL
Member original 1935 Old Globe Players and veteran of numerous productions for television, on and off-Broadway. Last Globe performances for Festival '83.

MARMALADE SOUFFLÉ

Servings
6
Planning
Serve
immediately
Preparing
40 minutes
Cooking
1 hour

SOUFFLÉ
3 large egg whites at room
    temperature, beaten
3 tablespoons sugar
2 tablespoons orange
    marmalade
1 teaspoon orange extract
½ cup chopped pecans or ½
    cup chopped fresh berries

SAUCE
3 large egg yolks, beaten
¾ cup powdered sugar
2 tablespoons brandy or rum
1 cup heavy cream, whipped

Utensils: straight-sided double-boiler, well-buttered; electric
mixer

For soufflé: Beat egg whites until stiff. Beat in sugar, one
tablespoon at a time, until whites are glossy; add orange extract.
In separate bowl mash marmalade with spoon; add 2-3
tablespoons egg white and blend gently. Fold mixture into
remaining egg whites. Gently spoon into well-buttered double boiler
top. Make sure boiling water just touches bottom of insert; cover.
Do not lift lid. Cook over low heat 1 hour or until a knife comes
out clean. Turn out on warm platter; sprinkle with pecans or
berries.

For sauce: Shortly before soufflé is done (15 minutes), beat egg
yolks until foamy; add powdered sugar and brandy or rum. Fold
whipped cream into yolk mixture. Serve generously over soufflé.

*Comment: A most unusual stove-top soufflé with intense orange
flavor, light texture. Delightful!*

ZABAGLIONE OVER SLICED PAPAYA

Servings
4
Planning
Serve
immediately
Preparing
15-20
minutes

6 egg yolks
6 tablespoons sugar
⅓ cup dry white wine

3 tablespoons brandy
2 papayas, peeled, seeded
and sliced into thirds

Utensils: heavy saucepan, rotary beater

Beat egg yolks over very low heat, stirring constantly. When light
yellow in color, gradually add sugar and continue to beat
constantly. Slowly add wine and brandy, beating until mixture
becomes thick and fluffy. (Do not let mixture reach boiling point or
it will separate.) Pour hot over sliced papaya and serve.

Comment: A custard cloak for a Hawaiian beauty.

BUTTERMILK SHERBET

Servings
4-6
Planning
Must make
ahead
Preparing
15 minutes
Chilling
3 hours
Storing
In freezer
several
days

4 cups buttermilk
½ cup granulated sugar
1½ cups corn syrup

2 lemons or 2 limes, juice
and grated rind

Utensil: 8 x 8 inch metal pan
Freezer

Mix together buttermilk, sugar, corn syrup, lemon juice and rind.
Pour into pan; freeze until firm around outer edges but slushy in
center, about 1 hour. Remove, pour into bowl and beat; return to
pan and freeze. Repeat procedure three times. Place in covered
container to store.

Comment: An interesting, tart summer dessert that's especially
attractive served in lemon or lime shells and garnished with
leaves.

Servings
6-8
Planning
Can make 8
hours ahead
Preparing
30-40
minutes
Baking
35 minutes

CAPIROTADA
(MEXICAN BREAD PUDDING)

¾ cup butter
9 ½-inch slices French
  bread, slightly stale, crusts
  trimmed
6 ounces cream cheese,
  chilled and crumbled
Whipped cream for garnish

FILLING
⅔ cup chopped pine nuts
½ cup raisins
1½ cups chopped Pippin
  apples, peeled and cored

SYRUP
1 cup brown sugar, firmly
  packed
⅔ cup water
2 tablespoons sherry
1 teaspoon aniseed
2 whole cloves
1 stick cinnamon

TOPPING
2 egg whites
⅓ cup chopped pine nuts
3 tablespoons brown sugar
1 tablespoon cinnamon

Utensils: small saucepan, strainer, large skillet; 1½-quart
soufflé dish, well buttered
Preheat oven to 350°

In skillet over medium heat, melt 5 tablespoons butter and sauté
bread, in batches, on both sides until just beginning to color (about
2 minutes total). Add more butter if needed. As each slice is done,
remove from skillet and set aside. Melt remaining butter.

Arrange ⅓ bread slices in dish. Cover with ⅓ filling, ⅓ cream
cheese and ⅓ syrup. Repeat layers. Pour remaining melted butter
on top and gently press down on bread layers. Spread topping
over pudding. Bake 35 minutes; turn off heat and let stand in oven
additional 15 minutes. Serve warm or at room temperature
garnished with whipped cream.

For filling: Combine pine nuts, raisins and apples.

For syrup: Combine brown sugar, water, sherry, aniseed, whole
cloves and cinnamon. Boil 1 minute; strain.

For topping: Beat egg whites until stiff; fold in nuts, brown sugar
and cinnamon.

Comment: A gold medal winner.

ORANGE BREAD PUDDING

Servings
4
Planning
Good warm
or cold
Preparing
15 minutes
Baking
45 minutes

2 egg yolks
2 tablespoons granulated
  sugar
¹/₈ teaspoon salt
1 tablespoon butter, melted
1 teaspoon grated orange
  rind
½ teaspoon grated lemon
  rind
¹/₃ cup orange juice

½ cup evaporated milk
1 cup day-old ½-inch bread
  cubes
¼ cup raisins
3 tablespoons currant jelly
1 orange, peeled and cut into
  segments
¾ cup heavy cream, whipped,
  optional

Utensil: 9 x 5 inch loaf pan, greased
Preheat oven to 350°

Beat egg yolks. Add sugar, salt, melted butter, orange and lemon
rinds, orange juice and milk. Pour over bread cubes, add raisins
and mix well. Pour into loaf pan and place in pan of warm water.
Bake 45 minutes or until inserted knife tests clean. Garnish with
jelly, orange segments and whipped cream, if desired.

*Comment: A quest for the best bread pudding produced this
California update of an old-time favorite.*

**So are you to my thoughts as food to life,
Or as sweet-seasoned showers are to the ground.**
                                        SONNET IXXV

THICK, CHEWY CHOCOLATE SAUCE

Yield
About 2½ cups
Planning
Can make ahead
Preparing
5 minutes
Cooking
20 minutes
Storing
Refrigerate

1 12-ounce package
  semisweet chocolate bits
2 tablespoons butter
1 cup clear corn syrup

¼ cup sugar
⅛ teaspoon salt
¼ cup water
½ teaspoon vanilla

Utensil: double-boiler

Melt chocolate in top part of double-boiler; add butter, corn syrup, sugar, salt, water and vanilla. Cook 10 minutes, stirring often. Place in glass jar and store in refrigerator (it will keep for several weeks). Sauce will thicken when cold. Before serving, reheat desired amount in microwave or top of double-boiler.

Comment: Warning! This is hard to resist even when cold.

FANCY SUNDAE BANANA SPLIT

Servings
2
Planning
Make fresh
Preparing
10 minutes
Cooking
3-5 minutes

2 tablespoons butter
3 tablespoons brown sugar,
  light or dark
¼ cup sliced or whole
  unsalted almonds
1 medium ripe banana, peeled
  and sliced

(or 1 ripe peach, peeled and
  sliced; or a combination)
1 ounce liqueur (combination
  of dark rum and Amaretto)
Dash cinnamon
Dash nutmeg
2 scoops vanilla ice cream

Utensil: 8-inch sauté pan, 2 ice cream dishes

Melt butter in pan over medium-high heat; add almonds and sauté 1 minute. Stir in brown sugar and cook until bubbly. Add banana or peach slices; sauté 1-2 minutes until heated. Add liqueur, stirring to blend; add dash of cinnamon and/or nutmeg to taste. Remove from heat; let cool a minute. Spoon over individual scoops of ice cream.

Comment: You'll never return to a plain banana split after this! For variety, experiment with different fruits, nuts and liqueurs.

PASSOVER CHOCOLATE NUT ROLL

6 extra large eggs
¾ cup sugar, divided
1½ cups ground walnuts or
  pecans

1 ounce unsweetened
  chocolate
3 tablespoons apricot
  preserves
Confectioners' sugar

FILLING
6 ounces bittersweet
  chocolate

Utensil: 10½ x 15½ inch jelly roll pan, lined with greased
wax paper
Preheat oven to 350°

Separate egg whites from egg yolks and place in separate bowls.
Beat egg whites until foamy, then gradually beat in ½ cup sugar
until a meringue is formed that is stiff and glossy. In second bowl
beat egg yolks with remaining ¼ cup sugar until light. Using a
rubber spatula, fold yolks into whites with ground nuts until well
combined. Spread evenly in prepared pan.

Bake 15-20 minutes until well browned and firm to the touch.
Remove from oven. Rinse a clean dish towel in cold water, wring
out and spread on counter top. Turn cake out on wet cloth and
peel off wax paper. Roll up warm cake in wet towel and set in
refrigerator to finish cooling.

To prepare filling: In the upper half of double boiler, melt both
chocolates over simmering water until well blended. Stir in apricot
preserves. Remove from heat and cool to room temperature.

When cake is cooled, lay a piece of wax paper on counter and
sprinkle with confectioners' sugar. Unroll cake on sugar and
spread with chocolate mixture. Roll up cake and finish with
confectioners' sugar, stirring it through a small strainer onto the
top surface of roll. To serve, cut in 1-inch thick slices, or serve two
or three slimmer slices with a ripe strawberry or two.

*...my favorite dessert which my mother makes every Passover. It
contains no flour and is totally sensational.*

DAVID SEGAL
Lighting designer. His designs have earned credits for Broadway productions, major opera companies,
noted resident theatres in addition to the Globe.

CHOCOLATE DECADENCE
BOOZE BOMBE

Servings
10-12
Planning
Must make
day ahead
Preparing
1 hour
Chilling
Overnight

1 pound unsalted butter,
  softened
2 cups sugar
12 eggs, separated
4 ounces unsweetened
  chocolate, melted
1 teaspoon vanilla
1 cup chopped pecans
24 split ladyfingers

1 cup bourbon or more, to
  taste
1½ cups heavy cream,
  whipped

OPTIONAL GARNISHES
Whipped cream
Fresh berries
Chocolate curls

Utensil: 10-inch spring-form pan, electric mixer

Cream butter and sugar until light and fluffy. Beat egg yolks until light; beat into creamed mixture. Stir in chocolate, vanilla and pecans. Beat egg whites until stiff but not dry; fold into mixture.

Line sides and bottom of pan with split ladyfingers that have been lightly dipped in bourbon. Spoon batter over ladyfingers and chill overnight. (No cooking or baking.)

To serve, remove sides of pan and decorate with choice of garnishes.

Comment: Sinfully rich, devastatingly decadent—in a word, wonderful!

Sweets grown common lose their dear delight.
SONNET CII

CHOCOLATE TRUFFLES

Yield
30-36
Planning
Must make
ahead
Preparing
Day 1: 20
minutes;
Day 2: 90
minutes
Baking
25 minutes
Chilling
As stated
Storing
2 weeks

FILLING
4 ounces premium quality
   semi-sweet chocolate
½ cup butter
¼ cup water
½ cup sugar
2 eggs
1 tablespoon Grand Marnier
   (or Cognac or Kahlua)

COATING
1 cup filberts (or almonds)

DIPPING COAT
12 ounces premium quality
   semi-sweet chocolate
¼ cup oil

Utensils: 2-3 quart heavy saucepan, 8-inch round pan, cookie sheet, wax paper
Preheat oven to 350°

For filling: Melt chocolate with butter, stirring constantly. Add water and sugar; beat in eggs and Grand Marnier. Spoon mixture into round pan. Bake at 350° no longer than 25 minutes. Refrigerate several days to allow flavors to mix.

For coating: Toast filberts at 350° for 15-20 minutes, stirring several times to prevent scorching. Remove skins from cooled nuts by rolling between hands until loose skins crumble and drop off. Chop until very fine.

When ready to prepare, shape refrigerated filling mixture into balls, 1 teaspoonful at a time. Work quickly with hands to keep mixture as cold as possible. Roll each ball through chopped filberts until well coated. Place on cookie sheet and chill several hours until firm before dipping.

For dipping coat: Melt chocolate and add oil, stirring constantly; cool to 90°. Dip truffles into chocolate, lift out and allow excess chocolate to drip back into pan. (Truffles can be dipped twice, if desired.)

Place dipped truffles on cookie sheet lined with wax paper; chill. May be kept chilled up to 2 weeks.

Comment: Smooth, elegant, wonderful and rich—a marvelous present.

PAKLAVA ARMENIAN STYLE

Servings
20-25
Planning
Must make
ahead
Preparing
1 hour
Baking
45 minutes

1 pound filo dough (about 24
  sheets)
¾ pound unsalted butter,
  melted

FILLING
1 pound walnuts, finely
  chopped
1 tablespoon sugar
1 teaspoon cinnamon

SYRUP TOPPING
3 cups sugar
1½ cups water
⅛ teaspoon lemon juice

**Utensils: 12 x 17 inch baking dish, large pastry brush,
saucepan
Preheat oven to 325°**

Lay filo between two damp towels to keep fresh; keep covered
when not using and do not allow to dry out. With pastry brush
spread butter on bottom of pan. Start layering filo in pan, 1 sheet
at a time, spreading butter evenly over each piece. When ½ dough
is used, spread with ¾ filling; reserve ¼ to sprinkle over top.
Continue layering and buttering until all filo is used. Spread
remaining butter over top and sprinkle with reserved filling.

Using a very sharp knife, cut pastry into 1½-inch rows the length
of the pan; then cut diagonal rows to form finger-size diamonds.
Bake approximately 45 minutes. Check to see if bottom is nicely
browned by slipping knife under side of pastry and lifting. Remove
from oven and cool overnight to let pastry become light and flaky.
The next day, add hot syrup and allow to soak into pastry several
hours before serving.

For filling: Combine walnuts, sugar and cinnamon.

For syrup: Combine sugar, water and lemon juice; bring to boil
over medium heat, stirring constantly. Continue boiling and stirring
until mixture becomes clear.

Comment: Exotic and aristocratic, the king of desserts.

PAVLOVA

Servings
8
Planning
*Can make 8
hours ahead*
Preparing
30 minutes
Baking
1½-2 hours

6 egg whites at room
temperature
2 cups granulated sugar
1 tablespoon cornstarch

1½ teaspoons white vinegar
1½ teaspoons vanilla
1 pint whipping cream
Fresh fruit in season

Utensil: 12 to 14 inch flat, oven-proof plate; cooking parchment
or wax paper

Oven directions follow

With gas oven: Preheat to 250° as you begin preparing recipe.
Place meringue on center shelf for 1½ hours. Remove and cool.

With electric oven: Do not preheat. Place meringue on lowest
shelf and turn oven to 200° and bake 45 minutes. Turn off heat
and leave in oven to cool.

With either kind of oven: Be aware that ovens are not all equal,
either in temperature or insulation, and that meringue may not
cook in time indicated. You may wish to cook longer, especially if
the humidity is high. Look for parchment color as sign of
doneness.

Using electric mixer beat egg whites at high speed until soft peaks
form. Gradually add sugar, 1 tablespoon at a time, beating at high
speed until all sugar is incorporated (1-2 tablespoons water may
be added to disolve sugar; avoid "weeping" by making certain
sugar is thoroughly dissolved). Add cornstarch and continue
beating. Add vinegar and vanilla. Beat until very stiff.

Cover plate with 1 sheet cooking parchment or 2 sheets waxed
paper and heap meringue onto it. Mound up sides and make a
slight depression in center with spatula. Bake. To serve, cover with
whipped cream and decorate with fresh cut-up fruit. (May be
stored briefly in airtight container before adding cream and fruit.)

*Comment: This came to the Old Globe via a Guilder friend in
Australia where Pavlova is regarded as the national dessert.*

Servings
8-10
Planning
Must make
ahead
Preparing
1 hour
Baking
15 minutes

SPICED PUMPKIN ROLL

BATTER
¾ cup all-purpose flour
2 teaspoons pumpkin pie
   spice
1 teaspoon baking powder
½ teaspoon salt

3 eggs
¾-1 cup granulated sugar
⅔ cup cooked or canned
   pumpkin
Powdered sugar for dusting

FILLING
2 3-ounce packages cream
   cheese
4 tablespoons butter

½ teaspoon vanilla
1 cup powdered sugar

Utensil: 10 x 15 inch jelly roll pan lined with wax paper
coated heavily with non-stick spray
Preheat oven to 375°

For batter: Sift together flour, spice, baking powder and salt; set
aside. With electric mixer beat eggs at high speed for 5 minutes;
gradually beat in sugar. Using low speed, add flour mixture and
pumpkin. Spread batter in pan and bake 15 minutes.

For filling: Combine cream cheese, butter and vanilla; beat in
powdered sugar.

Remove cake from oven and immediately invert onto a towel
dusted with powdered sugar. Remove wax paper. Roll cake and
towel into a cylinder; cool completely. Unroll cake, spread with
filling and reroll.

Comment: A festive fall dessert.

GREATEST VANILLA ICE CREAM

Yield
*See each
variation*
Planning
*Can make
ahead*
**Preparing
& Cooking**
1 hour
Chilling
Overnight
Storing
Freeze

1 cup plus 2 tablespoons
  half-and-half
6 large egg yolks
5½ tablespoons sugar
1 cup whipping cream

5½ tablespoons sugar
  (second addition)
1 whole vanilla bean, split
¼ cup butter
½ teaspoon vanilla extract

Utensil: ice cream maker

In small heavy saucepan slowly bring half-and-half to boil and remove from heat. Place in refrigerator overnight, or chill briefly in freezer without freezing.

Cream egg yolks with 5½ tablespoons sugar; set aside.

In 2-quart saucepan combine whipping cream, remaining sugar and vanilla bean; slowly bring to boil, stirring frequently. Remove bean. Using the point of a paring knife, scrape vanilla grains from inside hull into mixture. Use fingers to rub into mixture any vanilla grains or cream remaining on bean.

Slowly add cream mixture to yolks, whisking constantly. Pour into saucepan and, continuing constant whisking, cook to temperature just under boiling point. Remove from heat and whisk in butter. Immediately place pan in cold water or over ice to stop cooking. Stir frequently until cool.

Strain mixture through fine strainer or chinois. Beat in chilled half-and-half and vanilla. Place in ice cream maker; churn and freeze according to manufacturer's directions.

Makes 1 quart. (Recipe can be doubled and will fit 6-quart ice cream maker.)

Comment: A fantastic recipe from France's most famous pâtissier, Gaston Lenotre.

CHOCOLATE ICE CREAM

**1 recipe Greatest Vanilla Ice
Cream, omitting vanilla
bean
1½ ounces unsweetened
chocolate**

Make Greatest Vanilla Ice Cream according to directions, except add chocolate to half-and-half when bringing to boil. Churn and freeze. Makes 1 quart.

ROCKY ROAD ICE CREAM

**2 recipes Chocolate Ice
Cream
1 cup semisweet chocolate
pieces
3 cups coarsely chopped
toasted nuts
1 cup miniature
marshmallows**

After ice cream has been churned, fold in chocolate, nuts and marshmallows. Makes about 2 quarts.

BUTTERED PECAN ICE CREAM

**1 recipe Greatest Vanilla Ice
Cream
1 cup salted whole pecans**

Lightly sauté pecans, using the ¼ cup butter in recipe. Remove pecans with slotted spoon and set aside. Use butter remaining in skillet as directed in recipe (whisk into cream-yolk mixture). After churning, stir in pecans. Makes about 1 quart.

FRESH PEACH ICE CREAM

1 recipe Greatest Vanilla Ice
  Cream, omitting vanilla
  bean and extract
⅛ teaspoon almond extract,
  optional
4 very ripe peaches, peeled
  and finely chopped

Make Greatest Vanilla Ice Cream according to directions; add
almond extract if desired. Stir in peaches. Churn and freeze.
Makes about 1½ quarts.

PRALINE ICE CREAM TOPPING

1 cup blanched almonds
⅔ cups sugar
3 tablespoons water

Utensil: baking pan, lightly buttered
Preheat oven to 350°

Place almonds on cookie sheet and toast until light brown, 10-15
minutes, stirring occasionally.

In 1-quart saucepan heat sugar with water, stirring constantly,
until sugar caramelizes. Remove from heat when mixture turns
light to medium brown (it will continue to darken from its own
heat). Immediately stir in nuts. Return to heat and bring to boil.
Pour into prepared pan to cool.

To make praline, break into pieces and pulverize using blender or
food processor fitted with steel blade.

*Comment: Praline is delicious over ice cream or added to ice
cream before churning. It also can be used to flavor icings and
cake fillings.*

DESSERT CHEESE ROLL

Servings
6
Planning
Must make
ahead
Preparing
20 minutes
Chilling
24 hours

¼ cup chopped dried apricots
¼ cup chopped dates or figs
(or combination)
½ cup diced mixed candied
fruits
2 tablespoons port wine
2 tablespoons orange liqueur
1 8-ounce package cream
cheese, softened

½ cup grated imported white
Cheddar cheese
1 teaspoon grated orange
rind
¾ cup poppy seeds

Crackers
Grapes
Port wine

Utensils: electric mixer, wax paper

In bowl combine apricots, dates or figs and candied fruits; add
port wine and orange liqueur. Cover and marinate 2 hours. Beat
together cream and Cheddar cheeses; stir in orange rind and
marinated fruit mixture. Chill, covered, until firm. Using wax
paper, roll into log shape; coat with poppy seeds. Chill at least 24
hours. Serve with crackers, grapes and a good port wine.

Comment: Unusual and enjoyable. A fine finish to a festive meal.

Who riseth from a feast
With that keen appetite that he sits down?
THE MERCHANT OF VENICE

LEMON IN A GLASS

Servings
6-8
Planning
Make ahead
Preparing
45 minutes
Chilling
2 hours

2 3-ounce packages cream
  cheese, softened
½ cup yogurt
1 cup sour cream
5 egg yolks
¼ cup sugar
1 tablespoon quick-mixing
  flour

Yellow zest 2 lemons
¼ cup lemon juice
2 tablespoons sugar
½ pint whipping cream
2 cups blueberries,
  raspberries or sliced
  strawberries

Blend cream cheese, yogurt and sour cream together; set aside.
Mix egg yolks, ¼ cup sugar, flour, lemon zest and lemon juice;
cook over low heat stirring constantly until mixture thickens. Cool.
Add 2 tablespoons sugar to cream and whip until soft peaks form.
Fold cream cheese mixture into egg mixture; add whipped cream
and blend thoroughly.

To serve, layer alternately with fruit in wine glasses and
refrigerate at least 2 hours.

Comment: Rich and wonderful.

Be kind and courteous to this gentleman;
Hop in his walks and gambol in his eyes;
Feed him with apricocks and dewberries,
With purple grapes, green figs and mulberries.
                    A MIDSUMMER NIGHT'S DREAM

AUSTRIAN SPICED LINTZER TORTE

Servings
8-10
Planning
*Can make
1-2 days
ahead*
Preparing
30 minutes
Baking
1-1½ hours

1¼ cups unblanched
   almonds, ground
¾ cup butter, softened
½ cup sugar
2 egg yolks
1 cup all-purpose flour
Scant ¼ teaspoon ground
   cloves

Scant ¼ teaspoon cinnamon
Bread crumbs or flour as
   needed
1 8-ounce jar raspberry jam
Powdered sugar for topping

Utensils: 9-inch spring-form pan, buttered; blender
Preheat oven to 325°

Grind almonds in blender (or food processor). In large bowl
combine butter, sugar, egg yolks, almonds, flour, cloves and
cinnamon; mix by hand. Pat half the dough into pan and form an
edge about ½-inch high. (If dough is too soft and buttery, add a
little flour or a few plain bread crumbs.)

Spread raspberry jam over dough, leaving ½-inch space at edge.
Form narrow rolls with remaining dough; place over jam in a
lattice crisscross pattern. (Again, use extra flour if hard to handle.)
Bake 1-1½ hours or until torte turns light brown in color.
(Suggestion: place pan on cookie sheet when baking as butter may
drip). When cool, sift powdered sugar over top.

Comment: A classic Austrian recipe.

*The setting sun, and music at the close,
As the last taste of sweets, is sweetest last,
Writ in remembrance more than things long past.*
                                        RICHARD II

The Globe Guilders express their appreciation to the Old Globe Theatre's artists, subscribers and friends who contributed recipes for Cooks 'Round the Globe. Each regular recipe in this book has been tested at least twice. Celebrity recipes (denoted by * in the index) are printed in as close facsimile as possible to the artists' originals and, to preserve their integrity, have not been altered in any manner by the testers.

Artist-Contributors

Brian Bedford
Barry Bostwick
Michael Byers
Kandis Chappell
Charles Haid
Joseph Hardy
Linda Hart
Katherine Helmond
John Houseman
Beth Howland
Tom Lacy
Michael Learned
Marsha Mason
Amanda McBroom
Katherine McGrath
Jonathan McMurthy
Robert Morgan
Jack O'Brien
Christopher Reeve
Marion Ross
Gena Rowlands
Douglas W. Schmidt
David F. Segal
David Ogden Stiers
Bertram Tanswell
Irene Tedrow
Sada Thompson

Contributors

Ida E. Abbott
Celeste Abel
Jean Adams
Colleen Alessandra
Janice Alessandra
Millie MacArthur
  Alexander
Mary Allen
Maxine Allen
Jeane L. Ambrose
Nelma R. Anderson
Sue Francis Anderson
Beth Andinga
Mary Ann Arme
K. C. Armour

Marcia Baer
Ruth Elizabeth Baer
Carole Barklow
Barbara Barnes
David Barnes
Marianne Barnes
Nancy Bayer
Mary Bear
Ann Southard Beard
Tina Becharas
Sherrill Beck
Maurine Beinbrink
Ann O. Beinert
Gladys Beit-Ishoo
Laurie Ann Bell
Vi Bell
Inez Bellows
Kathryn S. Bemis
Kaye D. Benton
Lori Berberian
Christine Billet
Nancy Billhardt
Joy Bird
Deborah Black
Jerry Black
Katherine Black
Paul Black
Dick Blackington
Laurie Blackington
Betty Blankenship
Joanne B. Blankenship

Beth D. Blue
Anne Blumenfeld
Hermione Bodinson
Mary Nell Bohler
Julie Bohnsack
Mary E. Bowman
Nancy S. Bradshaw
Sue Braun
Mera C. Brazier
Tish Breihan
Sophie Brody
Melissa Brooks
Doris R. Brosnan
Joyce Brower
Dorothy Brown
Peggy Brown
Maureen Buckley
Arlene Bullis-Rice
Mark S. Burgess
Marge Burglund
Kathi Burke
Miriam Burstein
Mary Ruth Butts

Carole Cady
Jeanne Cady
Mary Cahill
Jean Callahan
Don Cameron
Lohme Canfield
Ina Cantrell
Bridget L. Cantu
Phyllis Carlson
Susan F. Carnot
Deborah N. Caruana
Joyce Casale
Jeff Casey
Elsie Chan
Anne Chapman
Susan Charles
Joan Chesner
Alice Churchill
Gail Clause
Ruth Cleveland
Bette Coates
Mary Jo Cogan
Pat Cologne

Mildred G. Conley
Irene Cooper
Karen Correy
Jane Cowgill
Marlou Crabtree
Warrine Cranston
Linda Cunningham
Nancy Curtiss
Lori Cushenberry

Darlene G. Davies
Patricia Davies
Janice Davis
Lorene May Day
Franco F. K.
  DeAlbuero III
Melanie C. Dean
Lois Dechant
Norma J. Decker
Joni Delucchi
Edie Denne
Liane Denton
Bonnie de Selm
Katy Dessent
Ginny Dewey
Madeline Dodge
Elizabeth F. Dornbusch
Camille Dozier
Dorothy Dring
Yvonne Drisko
Kathleen L. Dunn
Daphne Durant
Irma Sue Durr

Helen Edison
Brenda Edwards
Dick Edwards
Sue Edwards
Marianne Egger
Marion Eggertsen
Mary Ehmcke
Sherrie Elder
Barbara Elliott
Alice Englander
Helen H. Erickson
Jodi Estep
Patricia Eu
Gloria Ewbank

Shirley E. Fairbanks
Tom Fat
Marion Faulk
Beverly Fawcett
Susan Fefferman
Esther Felt
Janel Findley
Dale Fisher
Marilyn Fisher
Nancy Fitzwilliams
Carol Fleming
Gene Foster
Joan Foster
Lanie Fouch
Dorothy C. Fowlie
Dottye Foxworthy
Sandy Frederick
Sue Friedman
Pat Frost
Edy Frueh

Dessie Galland
Zita Gardner
Dorthy Gartz
Jane D. Gawronski
Sondra Gibson
Barbara Gilbert
Jo Gilchrist
Russell H. Ginns
Beulah Giovanazzi
Karsten K. Gjemre
Dee Grabitz
Monica Grage
D. J. Gramann II
June Green
Pam Grender
Mary Griffin
Sue Griffith
Janet Gross
Robert P. Grossman
Bunnie Guilbert
Diane Gustafson

Charlotte Haas
Dottie Haggerty
Barbara Haislip
Arline Haugen Hales
Susan L. Hall
Lee Hanson
Marilyn Hanson
Pat Palmer Hanson
Helen Hansson
Isabel Harmes
Peggy Harris
Susan Hartwig-Hood
Marian Harvey
Marjorie Hasch

Patricia Hay
Joan Hayes
Frances Hays
Linda Heald
Isaac Hecht
Lillian Hecht
Connie Hedges
Joyce Lindell Hein
Susan Heller
M. Gail Henson
Kathy Herring
Eleanor B. Herzman
Rosemary Hewicker
Evelyn T. Hill
Shelley Hindes
Bobbi Hirschkoff
Gene Hirschkoff
Nancy E. Holland
Amy Holmes
Jill Holmes
Linda Holmes
Michael W. Holmes
Edward B.
  Houghtaling
John Howard
Kathi Howard
Margie Howard
Marian Howard
Phyllis Howell
Ann Hoxsey
Andrea Hunter
Dolly Hunter
Joanne L. Hunter
Kathleen Hurder
Viletta Hutchinson
Leanore Hutler

Mary Ingle
Joseph William
  Ippolito
Barbara Iredale
Sonia Israel

Elizabeth Jackson
Helen Jamieson
Ruth Lynn Jaworski
Mary Jermanok
Carolyn Jodka
Karen E. Johnson
Nancy Johnston
Barbara Ann Jones
J. Edgar Joseph
Bunty Justin

Barbara J. Kahley
Katharine A. Kane
Mikie Katz

Anne Kay
Mitchell Kay
Bibs Kearney
Judy Keaton
Virginia Kell
Donna Keller
Pat Keller
Edythe Kenton
Mary Kinyon
Helen Klein
Joanne Klein
Jeanette Knobbe
Kathy Korkis
Gretchen Kramer
Caryl Waller Krueger
Helene Kruger
Rose Ruth Kuntz
Monette Kupiec

J. Spencer Lake
Jan Landau
Tina Fisher Latham
Dolores Laughlin
Mary Surrell Laurila
Pamela Lawlor
Luci B. Laws
Nancy Lawson
George A. Lazar
Rose Ellen
  Leavenworth
Wendy Ledford
Jerry Ledin
Donna Lee
Tomaline Lenox
Anne C. Lindsey
Sue Liston
Caroll Long
Milt Long
Betty Jo Lopez
Elizabeth Lorenz
Harriet Love
Linda Lowry
Ed Lucado
Lois M. Lucas
Mary M. Luecke
Laura Lusk
Betty Lux

Irma Macpherson
Anne Maharry
Naida Malchiodi
Raye Malouff
Gerald Marans
Anne Marshall
Leitha Marsolais
Dolores Marx
Ingrid Massee

Patricia A. Matthews
Luella Maxwell
John Mazur
Maggie Mazur
Nancy McCall
Linda McCauley
Jerry McCormick
Vi McCoy
Claire McDonald
Kimberly McIntyre
Helen McKinley
Billie McKnight
Jackie McMahon
Ethel L. McPhee
Ann Meeker
David Meeker
Vickie Mehalick
Jennifer Messersmith
Goldie Metzger
Laura Metzger
Arla Meyer
Ferne Michniewicz
Eleanor Mikkelsen
Dori Mikles
Dean Miller
Judy Miller
Cynthia Lynne Millsaps
Fran Miner
Irene Minihan
Ann Moats
Thelma Montag
June C. Moore
Suzanne Moore
V. Moores
Clara Morehouse
Charlotte Moreno
Marjorie Moss
Marion Moxley
Betty Mudge
Pat Mudge
Kay Murphy
Marjorie Murphy
Pamela Mucia
Sandy Myers

Joyce Nash
Jeanne Nelson
Lucinda Nerhood
Enid Newton
Kathy Newton
Ken Newton
Crickett Nickle
Barbara Nielsen
Cheryl Nielsen
Betty Nimits
Gwen Nobil
Ruth Noe

297

Marty Norman
Carol Novick

Marge O'Donnell
Kaletta R. Oliver
Ginny Ollis
Elizabeth Olsen
Holli Olson
Lillian Olson
Kathleen O'Neill
Gail Orell
Ann Orr
Beth Ott
Peg Overlund

Rita Packard
Curtis Parker
Shelia Parker
Nadine Parsell
Jeannine Passenheim
Mary Jane Passman
Joe Payson
Victoria Payson
Aldine Peebles
Carole Pence
LaRayne Penny
Clarice Perkins
Barbara Peters
Marian Pettigrew
Jessica Petty
Jean Phippen
Eliot Pierce
Virginia Piraino
Mary Plischke
Dolly Poet
Sally Poet
Joan Pollard
Helen Poppenheimer
Marge Potorff
Maritha Pottenger
Virginia Poust
Gail Lee Powell
Bunny Preston
Jane Prichard
Janie Prim
Richard Puetter

Deborah Quillan

Evelyn Radway
Mitchell Ramos
Pat Reeve
Robin Renert
Doris Reynolds
Jane Reynolds
Marky Reynolds
Vanita Reynolds

Dan Richmond
Susan F. Rick
Hilda Ridout
Wanda Richey Roach
Corrine Robbins
Jean Rock
Barbara Rohrbach
Fay L. Rossi
Mary Rowley
Elizabeth M. Ruch
Doris Ruffino
Nancy Russell
William Russell
Sarah Ryan

Kacy Sackett
Jo Samplawski
Joan Schaefer
Shirley Schaefer
Biddy Schall
Kim Schall
Harriette Schapiro
Rita Schiarrone
Charlotte Schriefer
Sue Schugar
Suzanne Schulman
Judy Schwartz
Margaret Sell
Gail Senteney
Georgina Sham
Francena L. Sherburne
Sharon Lynn Sherman
Joyce Shinn
Carol Sigelman
Kathi Sigelman
Kim Sigelman
Sonya M. Singer
Maureen Kelley Sipp
Marty Slawson
Christine Smead
Frederic G. Smith
Julie Smith
Winifred Smith
Karen E. Snipes
Pearl Solomon
Pamela Southard
Barbara Spaulding
Marje Spear
Barbara Sperling
Christine Stalder
Bob Stanley
Carol K. Stark
Jonathan Stark
Carla Stayboldt
Karl L. Steinhauser
Joni M. Steinman
Jane Stillman

Janet O'Brien Stillwell
Diane Fleming Stone
Kay Stone
Marion Strickler
Woodrow J. Strossen
Pat Sullivan
Cora Sweet

Emily Talbert
Wynne Tartre
Helen Taylor
Diane Thomas
Cheryl Thompson
Dorothy A. Thompson
Mackie Thompson
Marillynn Thompson
Elizabeth P. Thornton
Peg Thornton
Velma Ticknor
Bob Torrance
Kristin Tow
Joyce Trask
Marian Trevor
Dotty Turner
Jeri Turner
Pennie Turner
Suzie Turner

Dixie Unruh
Mary Jane Urlaub

Cathy Valerio
Marjorie Van Nuis
Kathleen Veinbergs
Nancy Verhage
Ethel Vetter
Fran Viertel
Judy Volm
Ria Vongehr
Harvey Von Wantoch
Jordine Von Wantoch

Libby Waggoner
Merle Wahl
Phil Wahl
Rusty Walker
Louise M. Ward
Helen Warfel
Isabelle Wasserman
Mary Wayne
Alma Webster
Mary Beth Wedberg
Patricia Wegner
Rosalie Weinberger
Lillian Weis
Pat Welsh
Sharon Western

Kathryn Whistler
Ginny Whitby
Mary Ellen White
Vera Wiernik
Martha B. Wiley
Penny Wilkes
Dorothy Wilkison
Carol Williams
Christin Williams
Jeanne Williams
Barbara Wilson
Rebekah Wilson
Lenora Witt
Elsie E. Wolf
Barbara Wolpert
Anne Wood

Carol Yorston

Floria Zeiler
Joyce Zillner
Elizabeth Zongker
Kita Mears Zucco
Harriette S. Zuckerman

INDEX

The asterisk * denotes recipes contributed by artists associated with the Old Globe Theatre.

302

The asterisk * denotes recipes contributed by artists associated with the Old Globe Theatre.

304

The asterisk * denotes recipes contributed by artists associated with the Old Globe Theatre.

The asterisk * denotes recipes contributed by artists associated with the Old Globe Theatre.

The asterisk * denotes recipes contributed by artists associated with the Old Globe Theatre.

308

The asterisk * denotes recipes contributed by artists associated with the Old Globe Theatre.

The asterisk * denotes recipes contributed by artists associated with the Old Globe Theatre.

The asterisk * denotes recipes contributed by artists associated with the Old Globe Theatre.

ORDER FORM

Cooks 'Round the Globe
Old Globe Theatre
P. O. Box 2171
San Diego, California 92112

Please send me_____copies of COOKS 'ROUND THE GLOBE cookbook
at $18.95 each $_____
California residents add 6½% sales tax at $1.23 each $_____
Shipping and handling at $2.50 each $_____

Total enclosed $_____

Enclosed is my check or money order or credit card information for the amount of
$_____payable to the OLD GLOBE THEATRE.

☐ Check or Money Order   ☐ Master Card   ☐ American Express   ☐ Visa

Account No. _____Expiration date _____

Signature_____

Send to:

Name _____

Address _____

City_____State_____Zip_____

ORDER FORM

Cooks 'Round the Globe
Old Globe Theatre
P. O. Box 2171
San Diego, California 92112

Please send me_____copies of COOKS 'ROUND THE GLOBE cookbook
at $18.95 each $_____
California residents add 6½% sales tax at $1.23 each $_____
Shipping and handling at $2.50 each $_____

Total enclosed $_____

Enclosed is my check or money order or credit card information for the amount of
$_____payable to the OLD GLOBE THEATRE.

☐ Check or Money Order   ☐ Master Card   ☐ American Express   ☐ Visa

Account No. _____Expiration date _____

Signature_____

Send to:

Name _____

Address _____

City_____State_____Zip_____